내공
중학영어듣기
모의고사 20회

DARAKWON

Structures & Features
이 책의 구성과 특징

실전 모의고사 20회

최근 시·도 교육청 영어듣기능력평가를 분석·반영하여 실전에 대비할 수 있도록
구성하였습니다. 실제 시험과 유사한 모의고사를 20회 풀어보게 하였으며, 매회
영국식 발음을 5문항씩 제공하여 다양한 발음에 노출되도록 합니다.

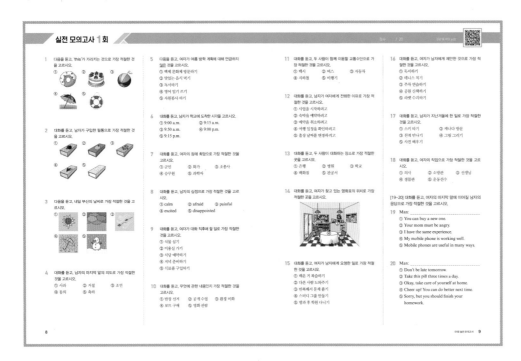

Listen and Check

모의고사를 다시 한 번 들은 후 들은
내용을 한 번 더 확인해 봅니다.

내공
중학영어듣기 ①
모의고사 20회

DARAKWON

저자 약력

김소원 체크체크(천재교육), EBS 변형문제(모자이크) 외 집필

서재교 EBS 수능변형문제 시리즈(모자이크), 맨처음 수능영어 독해모의고사(다락원) 외 집필
현) 대전 스카이피아 원장, 모자이크 EBS 변형문제 출제위원

이소영 EBS 변형문제(모자이크), 천기누설 EBS 고난도 변형문제(비투비) 외 집필
De La Salle University 교육 심리학과 졸

이연홍 맨처음 수능영어 독해모의고사(다락원), EBS 우수문항 고난도 변형문제(모자이크) 외 집필
현) 창원 명장학원 원장, 모자이크 EBS 변형문제 출제위원
경북대 졸

이건희 맨처음 수능영어[기본·완성·실력·독해모의고사], 내공[영문법·구문·단어·듣기](다락원)
체크체크, 싱크로드, 열공(천재교육), Grammar In(비상), EBS 변형문제(모자이크) 외 집필
인스타그램 http://instagram.com/gunee27

내공 **중학영어듣기 ①**
모의고사 20회

지은이 김소원, 서재교, 이소영, 이연홍, 이건희
펴낸이 정규도
펴낸곳 (주)다락원

초판 1쇄 발행 2019년 8월 19일
초판 6쇄 발행 2024년 6월 24일

편집 서민정, 정지인, 이동호
디자인 윤지영, 박선영
영문 감수 Michael A. Putlack

다락원 경기도 파주시 문발로 211
내용문의 (02)736-2031 내선 505, 506
구입문의 (02)736-2031 내선 250~252
Fax (02)732-2037
출판등록 1977년 9월 16일 제 406-2008-000007호

ISBN   978-89-277-0851-3 54740
        978-89-277-0850-6 54740 (set)

http://www.darakwon.co.kr
다락원 홈페이지를 방문하시면 상세한 출판 정보와 함께 동영상
강좌, MP3 자료 등 다양한 어학 정보를 얻으실 수 있습니다.

Dictation Test

모의고사 전 지문의 받아쓰기를 통해 다시 한번 내용을 확인하고 중요 표현들과 연음을 학습할 수 있습니다. 발음과 표현 팁을 통해 심층 학습을 할 수 있습니다.

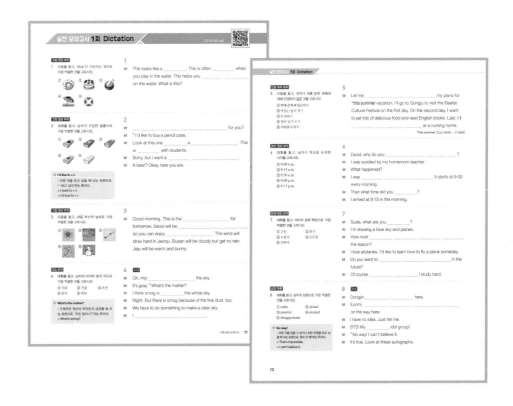

Vocabulary Test

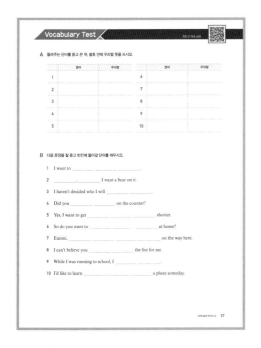

모의고사에 나온 단어를 듣고 영어 단어와 한글 뜻을 같이 써 보면서 어휘를 학습합니다. 또한, 모의고사에 나온 문장들을 다시 듣고 빈칸을 채우며 중요 표현을 복습합니다.

온라인 부가 자료 제공

www.darakwon.co.kr

MP3파일

미국식 발음 100%로 녹음된 파일과 영국식 발음 100%로 녹음된 파일 2종 MP3 파일을 제공합니다. 또한, 0.8배속/1.0배속/1.2배속 MP3 파일을 제공하여 실력에 따라 듣기 속도를 다르게 하여 학습할 수 있습니다.

미니 어휘 암기장

모의고사에 나온 단어와 표현을 정리한 휴대용 미니 암기장으로 언제 어디서든 학습이 가능합니다.

Contents
목차

실전 모의고사

1 다음을 듣고, 'this'가 가리키는 것으로 가장 적절한 것을 고르시오.

2 대화를 듣고, 남자가 구입한 필통으로 가장 적절한 것을 고르시오.

3 다음을 듣고, 내일 부산의 날씨로 가장 적절한 것을 고르시오.

4 대화를 듣고, 남자의 마지막 말의 의도로 가장 적절한 것을 고르시오.
① 사과   ② 거절   ③ 조언
④ 동의   ⑤ 축하

5 다음을 듣고, 여자가 여름 방학 계획에 대해 언급하지 **않은** 것을 고르시오.
① 백제 문화제 방문하기
② 맛있는 음식 먹기
③ 독서하기
④ 영어 일기 쓰기
⑤ 자원봉사 하기

6 대화를 듣고, 남자가 학교에 도착한 시각을 고르시오.
① 9:00 a.m.   ② 9:15 a.m.
③ 9:50 a.m.   ④ 9:00 p.m.
⑤ 9:15 p.m.

7 대화를 듣고, 여자의 장래 희망으로 가장 적절한 것을 고르시오.
① 군인   ② 화가   ③ 조종사
④ 승무원   ⑤ 과학자

8 대화를 듣고, 남자의 심정으로 가장 적절한 것을 고르시오.
① calm   ② afraid   ③ painful
④ excited   ⑤ disappointed

9 대화를 듣고, 여자가 대화 직후에 할 일로 가장 적절한 것을 고르시오.
① 식물 심기
② 미용실 가기
③ 식당 예약하기
④ 저녁 준비하기
⑤ 식료품 구입하기

10 대화를 듣고, 무엇에 관한 내용인지 가장 적절한 것을 고르시오.
① 반장 선거   ② 공개 수업   ③ 환경 미화
④ 보트 구매   ⑤ 영화 관람

11 대화를 듣고, 두 사람이 함께 이용할 교통수단으로 가장 적절한 것을 고르시오.
① 택시   ② 버스   ③ 자동차
④ 지하철   ⑤ 비행기

12 대화를 듣고, 남자가 여자에게 전화한 이유로 가장 적절한 것을 고르시오.
① 사업을 시작하려고
② 숙박을 예약하려고
③ 예약을 취소하려고
④ 여행 일정을 확인하려고
⑤ 출장 날짜를 변경하려고

13 대화를 듣고, 두 사람이 대화하는 장소로 가장 적절한 곳을 고르시오.
① 은행   ② 병원   ③ 학교
④ 백화점   ⑤ 관공서

14 대화를 듣고, 여자가 찾고 있는 영화표의 위치로 가장 적절한 곳을 고르시오.

15 대화를 듣고, 여자가 남자에게 요청한 일로 가장 적절한 것을 고르시오.
① 배운 거 복습하기
② 다른 사람 도와주기
③ 반복해서 문제 풀기
④ 스터디 그룹 만들기
⑤ 방과 후 학원 다니기

16 대화를 듣고, 여자가 남자에게 제안한 것으로 가장 적절한 것을 고르시오.
① 독서하기
② 테니스 치기
③ 주차 연습하기
④ 공원 산책하기
⑤ 라켓 수리하기

17 대화를 듣고, 남자가 지난겨울에 한 일로 가장 적절한 것을 고르시오.
① 스키 타기   ② 캐나다 방문
③ 친척 만나기   ④ 그림 그리기
⑤ 사진 배우기

18 대화를 듣고, 여자의 직업으로 가장 적절한 것을 고르시오.
① 의사   ② 소방관   ③ 선생님
④ 경찰관   ⑤ 운동선수

[19-20] 대화를 듣고, 여자의 마지막 말에 이어질 남자의 응답으로 가장 적절한 것을 고르시오.

19 Man: _____
① You can buy a new one.
② Your mom must be angry.
③ I have the same experience.
④ My mobile phone is working well.
⑤ Mobile phones are useful in many ways.

20 Man: _____
① Don't be late tomorrow.
② Take this pill three times a day.
③ Okay, take care of yourself at home.
④ Cheer up! You can do better next time.
⑤ Sorry, but you should finish your homework.

Listen and Check

대화를 다시 듣고, 알맞은 것을 고르시오.

1 This helps you sink into the water.
- [ ] True
- [ ] False

2 What kind of shape does he want for his pencil case?
- [ ] a heart shape
- [ ] a bear shape

3 Will it rain in Seoul tomorrow?
- [ ] Yes
- [ ] No

4 The sky looks gray because of the fine dust.
- [ ] True
- [ ] False

5 What will she do during summer vacation?
- [ ] volunteer work
- [ ] overseas trip

6 He arrived at school at 9:50 a.m.
- [ ] True
- [ ] False

7 What does she want to be?
- [ ] a painter
- [ ] a pilot

8 He saw his favorite idol group by chance.
- [ ] True
- [ ] False

9 What will they buy for dinner?
- [ ] meat
- [ ] vegetables

10 Does he tell her who he'll vote for?
- [ ] Yes
- [ ] No

11 He doesn't care about driving on a busy street.
- [ ] True
- [ ] False

12 Why does he have to cancel the reservation?
- [ ] a business trip
- [ ] a family event

13 He went to school to open an account.
- [ ] True
- [ ] False

14 Where are they now?
- [ ] in a restaurant
- [ ] in a theater

15 Did she review her notes after school?
- [ ] Yes
- [ ] No

16 What will they play after this dialogue?
- [ ] tennis
- [ ] badminton

17 Where did she go last winter?
- [ ] Canada
- [ ] Jeju Island

18 Why did she run into the fire?
- [ ] to save the man
- [ ] to pick up a wallet

19 Did she lose her mobile phone?
- [ ] Yes
- [ ] No

20 She wants to go home to get some rest.
- [ ] True
- [ ] False

1 다음을 듣고, 'this'가 가리키는 것으로 가장 적절한 것을 고르시오.

① ② ③

④ ⑤

1

M This looks like a _____. This is often _____ when you play in the water. This helps you _____ _____ on the water. What is this?

2 대화를 듣고, 남자가 구입한 필통으로 가장 적절한 것을 고르시오.

① ② ③

④ ⑤

2

W _____ _____ _____ _____ for you?
M ♥I'd like to buy a pencil case.
W Look at this one _____ a _____ _____. This is _____ with students.
M Sorry, but I want a _____ _____ _____.
W A bear? Okay, here you are.

> ♥ **I'd like to + v**
> : 어떤 것을 하고 싶을 때 쓰는 표현으로, '～하고 싶다'라는 뜻이다.
> = I want to + v
> = I'd love to + v

3 다음을 듣고, 내일 부산의 날씨로 가장 적절한 것을 고르시오.

① ② ③

④ ⑤

3

W Good morning. This is the _____ _____ for tomorrow. Seoul will be _____ _____ _____, so you can enjoy _____ _____. The wind will blow hard in Jeonju. Busan will be cloudy but get no rain. Jeju will be warm and sunny.

4 대화를 듣고, 남자의 마지막 말의 의도로 가장 적절한 것을 고르시오.
① 사과　② 거절　③ 조언
④ 동의　⑤ 축하

> ♥ **What's the matter?**
> : 구체적인 원인이 무엇인지 궁금할 때 쓰는 표현으로, '무슨 일이니?'라는 뜻이다.
> = What's wrong?

4 🇬🇧

W Oh, my! _____ _____ the sky.
M It's gray. ♥What's the matter?
W I think smog is _____ the whole sky.
M Right. But there is smog because of the fine dust, too.
W We have to do something to make a clear sky.
M I _____ _____ _____.

언급 유무 파악

5 다음을 듣고, 여자가 여름 방학 계획에 대해 언급하지 **않은** 것을 고르시오.

① 백제 문화제 방문하기
② 맛있는 음식 먹기
③ 독서하기
④ 영어 일기 쓰기
⑤ 자원봉사 하기

5

W Let me _____ _____ _____ my plans for *this summer vacation. I'll go to Gongju to visit the Baekje Cultural Festival on the first day. On the second day, I want to eat lots of delicious food and read English books. Last, I'll _____ _____ _____ at a nursing home.

*this summer [디스] [써머] → [디써머]

숫자 정보 파악

6 대화를 듣고, 남자가 학교에 도착한 시각을 고르시오.

① 9:00 a.m.
② 9:15 a.m.
③ 9:50 a.m.
④ 9:00 p.m.
⑤ 9:15 p.m.

6

W David, why do you _____ _____ _____?
M I was scolded by my homeroom teacher.
W What happened?
M I was _____ _____ _____. It starts at 9:00 every morning.
W Then what time did you _____?
M I arrived at 9:15 in the morning.

장래 희망 파악

7 대화를 듣고, 여자의 장래 희망으로 가장 적절한 것을 고르시오.

① 군인　　② 화가
③ 조종사　　④ 승무원
⑤ 과학자

7

M Susie, what are you _____?
W I'm drawing a blue sky and planes.
M How nice! _____ _____ _____ the reason?
W I love airplanes. I'd like to learn how to fly a plane someday.
M Do you want to _____ _____ _____ in the future?
W Of course. _____ _____ I study hard.

심정 추론

8 대화를 듣고, 남자의 심정으로 가장 적절한 것을 고르시오.

① calm　　② afraid
③ painful　　④ excited
⑤ disappointed

♥ **No way!**
: 어떤 것을 믿을 수 없거나 강한 부정을 하고 싶을 때 쓰는 표현으로, '말도 안 돼'라는 뜻이다.
= That's impossible.
= I can't believe it.

8 🇬🇧

W Dongjin, _____ _____ here.
M Eunmi, _____ _____ _____ _____ _____ on the way here.
W I have no idea. Just tell me.
M BTS! My _____ idol group!
W ♥No way! I can't believe it.
M It's true. Look at these autographs.

할 일 파악

9 대화를 듣고, 여자가 대화 직후에 할 일로 가장 적절한 것을 고르시오.

① 식물 심기
② 미용실 가기
③ 식당 예약하기
④ 저녁 준비하기
⑤ 식료품 구입하기

9

M Mom, _____ _____ _____ a hair salon together.

W A hair salon?

M Yes, I want to get my hair cut shorter.

W That's a good idea. But I need to _____ _____ _____ for dinner.

M Okay. Then let's go _____ _____ first.

W Thank you for understanding.

화제·주제 파악

10 대화를 듣고, 무엇에 관한 내용인지 가장 적절한 것을 고르시오.

① 반장 선거
② 공개 수업
③ 환경 미화
④ 보트 구매
⑤ 영화 관람

10

M Today is _____ _____ for _____ _____.

W I know. I *haven't decided who I will _____ _____.

M I think Seongho is the _____ _____.

W Don't tell me. It's a secret election system.

M Sorry. I forgot.

W People should vote secretly in every election.

*haven't decided [헤븐트] [디사이디드] → [헤븐디사이디드]

교통수단 파악

11 대화를 듣고, 두 사람이 함께 이용할 교통수단으로 가장 적절한 것을 고르시오.

① 택시
② 버스
③ 자동차
④ 지하철
⑤ 비행기

♥ **You're right.**
: 상대방의 의견에 동의할 때 쓰는 표현으로, '네 말이 맞아.'라는 뜻이다.
= That's right.
= That's correct.

11 🇬🇧

M _____ _____ _____ _____ to Grandma's house this Friday?

W We can take the subway. It'll take forty minutes.

M Wait! We have to carry _____ _____ _____ baggage there.

W ♥You're right. I think driving your car is the only way.

M [*Sigh*] I hate driving on _____ streets. But all right.

이유 추론

12 대화를 듣고, 남자가 여자에게 전화한
이유로 가장 적절한 것을 고르시오.
① 사업을 시작하려고
② 숙박을 예약하려고
③ 예약을 취소하려고
④ 여행 일정을 확인하려고
⑤ 출장 날짜를 변경하려고

12

[*Telephone rings.*]

M　Hello. May I _____ _____ the manager?

W　This is she speaking. _____ _____ _____
　　_____ for you?

M　I reserved two double rooms yesterday, but I have to
　　_____ my reservation.

W　Can I ask you why?

M　I have to _____ _____ _____ _____
　　_____ on the same day.

W　Ah, I got it. I'll help you to cancel your reservation.

장소 추론

13 대화를 듣고, 두 사람이 대화하는 장소로
가장 적절한 곳을 고르시오.
① 은행
② 병원
③ 학교
④ 백화점
⑤ 관공서

13 🇬🇧

W　Good afternoon. _____ _____ _____
　　_____?

M　Yes, please. I want to open an account.

W　Okay. Could you fill out this form?

M　Sure. I'd also like to _____ _____ _____
　　into my account.

W　_____ _____ do you want to deposit?

M　Fifty thousand won, please.

그림 정보 파악

14 대화를 듣고, 여자가 찾고 있는 영화표의
위치로 가장 적절한 곳을 고르시오.

14

M　It was the best pizza in the world.

W　Totally! _____ _____ _____ _____ a
　　movie now. [*Pause*] Where are the movie tickets?

M　Did you _____ _____ on the counter?

W　No, I ★carried them to the table.

M　I can't see any tickets on the table.

W　Oh, I found them. They are _____ _____
　　_____.

★carried them [캐리드] [뎀] → [캐리뎀]

요청한 것 파악

15 대화를 듣고, 여자가 남자에게 요청한 일로 가장 적절한 것을 고르시오.

① 배운 거 복습하기
② 다른 사람 도와주기
③ 반복해서 문제 풀기
④ 스터디 그룹 만들기
⑤ 방과 후 학원 다니기

♥ **Why don't we + v ~?**
: 어떤 것을 함께 하자고 제안할 때 쓰는 표현으로, '~는 어때?'라는 뜻이다.
= How about + -ing?
= Let's + v

15

W I think this problem is _____ _____ _____.

M Did you _____ your notes after school?

W No, I didn't.

M You should review them. You can't remember something forever.

W ♥Why don't we make a study group together?

M That's a _____. It will help.

제안한 것 파악

16 대화를 듣고, 여자가 남자에게 제안한 것으로 가장 적절한 것을 고르시오.

① 독서하기
② 테니스 치기
③ 주차 연습하기
④ 공원 산책하기
⑤ 라켓 수리하기

16

W I feel bored. Is there _____ _____ to do?

M Why don't you read a book?

W I prefer outdoor activities.

M Then let's _____ _____ _____ in the park.

W Maybe *next time. How about _____ _____?

M Sure, I'll bring my tennis rackets.

*next time [넥스트] [타임] → [넥스타임]

한 일 파악

17 대화를 듣고, 남자가 지난겨울에 한 일로 가장 적절한 것을 고르시오.

① 스키 타기
② 캐나다 방문
③ 친척 만나기
④ 그림 그리기
⑤ 사진 배우기

17 🇬🇧

M Hyewon, what did you do last winter?

W I went to Canada _____ _____ _____ with my family.

M _____ _____ you had fun there.

W I bet. What did you do, Junsu?

M I learned _____ _____ _____ nice pictures on Jeju Island.

W Really? Will you take a picture of me?

직업 추론

18 대화를 듣고, 여자의 직업으로 가장 적절한 것을 고르시오.

① 의사
② 소방관
③ 선생님
④ 경찰관
⑤ 운동선수

18

M Thank you for _____ _____ _____.

W I'm happy to see you safe.

M I can't believe you ran into the fire for me.

W As you know, that's my job.

M You are _____ _____. I want to be a _____ like you.

W It's kind of you to say that.

적절한 응답 찾기

[19~20] 대화를 듣고, 여자의 마지막 말에 이어질 남자의 응답으로 가장 적절한 것을 고르시오.

19 Man: _____

① You can buy a new one.
② Your mom must be angry.
③ I have the same experience.
④ My mobile phone is working well.
⑤ Mobile phones are useful in many ways.

♥ **What do you mean?**
: 이해가 되지 않아 추가적인 설명이 필요할 때 쓰는 표현으로, '무슨 의미니?'라는 뜻이다.
= What exactly is it?
= Can you explain it?

19

M Sohee, you _____ _____ _____. Are you okay?

W My mobile phone is _____.

M How *did that happen?

W While I was running to school, I dropped it.

M Look on the _____ _____.

W ♥What do you mean?

M You can buy a new one.

*did that [디드] [뎃] → [디뎃]

적절한 응답 찾기

20 Man: _____

① Don't be late tomorrow.
② Take this pill three times a day.
③ Okay, take care of yourself at home.
④ Cheer up! You can do better next time.
⑤ Sorry, but you should finish your homework.

20

W Do you _____ _____ _____, sir?

M Sure. _____ _____.

W I have a bad cough and a runny nose.

M Did you _____ _____ _____?

W Yes, I did, but it didn't work.

M So do you want to get some rest at home?

W Yes. I think I should go home.

M Okay, take care of yourself at home.

16

A 들려주는 단어를 듣고 쓴 뒤, 괄호 안에 우리말 뜻을 쓰시오.

	영어	우리말			영어	우리말
1				6		
2				7		
3				8		
4				9		
5				10		

B 다음 문장을 잘 듣고 빈칸에 들어갈 단어를 채우시오.

1 I want to _____ _____ _____.

2 _____, _____ I want a bear on it.

3 I haven't decided who I will _____ _____.

4 Did you _____ _____ on the counter?

5 Yes, I want to get _____ _____ _____ shorter.

6 So do you want to _____ _____ _____ at home?

7 Eunmi, _____ _____ _____ _____ on the way here.

8 I can't believe you _____ _____ the fire for me.

9 While I was running to school, I _____ _____.

10 I'd like to learn _____ _____ _____ a plane someday.

1 다음을 듣고, 'I'가 무엇인지 가장 적절한 것을 고르시오.

①   ②   ③

④   ⑤

2 대화를 듣고, 남자가 구입할 담요로 가장 적절한 것을 고르시오.

①   ②   ③

④   ⑤

3 다음을 듣고, 시카고의 내일 날씨로 가장 적절한 것을 고르시오.

①   ②   ③

④   ⑤

4 대화를 듣고, 여자가 한 마지막 말의 의도로 가장 적절한 것을 고르시오.
① 격려   ② 축하   ③ 항의
④ 찬성   ⑤ 거절

5 다음을 듣고, 여자가 친구에 대해 언급하지 <u>않은</u> 것을 고르시오.
① 고향   ② 나이   ③ 직업
④ 외모   ⑤ 성격

6 대화를 듣고, 두 사람이 만날 시각을 고르시오.
① 4:00 p.m.   ② 4:30 p.m.
③ 5:00 p.m.   ④ 5:30 p.m.
⑤ 6:00 p.m.

7 대화를 듣고, 남자의 장래 희망으로 가장 적절한 것을 고르시오.
① 요리사   ② 간호사   ③ 선생님
④ 미식가   ⑤ 건축가

8 대화를 듣고, 남자의 심정으로 가장 적절한 것을 고르시오.
① tired   ② scared
③ excited   ④ sad
⑤ relieved

9 대화를 듣고, 남자가 대화 직후에 할 일로 가장 적절한 것을 고르시오.
① 책 구입하기
② 샌드위치 만들기
③ 오렌지 주스 사기
④ 가게에서 기다리기
⑤ 공원에서 산책하기

10 대화를 듣고, 무엇에 관한 내용인지 가장 적절한 것을 고르시오.
① 물건 교환   ② 봉사 활동
③ 벼룩시장   ④ 과소비 습관
⑤ 정기 할인 판매

11 대화를 듣고, 남자가 이용할 교통수단으로 가장 적절한
    것을 고르시오.
    ① 택시   ② 버스   ③ 자전거
    ④ 지하철   ⑤ 비행기

12 대화를 듣고, 남자가 여자를 도와줄 수 없는 이유로 가
    장 적절한 것을 고르시오.
    ① 다른 계획이 있어서
    ② 친구를 도와야 해서
    ③ 무대 공포증이 있어서
    ④ 찾아야 할 사람이 있어서
    ⑤ 노래를 잘 부르지 못해서

13 대화를 듣고, 두 사람의 관계로 가장 적절한 것을 고르
    시오.
    ① 선생님 – 학생   ② 승무원 – 승객
    ③ 시청 직원 – 시민   ④ 자동차 판매원 – 고객
    ⑤ 버스 운전기사 – 승객

14 대화를 듣고, 약국의 위치로 가장 적절한 곳을 고르시
    오.

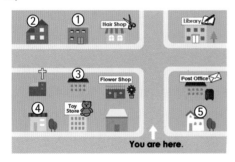

15 대화를 듣고, 남자가 여자에게 부탁한 일로 가장 적절
    한 것을 고르시오.
    ① 여행 갈 짐 꾸리기
    ② 집에 일찍 도착하기
    ③ 근사한 저녁 준비하기
    ④ 공항에서 부모님 모셔오기
    ⑤ 부모님과 즐거운 시간 보내기

16 대화를 듣고, 여자가 남자에게 제안한 것으로 가장 적
    절한 것을 고르시오.
    ① 조용히 하기
    ② 아픔을 견디기
    ③ 윗집 방문하기
    ④ 이웃과 잘 지내기
    ⑤ 일찍 잠자리에 들기

17 대화를 듣고, 두 사람이 구입할 옷을 고르시오.
    ① 셔츠   ② 치마   ③ 조끼
    ④ 바지   ⑤ 스웨터

18 대화를 듣고, 남자의 직업으로 가장 적절한 것을 고르
    시오.
    ① 기자   ② 경찰관
    ③ 사진작가   ④ 호텔 관리자
    ⑤ 관광 안내소 직원

[19-20] 대화를 듣고, 남자의 마지막 말에 이어질 여자의
응답으로 가장 적절한 것을 고르시오.

19 Woman: _____
    ① It opens at 7:00 p.m.
    ② Four times a week.
    ③ I'm heading to a concert.
    ④ Can I taste the garlic pizza?
    ⑤ It's hard to practice every day.

20 Woman: _____
    ① Of course. Be my guest.
    ② I can call a taxi for you.
    ③ You can buy another one.
    ④ Do I have your phone number?
    ⑤ We should go to the service center.

Listen and Check

● 대화를 다시 듣고, 알맞은 것을 고르시오.

1 Because I have two wings, I can fly.
- [ ] True
- [ ] False

2 Which blanket does he choose?
- [ ] the one with stripes
- [ ] the one with little stars

3 How will the weather in Los Angeles be tomorrow?
- [ ] sunny
- [ ] rainy

4 Do the toys belong to her sister?
- [ ] Yes
- [ ] No

5 What is Jessica's hobby?
- [ ] drawing people
- [ ] painting houses

6 They will meet in the shopping mall.
- [ ] True
- [ ] False

7 What is he making for dinner?
- [ ] fried chicken
- [ ] beef stew

8 They saw nothing in the forest.
- [ ] True
- [ ] False

9 What is she expected to buy?
- [ ] sandwiches
- [ ] orange juice

10 He bought a sweater at the flea market.
- [ ] True
- [ ] False

11 Will he ride his bicycle to school today?
- [ ] Yes
- [ ] No

12 They will sing together at the school festival.
- [ ] True
- [ ] False

13 Where does he want to go?
- [ ] City Hall
- [ ] a concert hall

14 Will he go to the flower shop?
- [ ] Yes
- [ ] No

15 She'll prepare a nice dinner.
- [ ] True
- [ ] False

16 What made him stay awake last night?
- [ ] loud noises
- [ ] a visit from friends

17 They decide to buy pants for a baby.
- [ ] True
- [ ] False

18 Is it her second time to visit Korea?
- [ ] Yes
- [ ] No

19 What will he buy at the food market?
- [ ] carrots
- [ ] garlic

20 Where does he think he lost his mobile phone?
- [ ] in a taxi
- [ ] in his room

정답 및 해설 *p.06*

그림 정보 파악

1 다음을 듣고, 'I'가 무엇인지 가장 적절한 것을 고르시오.

① ② ③
④ ⑤

1

W | I have two short _____ and two _____. I cannot fly, but I can swim very well. I have dark skin with a white belly. I also have a strong beak. It helps me to _____ _____. I live both on land and _____ _____ _____. I'm usually found at the South Pole. What am I?

그림 정보 파악

2 대화를 듣고, 남자가 구입할 담요로 가장 적절한 것을 고르시오.

① ② ③
④ ⑤

♥ **How about ~?**
: 어떤 것을 제안할 때 쓰는 표현으로, '~는 어때?'라는 뜻이다.
= What about ~?
= Why don't you ~?

2 🇬🇧

W | Welcome. What can I do for you?
M | I need a blanket for a camping trip.
W | The blanket _____ _____ is a hot item.
M | I don't like stripes. Do you _____ _____ _____?
W | ♥How about this blanket with little stars?
M | It looks nice. I'll _____ it.

그림 정보 파악

3 다음을 듣고, 시카고의 내일 날씨로 가장 적절한 것을 고르시오.

① ② ③
④ ⑤

3

M | Here is the _____ _____ for tomorrow. New York will be _____ _____ _____. Please wear a muffler when you go out. You can expect to see _____ in Chicago. In Los Angeles, it will be sunny and warm. It will be a perfect day _____ _____. However, there will be strong winds and heavy rain in Seattle.

의도 파악

4 대화를 듣고, 여자가 한 마지막 말의 의도로 가장 적절한 것을 고르시오.

① 격려 ② 축하 ③ 항의
④ 찬성 ⑤ 거절

4

M | _____ _____ _____ your sister.
W | I'm sorry, Dad. But she keeps taking my toys.
M | Your sister is _____ _____ than toys.
W | Those are my favorites!
M | You are an older sister. Just _____ _____ to her.
W | That's _____.

언급 유무 파악

5 다음을 듣고, 여자가 친구에 대해 언급하지 않은 것을 고르시오.

① 고향　　　　② 나이
③ 직업　　　　④ 외모
⑤ 성격

---

5 🇬🇧

W　I want to _____ my friend Jessica. She _____ _____ Canada and is here with her family. She is 14 years old, and she is a student _____ _____. Her _____ is drawing people on the street. She is quiet and shy but polite to people.

숫자 정보 파악

6 대화를 듣고, 두 사람이 만날 시각을 고르시오.

① 4:00 p.m.　　② 4:30 p.m.
③ 5:00 p.m.　　④ 5:30 p.m.
⑤ 6:00 p.m.

> ♥ **Do you mind if I~?**
> : 상대방에게 허락을 구할 때 쓰는 표현으로, '~하면 신경 쓰이니?'라는 뜻이다.
> = May/Can I ~?
> = Is it all right if I ~?

6

[*Telephone rings.*]

W　Do you know _____ is Mom's birthday?

M　Of course. I _____ _____ my allowance for it.

W　Good job. Meet me at 4:00 p.m. in the shopping mall.

M　♥Do you mind if I arrive there 30 _____ _____? I'm still home.

W　Okay. Then let's _____ _____ 4:30.

M　See you soon.

장래 희망 파악

7 대화를 듣고, 남자의 장래 희망으로 가장 적절한 것을 고르시오.

① 요리사　　　② 간호사
③ 선생님　　　④ 미식가
⑤ 건축가

7

W　_____ _____. What are you doing, Mike?

M　I'm making beef stew for dinner.

W　Beef stew? _____ _____ _____?

M　Sure! Mom, want to _____ _____?

W　It's so delicious! You could sell this at a restaurant.

M　That's my dream. Someday, I want to open my own restaurant.

W　You will become an amazing cook.

심정 추론

8 대화를 듣고, 남자의 심정으로 가장 적절한 것을 고르시오.

① tired　　　　② scared
③ excited　　　④ sad
⑤ relieved

> ♥ **I totally agree with you.**
> : 상대방의 의견에 동의할 때 쓰는 표현으로, '난 너에게 완전히 동의해.'라는 뜻이다.
> = I think so.
> = Same here.

8

M　It's _____ _____ here. I can see almost nothing.

W　The sun is going down. We should hurry.

M　♥I totally agree with you. Or we might _____ _____ in the forest.

W　Wait! I saw _____ _____ in the tree.

M　*Is it a ghost? Run! We should get out of here.

*Is it [이즈] [잇] → [이짓]

할 일 파악

9 대화를 듣고, 남자가 대화 직후에 할 일로 가장 적절한 것을 고르시오.

① 책 구입하기
② 샌드위치 만들기
③ 오렌지 주스 사기
④ 가게에서 기다리기
⑤ 공원에서 산책하기

9 🏴

W It's perfect weather for _____ _____ _____.

M Right. But I think I'm hungry.

W Me, too. I need something to eat.

M There's a sandwich shop _____ _____ _____.

W I'll go there and buy two sandwiches for us.

M Okay. Should I _____ _____ _____ here?

W Hmm... What about buying some orange juice?

M That's a good idea.

화제·주제 파악

10 대화를 듣고, 무엇에 관한 내용인지 가장 적절한 것을 고르시오.

① 물건 교환
② 봉사 활동
③ 벼룩시장
④ 과소비 습관
⑤ 정기 할인 판매

10

W Look at this sweater. I *bought this for only ten dollars.

M It _____ _____ _____ you. Where did you get it?

W At the flea market.

M That place is amazing. We can buy nice things _____ _____ _____.

W We can also sell our unwanted stuff.

M I should go there this Saturday.

*bought this [보우트] [디스] → [보웃디스]

교통수단 파악

11 대화를 듣고, 남자가 이용할 교통수단으로 가장 적절한 것을 고르시오.

① 택시
② 버스
③ 자전거
④ 지하철
⑤ 비행기

11

M Oh, no! My alarm clock didn't go off.

W _____ _____, or you will be _____ _____ _____.

M Mom, where is my bicycle helmet?

W Honey, it's _____ to ride your bike when you are nervous.

M I agree. I should call a taxi.

이유 추론

12 대화를 듣고, 남자가 여자를 도와줄 수 없는 이유로 가장 적절한 것을 고르시오.

① 다른 계획이 있어서
② 친구를 도와야 해서
③ 무대 공포증이 있어서
④ 찾아야 할 사람이 있어서
⑤ 노래를 잘 부르지 못해서

♥ **I am sorry. I can't.**

: 상대방의 의견이나 제안을 거절할 때 쓰는 표현으로, '미안해. 나는 못할 것 같아.'라는 뜻이다.
= I'm afraid that I can't.
= Thank you, but I can't.

12

W Justin, can you _____ _____ _____ at the school festival?

M Thanks for asking me. But ♥I'm sorry. I can't.

W Do you have other plans?

M No. In fact, I'm _____ _____ being on stage.

W Oh, I didn't know that.

M Sorry, but I can help you _____ _____.

W Can you? I'm _____ _____ _____ that.

관계 추론

13 대화를 듣고, 두 사람의 관계로 가장 적절한 것을 고르시오.

① 선생님 – 학생
② 승무원 – 승객
③ 시청 직원 – 시민
④ 자동차 판매원 – 고객
⑤ 버스 운전기사 – 승객

♥ **Don't worry.**

: 낙담하고 있는 상대방을 격려하기 위해서 쓰는 표현으로, '걱정하지 마.'라는 뜻이다.
= Cheer up!
= Don't be disappointed.

13

M Excuse me. Does this bus go to City Hall?

W Yes. Please _____ _____ the bus.

M _____ _____ _____ is it to City Hall?

W It is five stops.

M Can I _____ _____ at the right stop?

W ♥Don't worry. I'll let you know when to get off.

M Thank you. I'm a stranger here.

그림 정보 파악

14 대화를 듣고, 약국의 위치로 가장 적절한 곳을 고르시오.

14

W Yejun, what's wrong with your leg? It's bleeding.

M I _____ _____ the stairs.

W Tell me where a drugstore is. I'll go there to get some medicine.

M Go straight one block and turn left.

W And then?

M It'll be _____ _____ _____ between the church and the flower shop.

W Okay. I *got it.

M Thank you very much.

*got it [가트] [잇] → [가릿]

부탁한 것 파악

15 대화를 듣고, 남자가 여자에게 부탁한 일로
가장 적절한 것을 고르시오.

① 여행 갈 짐 꾸리기
② 집에 일찍 도착하기
③ 근사한 저녁 준비하기
④ 공항에서 부모님 모셔오기
⑤ 부모님과 즐거운 시간 보내기

15

M Hyeonseo, do you have any plans for today?

W Not really. Is there anything I can _____ _____ you?

M I need you to _____ _____ my parents at the airport.

W No problem. _____ _____ should I arrive at the airport?

M By 4 o'clock. I'll _____ a nice dinner.

W Okay. I'll come back _____ _____ _____.

제안한 것 파악

16 대화를 듣고, 여자가 남자에게 제안한
것으로 가장 적절한 것을 고르시오.

① 조용히 하기
② 아픔을 견디기
③ 윗집 방문하기
④ 이웃과 잘 지내기
⑤ 일찍 잠자리에 들기

16

M I couldn't sleep at night. I lay in bed for hours _____ _____.

W What was the reason?

M Loud noises were coming from upstairs _____ _____ _____.

W That's terrible. Why don't you visit your _____ neighbors?

M I think that's a good idea.

W Yeah. They *need to _____ _____ your pain.

*need to [니드] [투] → [니투]

특정 정보 파악

17 대화를 듣고, 두 사람이 구입할 옷을
고르시오.

① 셔츠
② 치마
③ 조끼
④ 바지
⑤ 스웨터

17

M Did you hear our English teacher _____ _____ _____ last week?

W Of course. I saw _____ _____ _____ her baby. She's so cute.

M How about buying some clothes for the baby?

W Nice. I think this yellow skirt looks _____ _____.

M But pants are _____ _____ a skirt for a baby.

W You're right. Babies need to be warm.

18 대화를 듣고, 남자의 직업으로 가장 적절한 것을 고르시오.

① 기자
② 경찰관
③ 사진작가
④ 호텔 관리자
⑤ 관광 안내소 직원

♥ **How may I help you?**
: 상대방에게 도움을 주려고 먼저 물어볼 때 쓰는 표현으로, '어떻게 도와 드릴까요?'라는 뜻이다.

18

M Welcome. ♥How may I help you?

W Hello. This is my first time _____ _____ _____.

M Then here's a _____ _____ nearby hotels and restaurants.

W It _____ _____.

M You also need this subway map. It's for tourists.

W You are so kind. Thank you very much.

M When you need help, _____ _____ to *contact us.

★contact us [컨텍트] [어스] → [컨텍터스]

적절한 응답 찾기

[19~20] 대화를 듣고, 남자의 마지막 말에 이어질 여자의 응답으로 가장 적절한 것을 고르시오.

19 Woman: _____

① It opens at 7:00 p.m.
② Four times a week.
③ I'm heading to a concert.
④ Can I taste the garlic pizza?
⑤ It's hard to practice every day.

19 🇬🇧

W Jaeyoung, _____ _____ _____ _____ _____?

M I'm going to a food market to buy some garlic and onions. And you?

W I'm going to the music hall.

M For what?

W I have to _____ _____ the violin.

M _____ _____ do you practice?

W Four times a week.

적절한 응답 찾기

20 Woman: _____

① Of course. Be my guest.
② I can call a taxi for you.
③ You can buy another one.
④ Do I have your phone number?
⑤ We should go to the service center.

20

W You have _____ _____ _____. What's the matter with you?

M I _____ my mobile phone. I bought it yesterday.

W Oh, my! Where did you put it?

M I'm not sure, but I think I _____ _____ in a taxi.

W _____ don't you _____ _____ _____ phone number?

M Good idea. Can I use your mobile phone?

W Of course. Be my guest.

정답 및 해설 *p.11*

A 들려주는 단어를 듣고 쓴 뒤, 괄호 안에 우리말 뜻을 쓰시오.

	영어	우리말		영어	우리말
1			6		
2			7		
3			8		
4			9		
5			10		

B 다음 문장을 잘 듣고 빈칸에 들어갈 단어를 채우시오.

1 It _____ _____ _____ you.

2 I live both _____ _____ and _____ _____ _____.

3 Or we might _____ _____ _____ the forest.

4 In fact, I'm _____ _____ being on stage.

5 This is _____ _____ _____ to visit Korea.

6 Your sister is _____ _____ than toys.

7 How about this _____ _____ _____ _____?

8 _____ _____ _____ I arrive at the airport?

9 Why don't you visit your _____ _____?

10 Honey, it's _____ _____ _____ your bike when you are nervous.

1 다음을 듣고, 'this'가 가리키는 것으로 가장 적절한 것을 고르시오.

①   ②   ③

④   ⑤

2 대화를 듣고, 여자가 사려는 공책으로 가장 적절한 것을 고르시오.

①   ②   ③

④   ⑤

3 다음을 듣고, 수요일 날씨로 가장 적절한 것을 고르시오.

①   ②   ③

④   ⑤

4 대화를 듣고, 여자의 마지막 말의 의도로 가장 적절한 것을 고르시오.
① 충고 ② 위로 ③ 거절
④ 제안 ⑤ 축하

5 다음을 듣고, 여자가 불꽃 축제에 대해 언급하지 않은 것을 고르시오.
① 축제 목적 ② 축제 장소
③ 축제 시간 ④ 축제 규칙
⑤ 축제 준비물

6 대화를 듣고, 두 사람이 운동할 시각을 고르시오.
① 5:00 ② 5:30
③ 6:00 ④ 6:30
⑤ 7:00

7 대화를 듣고, 여자의 장래 희망으로 가장 적절한 것을 고르시오.
① 카페 주인 ② 회사 경영인
③ 쇼콜라티에 ④ 학원 선생님
⑤ 커피 원두 감별사

8 대화를 듣고, 남자의 심정으로 가장 적절한 것을 고르시오.
① lonely ② nervous
③ scared ④ annoyed
⑤ depressed

9 대화를 듣고, 여자가 대화 직후에 할 일로 가장 적절한 것을 고르시오.
① 요리하기 ② 손님 초대하기
③ 슈퍼마켓 가기 ④ 친구 만나러 가기
⑤ 새집으로 이사하기

10 대화를 듣고, 무엇에 관한 내용인지 가장 적절한 것을 고르시오.
① 표시의 중요성 ② 야생 동물 보호
③ 동물 카페 ④ 동물 보호 단체
⑤ 동물권 캠페인

11 대화를 듣고, 두 사람이 함께 이용할 교통수단으로 가장 적절한 것을 고르시오.
① 택시   ② 버스   ③ 지하철
④ 비행기   ⑤ 유람선

12 대화를 듣고, 남자가 여자를 위로하는 이유로 가장 적절한 것을 고르시오.
① 시험 성적으로 낙담하고 있기 때문에
② 연설에 대해 두려움을 느끼기 때문에
③ 사람들을 돕지 못해 슬퍼하기 때문에
④ 사람들의 부정적인 시선이 두렵기 때문에
⑤ 친구의 부탁을 거절한 것이 미안하기 때문에

13 대화를 듣고, 두 사람이 대화하는 장소로 가장 적절한 곳을 고르시오.
① 카페   ② 언덕   ③ 기차
④ 학교   ⑤ 공원

14 대화를 듣고, 여자가 찾고 있는 책의 위치로 가장 적절한 곳을 고르시오.

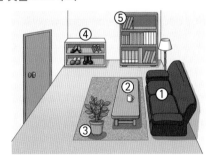

15 대화를 듣고, 남자가 여자에게 부탁한 일로 가장 적절한 것을 고르시오.
① 그림 가르쳐 주기
② 동물 가면 색칠해 주기
③ 미술 수업 함께 듣기
④ 동물 가면 그려 주기
⑤ 함께 취미 활동 하기

16 대화를 듣고, 여자가 남자에게 제안한 것으로 가장 적절한 것을 고르시오.
① 숙제 제출하기
② 각자 정보 찾기
③ 관련 영화 보기
④ 도서관에 가기
⑤ 오늘 밤까지 숙제 끝내기

17 대화를 듣고, 여자가 어제 한 일로 가장 적절한 것을 고르시오.
① 약국에 가기   ② 휴식 취하기
③ 의사 진료 받기   ④ 두통약 먹기
⑤ 두통의 원인 검색하기

18 대화를 듣고, 여자의 직업으로 가장 적절한 것을 고르시오.
① 목수   ② 건축가
③ 삽화가   ④ 페인트 코디네이터
⑤ 인테리어 디자이너

[19-20] 대화를 듣고, 남자의 마지막 말에 이어질 여자의 응답으로 가장 적절한 것을 고르시오.

19 Woman: _____
① I visited them last Saturday.
② I usually talk about my school life.
③ My grandparents love me so much.
④ I suggest you call them more often.
⑤ Making a call feels harder than texting.

20 Woman: _____
① I know time is gold.
② I'm leaving at 9:00 a.m.
③ Sorry, but I can't tell you that.
④ Skiing is my favorite winter sport.
⑤ You can call me tomorrow morning.

Listen and Check

● 대화를 다시 듣고, 알맞은 것을 고르시오.

1 People buy this for different purposes.
☐ True   ☐ False

2 The woman prefers a plain notebook.
☐ True   ☐ False

3 Will the weather be better on Thursday?
☐ Yes   ☐ No

4 What is their plan for the first day?
☐ to go sightseeing   ☐ to go shopping

5 The fireworks festival takes place every month.
☐ True   ☐ False

6 Why do they meet at 7:00?
☐ to have dinner   ☐ to exercise

7 Does the woman manage the café now?
☐ Yes   ☐ No

8 They feel scared about advanced robots.
☐ True   ☐ False

9 Why did the woman invite the man to her house?
☐ to clean the house   ☐ to have dinner

10 Does the man support protecting animals?
☐ Yes   ☐ No

11 What makes them take the subway?
☐ the low subway fare   ☐ the heavy traffic

12 The woman feels nervous about making a speech.
☐ True   ☐ False

13 Do they like to go up to the top of the hill?
☐ Yes   ☐ No

14 Where did the woman put the book last?
☐ on the table   ☐ next to the door

15 The man is talented at drawing pictures.
☐ True   ☐ False

16 Did they decide to search separately?
☐ Yes   ☐ No

17 The man will take the woman to a hospital.
☐ True   ☐ False

18 What interior style does the man want?
☐ luxurious   ☐ simple

19 Does the woman call her grandparents often?
☐ Yes   ☐ No

20 The woman plans to go skiing.
☐ True   ☐ False

그림 정보 파악

1 다음을 듣고, 'this'가 가리키는 것으로 가장 적절한 것을 고르시오.

① ② ③
④ ⑤

1 🇬🇧

M People buy this to _____ special days. They can express their true mind with this. There are various _____ _____ _____ of this. Sometimes people use this to _____ their houses. This _____ really _____. This makes people happy and relaxed.

그림 정보 파악

2 대화를 듣고, 여자가 사려는 공책으로 가장 적절한 것을 고르시오.

① ② ③
④ ⑤

2

W Jack, _____ _____ _____ looks pretty?
M I like the one with some space to _____ _____ _____ on the notebook.
W Okay. That will be better.
M Which one do you want to buy?
W I want to have one _____ _____ _____ on it. I'll buy this one with the _____.

그림 정보 파악

3 다음을 듣고, 수요일 날씨로 가장 적절한 것을 고르시오.

① ② ③
④ ⑤

3 🇬🇧

M Good evening. This is the _____ _____ for the next week. It will be windy on Monday. From Tuesday to Thursday, there may be _____ _____ _____. On Friday, the weather will _____ _____. On the weekend, it will be sunny. You can _____ the warm sunshine and go out with your loved ones.

의도 파악

4 대화를 듣고, 여자의 마지막 말의 의도로 가장 적절한 것을 고르시오.
① 충고   ② 위로   ③ 거절
④ 제안   ⑤ 축하

4

W Honey, will it be 6 o'clock in the morning when _____ _____ _____ Beijing?
M Yes, that's right. We may be tired because we have to _____ _____ the airport in the early morning.
W What is our schedule for the _____ _____ in Beijing?
M We are going sightseeing in the city.
W Then why don't we get some sleep before we start the tour in Beijing?

언급 유무 파악

5 다음을 듣고, 여자가 불꽃 축제에 대해 언급하지 <u>않은</u> 것을 고르시오.

① 축제 목적　　② 축제 장소
③ 축제 시간　　④ 축제 규칙
⑤ 축제 준비물

5

W　The fireworks festival *is a _____ yearly _____.
This festival is to _____ New Year's Day. It takes place in
Sunset Park at 11:55 p.m. You can see the beautiful fireworks
for five minutes. You can come and enjoy the festival, but you
should _____ _____ _____ _____
_____.

*is a [이즈] [어] → [이저]

숫자 정보 파악

6 대화를 듣고, 두 사람이 운동할 시각을 고르시오.

① 5:00　　② 5:30　　③ 6:00
④ 6:30　　⑤ 7:00

♥ **What about -ing ?**
: 상대방에게 무언가를 할 것을 권하거나 제안할 때 쓰는 표현으로, '~하는 건 어때?'라는 뜻이다.
= How about -ing?

6

W　Nathan, did you _____ _____ what to do for
exercise?

M　♥What about going to _____ _____ _____?

W　I *like it. Should we go at 6:30?

M　But my work _____ _____ 5:30.

W　Then how about _____ at 7:00?

M　Great! Let's do our best!

*like it [라이크] [잇] → [라이킷]

장래 희망 파악

7 대화를 듣고, 여자의 장래 희망으로 가장 적절한 것을 고르시오.

① 카페 주인
② 회사 경영인
③ 쇼콜라티에
④ 학원 선생님
⑤ 커피 원두 감별사

7

M　What do you want to drink, Jenny?

W　I want to drink a cup of café latte.

M　You _____ _____ _____.

W　I really love coffee. I'm going to a coffee academy now.

M　That's awesome!

W　I hope to _____ _____ _____ _____
someday.

M　I believe you can do it.

심정 추론

8 대화를 듣고, 남자의 심정으로 가장 적절한 것을 고르시오.

① lonely　　② nervous
③ scared　　④ annoyed
⑤ depressed

♥ **I agree with you.**
: 상대방의 의견에 동의를 나타내는 표현으로, '당신의 의견에 동의해요.'라는 뜻이다.
= You can say that again.

8

W　Mark, I saw a jumping _____ on the Internet.

M　Really? How is that possible?

W　I think robots will _____ _____ _____
humans in the near future.

M　I can't believe it! That's _____ _____ _____.

W　♥I agree with you.

9 대화를 듣고, 여자가 대화 직후에 할 일로 가장 적절한 것을 고르시오.

① 요리하기
② 손님 초대하기
③ 슈퍼마켓 가기
④ 친구 만나러 가기
⑤ 새집으로 이사하기

💜 **All right.**

: 상대방의 말을 받아들일 때 사용하는 표현으로, '좋아요.', '괜찮아요.', '알겠어요.'라는 뜻이다.
= Okay.
= I'm fine with that.

9

M   Amy, should I _____ _____ your house _____ at 7:00?

W   Yes! I need to clean this new house before you come here.

M   Isn't it hard for you to _____ _____ _____?

W   Not at all. I think I have to go to the supermarket to buy some ingredients first.

M   💜 All right. I'm _____ _____ _____ dinner!

W   Okay. See you later!

---

10 대화를 듣고, 무엇에 관한 내용인지 가장 적절한 것을 고르시오.

① 표시의 중요성
② 야생 동물 보호
③ 동물 카페
④ 동물 보호 단체
⑤ 동물권 캠페인

10 🇬🇧

W   Peter, what is _____ _____ _____?

M   I guess it is telling us _____ _____ _____ _____.

W   Why do you think the sign is here?

M   It may be trying to protect the wild animals.

W   What do you think about protecting animals?

M   Well, it's very important because we live together and _____ _____ _____.

W   I think I should *take an interest in _____ _____.

M   That's a good idea!

*take an [테이크] [언] → [테이컨]

---

11 대화를 듣고, 두 사람이 함께 이용할 교통수단으로 가장 적절한 것을 고르시오.

① 택시
② 버스
③ 지하철
④ 비행기
⑤ 유람선

11

M   We should hurry. The play _____ _____ _____ _____.

W   I know. How should we go there?

M   It takes forty minutes by bus, but it takes only fifteen minutes by taxi.

W   It's _____ _____. Traffic must be heavy now.

M   Then what about _____ _____ _____?

W   Yes! That will be _____ _____ _____ a taxi.

M   Let's go!

이유 추론

12 대화를 듣고, 남자가 여자를 위로하는
이유로 가장 적절한 것을 고르시오.

① 시험 성적으로 낙담하고 있기 때문에
② 연설에 대해 두려움을 느끼기 때문에
③ 사람들을 돕지 못해 슬퍼하기 때문에
④ 사람들의 부정적인 시선이 두렵기 때문에
⑤ 친구의 부탁을 거절한 것이 미안하기 때문에

12

W   Johann, I'm _____ _____.

M   Why? What's wrong?

W   I'm making a _____ tomorrow. I don't think I can speak in front of people.

M   _____ _____ _____. I'll help you with it!

W   Thanks, but how?

M   _____ _____ _____ _____ the audience when you practice your speech.

장소 추론

13 대화를 듣고, 두 사람이 대화하는 장소로
가장 적절한 곳을 고르시오.

① 카페
② 언덕
③ 기차
④ 학교
⑤ 공원

13 🇬🇧

M   I really like _____ _____.

W   Like what?

M   I feel so calm when I _____ _____ _____ _____.

W   That's right. I like to feel the wind and to _____ _____ _____.

M   Me, too!

그림 정보 파악

14 대화를 듣고, 여자가 찾고 있는 책의
위치로 가장 적절한 곳을 고르시오.

14

W   Dad, *did you see a book on the table in the living room?

M   No, I didn't. _____ _____ _____ _____ _____ after you studied last night?

W   I remember I put it on this table.

M   Didn't you _____ _____ _____? Think carefully about it.

W   Oh, yes! Now I remember! I placed it on the shoe shelf _____ _____ _____ _____ _____.

M   Take good care of your things.

*did you [디드] [유] → [디쥬]

15 대화를 듣고, 남자가 여자에게 부탁한 일로
가장 적절한 것을 고르시오.

① 그림 가르쳐 주기
② 동물 가면 색칠해 주기
③ 미술 수업 함께 듣기
④ 동물 가면 그려 주기
⑤ 함께 취미 활동 하기

15

M   Maria, can I _____ _____ _____
    _____?

W   Sure. What is it?

M   I have to draw an animal mask, but I am _____
    _____ art.

W   Okay, what do you want me to draw?

M   Please draw me a _____ _____.

W   That _____ _____!

M   Thanks!

16 대화를 듣고, 여자가 남자에게 제안한
것으로 가장 적절한 것을 고르시오.

① 숙제 제출하기
② 각자 정보 찾기
③ 관련 영화 보기
④ 도서관에 가기
⑤ 오늘 밤까지 숙제 끝내기

♥ **How + 형용사!**
: 감탄을 나타낼 때 사용하는 표현으로, '~하
구나!'라는 뜻이다.

16

W   There's too much information _____ _____ _____.

M   Do you think we can finish our homework by tomorrow?

W   I'm not sure. It would be _____ _____ search
    separately and to combine the data we find.

M   ♥How smart!

W   Then I'll _____ _____ more causes of global
    warming.

M   All right. I'll take the effects then.

W   We can _____ _____ _____ _____
    later.

17 대화를 듣고, 여자가 어제 한 일로 가장
적절한 것을 고르시오.

① 약국에 가기
② 휴식 취하기
③ 의사 진료 받기
④ 두통약 먹기
⑤ 두통의 원인 검색하기

17 🇬🇧

M   Lisa, do you _____ _____ _____ _____?

W   Yes. And it's getting worse.

M   I wonder if you should go to _____ _____ _____.

W   I already did yesterday. I'll feel better if I get some rest today.

M   Okay.

정답 및 해설 *p.15*

직업 추론

18 대화를 듣고, 여자의 직업으로 가장 적절한 것을 고르시오.

① 목수
② 건축가
③ 삽화가
④ 페인트 코디네이터
⑤ 인테리어 디자이너

18

W Hi. How can I help you?

M I'd like to _____ _____ _____ to my old house.

W _____ _____ _____ _____ *would you like?

M I want a black and white interior. It looks simple.

W Okay. We can select some furniture for you. It will _____ _____ _____ your house.

M Sounds great! I can't wait to see my new house.

W The interior work will finish soon.

*would you [우드] [유] → [우쥬]

적절한 응답 찾기

[19~20] 대화를 듣고, 남자의 마지막 말에 이어질 여자의 응답으로 가장 적절한 것을 고르시오.

19 Woman: _____

① I visited them last Saturday.
② I usually talk about my school life.
③ My grandparents love me so much.
④ I suggest you call them more often.
⑤ Making a call feels harder than texting.

♥ **What about you?**
: 상대방의 의사를 물어볼 때 사용하는 표현으로, '네 생각은 어때?'라는 뜻이다.
= What do you think?
= How about you?

19

M Linda, _____ _____ do you call your grandparents?

W I call them once a week.

M You _____ _____ very often.

W ♥What about you?

M I call them _____ _____ _____ _____.

W I suggest you call them more often.

적절한 응답 찾기

20 Woman: _____

① I know time is gold.
② I'm leaving at 9:00 a.m.
③ Sorry, but I can't tell you that.
④ Skiing is my favorite winter sport.
⑤ You can call me tomorrow morning.

20

M What are you _____ _____ _____ this Friday?

W I'm planning to _____ _____.

M That sounds fun! Can I join you?

W Sure. _____ _____?

M What time are you leaving that day?

W I'm leaving at 9:00 a.m.

A 들려주는 단어를 듣고 쓴 뒤, 괄호 안에 우리말 뜻을 쓰시오.

	영어	우리말			영어	우리말
1				6		
2				7		
3				8		
4				9		
5				10		

B 다음 문장을 잘 듣고 빈칸에 들어갈 단어를 채우시오.

1 We can put it _____ _____ later.

2 _____ _____ _____ style would you like?

3 Isn't it _____ _____ _____ to cook dinner today?

4 I don't think I can speak _____ _____ _____ people.

5 I want to have one with some patterns _____ _____.

6 The fireworks festival is a popular _____ _____.

7 Nathan, did you think of _____ _____ _____ for exercise?

8 _____ _____ _____ _____ after you studied last night?

9 I think I should _____ _____ _____ _____ animal protection.

10 Robots will _____ _____ actual humans in the near future.

1 다음을 듣고, 'I'가 무엇인지 가장 적절한 것을 고르시오.

①   ②   ③

④   ⑤

2 대화를 듣고, 여자가 구입하려는 컵으로 가장 적절한 것을 고르시오.

①   ②   ③

④   ⑤

3 다음을 듣고, 대구의 날씨로 가장 적절한 것을 고르시오.

①   ②   ③

④   ⑤

4 대화를 듣고, 남자의 마지막 말의 의도로 가장 적절한 것을 고르시오.
① 요청 ② 위로 ③ 축하
④ 동의 ⑤ 거절

5 다음을 듣고, 남자가 방학 일과로 언급하지 <u>않은</u> 것을 고르시오.
① 일어나는 시간
② 친구들과의 만남
③ 아침에 하는 운동
④ 학원에서 듣는 수업
⑤ 좋아하는 TV 프로그램 시청

6 대화를 듣고, 두 사람이 만날 시각을 고르시오.
① 6:00 ② 7:00 ③ 8:00
④ 9:00 ⑤ 10:00

7 대화를 듣고, 여자의 장래 희망으로 가장 적절한 것을 고르시오.
① 작가 ② 기자
③ 통역사 ④ 영어 선생님
⑤ 책 표지 디자이너

8 대화를 듣고, 남자의 심정으로 가장 적절한 것을 고르시오.
① excited ② worried
③ surprised ④ ashamed
⑤ disappointed

9 대화를 듣고, 여자가 대화 직후에 할 일로 가장 적절한 것을 고르시오.
① 서비스 직원 부르기
② 친구의 도움 받기
③ 서비스 센터 찾아가기
④ 서비스 센터 전화하기
⑤ 새로운 컴퓨터 구입하기

10 대화를 듣고, 무엇에 관한 내용인지 가장 적절한 것을 고르시오.
① 자기 계발 ② 자원봉사
③ 감사 일기 ④ 동아리 홍보
⑤ 어르신 공경

11 대화를 듣고, 두 사람이 함께 이용할 교통수단으로 가장 적절한 것을 고르시오.
① 택시　　　② 버스　　　③ 지하철
④ 자전거　　⑤ 비행기

12 대화를 듣고, 남자가 고민을 하는 이유로 가장 적절한 것을 고르시오.
① 여행지를 정하지 못했기 때문에
② 사려는 물건이 너무 비싸기 때문에
③ 다툼의 해결책을 찾지 못했기 때문에
④ 어떤 귀걸이를 사야 할지 모르기 때문에
⑤ 아내에게 무엇을 선물할지 모르기 때문에

13 대화를 듣고, 두 사람의 관계로 가장 적절한 것을 고르시오.
① 상사 – 직원　　　　② 은행원 – 고객
③ 선생님 – 학생　　　④ 사진작가 – 손님
⑤ 운동선수 – 코치

14 대화를 듣고, 여자가 가려고 하는 장소로 가장 적절한 곳을 고르시오.

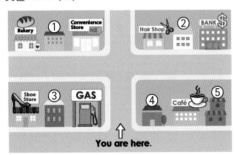

15 대화를 듣고, 남자가 여자에게 부탁한 일로 가장 적절한 것을 고르시오.
① 책상 정리해 주기
② 학교로 데리러 오기
③ 과학책 가져다 주기
④ 교실까지 부축해 주기
⑤ 잃어버린 물건 찾아 주기

16 대화를 듣고, 여자가 남자에게 제안한 것으로 가장 적절한 것을 고르시오.
① 급여 인상해 주기
② 관리자 직책 맡기
③ 마케팅 부서 늘리기
④ 회의 시간 조절하기
⑤ 회사 행사에 참여하기

17 대화를 듣고, 남자가 빌리려는 물건으로 가장 적절한 것을 고르시오.
① 종이　　　② 연필　　　③ 볼펜
④ 지우개　　⑤ 휴대폰

18 대화를 듣고, 여자의 직업으로 가장 적절한 것을 고르시오.
① 학교 선생님　　　② 군인
③ 회사원　　　　　④ 육상 선수
⑤ 엔지니어

[19~20] 대화를 듣고, 여자의 마지막 말에 이어질 남자의 응답으로 가장 적절한 것을 고르시오.

19 Man: _____
① I wish music were helpful.
② I know getting a good night's sleep is important.
③ Okay, maybe I should try doing that.
④ Sorry, but you're not helping at all.
⑤ What do you do to manage your stress?

20 Man: _____
① I don't think that's a good idea.
② Blooming flowers look so beautiful.
③ I'd love to do whatever you want.
④ I'm happy to go to the park together with you.
⑤ Well, it's hard to grow flowers inside the house.

Listen and Check

정답 및 해설 p.20

대화를 다시 듣고, 알맞은 것을 고르시오.

1 I am a quiet animal.

☐ True   ☐ False

2 What design does the woman want to buy?

☐ one with images   ☐ one with letters

3 Will the sky be clear in Daejeon?

☐ Yes   ☐ No

4 They will watch a musical together.

☐ True   ☐ False

5 What time does the man go jogging?

☐ 8:30   ☐ 9:00

6 What makes the woman delay the meeting time?

☐ the bus schedule   ☐ her homework

7 The man thinks reading English books is hard.

☐ True   ☐ False

8 Did the man buy the black T-shirt?

☐ Yes   ☐ No

9 What does the man tell the woman to do?

☐ fix it herself   ☐ call the center

10 They will do volunteer work for old people.

☐ True   ☐ False

11 How long does it take to go to the destination by bus?

☐ half an hour   ☐ an hour

12 Does the man know what his wife likes?

☐ Yes   ☐ No

13 Why did the woman visit the bank?

☐ to open a bank account

☐ to make a credit card

14 The post office is far from where the woman is.

☐ True   ☐ False

15 Will the woman bring the book for the man?

☐ Yes   ☐ No

16 Is the woman the manager of the marketing team?

☐ Yes   ☐ No

17 What does the woman tell the man not to forget to write down?

☐ his address   ☐ his name

18 Is the woman proud of her job?

☐ Yes   ☐ No

19 The man prefers relaxing indoors.

☐ True   ☐ False

20 Why does the woman want to buy flowers?

☐ to decorate a garden

☐ to celebrate

그림 정보 파악

1 다음을 듣고, 'I'가 무엇인지 가장 적절한
것을 고르시오.

① ② ③
④ ⑤

1

M   People like to have me _____ _____ _____.

I have _____ _____ and _____ _____.

The common colors of my fur are gray and white. I make little
sound. I hop around the place. I can be small or big. What am
I?

그림 정보 파악

2 대화를 듣고, 여자가 구입하려는 컵으로
가장 적절한 것을 고르시오.

① ② ③
④ coffee ⑤ LOVE

2

W   Hi. Could you _____ a mug for me, please?

M   Is there a particular mug design you want?

W   I want a simple one _____ _____ _____ on
it.

M   Then what about this one with _____ _____
_____ "Love" on it?

W   That's pretty! I'll *take it.

M   Here you are.

*take it [테이크] [잇] → [테이킷]

그림 정보 파악

3 다음을 듣고, 대구의 날씨로 가장 적절한
것을 고르시오.

① ② ③
④ ⑤

3   🇬🇧

M   Good evening. This is the weather forecast for tomorrow. It'll
rain hard in Seoul. In Daejeon and Daegu, it'll be _____
and _____. But the weather will be sunny, and
_____ _____ will be _____ in Busan. It'll be
perfect to _____ _____ _____ _____.

의도 파악

4 대화를 듣고, 남자의 마지막 말의 의도로
가장 적절한 것을 고르시오.

① 요청   ② 위로   ③ 축하
④ 동의   ⑤ 거절

♥ **Why don't we ~?**
: 상대방에게 무언가를 같이 하기를 권하거나
제안할 때 쓰는 표현으로, '우리 ~하는 게 어
때?'라는 뜻이다.
= Let's ~
= Shall we ~?

4

W   Ethan, do you _____ _____ _____ this
Saturday?

M   Nothing special. Why?

W   I have two free tickets to a musical. ♥Why don't we watch
together?

M   Sorry, but I'm _____ _____ _____
_____.

언급 유무 파악

5 다음을 듣고, 남자가 방학 일과로 언급하지 <u>않은</u> 것을 고르시오.

① 일어나는 시간
② 친구들과의 만남
③ 아침에 하는 운동
④ 학원에서 듣는 수업
⑤ 좋아하는 TV 프로그램 시청

5 🇬🇧

M I _____ _____ at 8:00 in the morning. I have breakfast at 8:30 and _____ _____ at 9:00. I usually have lunch at 12:00. After lunch, I go to an academy to take an English class. When I come back home, I _____ _____ _____. In the evening, I watch my favorite TV programs and _____ _____ _____ at 10:00.

숫자 정보 파악

6 대화를 듣고, 두 사람이 만날 시각을 고르시오.

① 6:00 　　② 7:00
③ 8:00 　　④ 9:00
⑤ 10:00

💗 **How about -ing?**
: 상대방에게 무언가를 할 것을 권하거나 제안할 때 쓰는 표현으로, '~하는 건 어때?'라는 뜻이다.
= What about -ing?

6

[*Telephone rings.*]

W Jack, what time are we meeting tomorrow?

M We're meeting at 8:00 in the morning. The amusement park _____ _____ 9:00.

W There's an _____ that I have to finish tonight. Can we delay our meeting time _____ _____ _____?

M Oh, I see. 💗 How about meeting at 9:00 then?

W Sounds good. Should I _____ _____ at the bus stop?

M Yes. I'll see you then!

장래 희망 파악

7 대화를 듣고, 여자의 장래 희망으로 가장 적절한 것을 고르시오.

① 작가
② 기자
③ 통역사
④ 영어 선생님
⑤ 책 표지 디자이너

7

M Do you _____ all _____ _____ every day?

W Yes, I do. I like reading books.

M But they are all _____ _____ _____! Aren't they hard to understand?

W Not really. I love English very much. I hope to _____ _____ English when I grow up.

M I believe you can become a great English teacher.

심정 추론

8 대화를 듣고, 남자의 심정으로 가장 적절한 것을 고르시오.

① excited 　　② worried
③ surprised 　　④ ashamed
⑤ disappointed

8

W Hi. What are you _____ _____?

M I'm looking for a T-shirt.

W _____ _____ do you want?

M I want a _____ _____. Oh, this looks good. Do you have this _____ _____?

W Sorry, but we only have that T-shirt in black.

M Well, I'll have to think about it then. Thank you.

할 일 파악

9 대화를 듣고, 여자가 대화 직후에 할 일로
가장 적절한 것을 고르시오.

① 서비스 직원 부르기
② 친구의 도움 받기
③ 서비스 센터 찾아가기
④ 서비스 센터 전화하기
⑤ 새로운 컴퓨터 구입하기

♥ **You'd better ~**
: 상대방에게 무언가를 조언하거나 충고를 할
때 사용하는 표현으로, '너는 ~하는 게 좋겠
다'라는 뜻이다.

9 🇬🇧

M Angela, what's wrong?

W The computer isn't _____ _____.

M Let me see. I think it *has a virus. ♥ You'd better go to the
service center to get it repaired.

W Should I just bring the computer there?

M You can call the center and _____ someone there
_____ _____ _____.

W Okay, I'll _____ _____ _____ _____.

*has a [헤스] [어] → [헤서]

화제·주제 파악

10 대화를 듣고, 무엇에 관한 내용인지 가장
적절한 것을 고르시오.

① 자기 계발   ② 자원봉사
③ 감사 일기   ④ 동아리 홍보
⑤ 어르신 공경

10

W Jess, did you _____ the bulletin board?

M No, I didn't. What was posted on it?

W There is a notice about the _____ work we are going
to do this Thursday. There is _____ _____
_____ activities we'll do.

M What activities are we doing?

W There are two. One is to listen to what _____
_____ say, and the other is to massage their hands.

M I hope we can _____ their day _____.

교통수단 파악

11 대화를 듣고, 두 사람이 함께 이용할
교통수단으로 가장 적절한 것을 고르시오.

① 택시   ② 버스
③ 지하철   ④ 자전거
⑤ 비행기

11

M So where is our next _____?

W It's the national museum. It _____ _____
_____ to get there by bus.

M What about _____ _____ _____?

W We can take the subway. But taking the bus is better
_____ _____ around at places.

M All right.

이유 추론

12 대화를 듣고, 남자가 고민을 하는 이유로 가장 적절한 것을 고르시오.

① 여행지를 정하지 못했기 때문에
② 사려는 물건이 너무 비싸기 때문에
③ 다툼의 해결책을 찾기 못했기 때문에
④ 어떤 귀걸이를 사야 할지 모르기 때문에
⑤ 아내에게 무엇을 선물할지 모르기 때문에

12

W Andrew, you look worried. What's the matter?

M It's _____ _____ _____ _____ . I don't know what to buy for my wife.

W What _____ _____ _____ does she like?

M Well, let me think. She likes accessories.

W Why don't you buy _____ _____ _____ _____ ?

M Okay! That sounds good.

관계 추론

13 대화를 듣고, 두 사람의 관계로 가장 적절한 것을 고르시오.

① 상사 – 직원
② 은행원 – 고객
③ 선생님 – 학생
④ 사진작가 – 손님
⑤ 운동선수 – 코치

13

M Good afternoon. How may I help you?

W I'd like to _____ _____ _____ _____ .

M Are you an office worker?

W Yes, I am.

M We have different cards for different _____ .

W I _____ spend the most money on shopping.

M Okay. Then I _____ _____ _____ .

그림 정보 파악

14 대화를 듣고, 여자가 가려고 하는 장소로 가장 적절한 곳을 고르시오.

14

W Excuse me. It's _____ _____ _____ to this town. Do you know if there's a post office near here?

M Sure, I do. It's _____ _____ _____ .

W How can I get there?

M _____ _____ one block. Then, turn left.

W Okay.

M You will see the convenience store _____ _____ _____ . It's between the store and the bakery.

W Thank you very much.

부탁한 것 파악

15 대화를 듣고, 남자가 여자에게 부탁한 일로 가장 적절한 것을 고르시오.

① 책상 정리해 주기
② 학교로 데리러 오기
③ 과학책 가져다 주기
④ 교실까지 부축해 주기
⑤ 잃어버린 물건 찾아 주기

15

[*Telephone rings.*]

M Katie, are you home now?

W Yes. I'm about to _____ _____ _____

_____ . Why?

M I forgot to _____ _____ _____ _____ .

It's on the *desk in my room.

W Wait. Let me check. Oh, I found it.

M Can you _____ _____ _____ _____ ?

My classroom is on the third floor.

W Okay. I'll _____ _____ _____ _____ .

M You're such a great sister.

*desk in [데스크] [인] → [데스킨]

제안한 것 파악

16 대화를 듣고, 여자가 남자에게 제안한 것으로 가장 적절한 것을 고르시오.

① 급여 인상해 주기
② 관리자 직책 맡기
③ 마케팅 부서 늘리기
④ 회의 시간 조절하기
⑤ 회사 행사에 참여하기

♥ **No problem.**

: 상대방이 감사한 마음을 표시할 때, 그에 대한 답변으로 괜찮다는 마음을 나타낼 때 사용하는 표현으로, '괜찮아요.', '별 말씀을요.'라는 뜻이다.

= Don't mention it.

= No worries.

16

W Hello, Mr. Park. _____ _____ _____

_____ .

M ♥No problem. What can I do for you?

W I want you to _____ the marketing team. I'm sure you

will be a good manager.

M That's _____ _____ _____ _____ .

W I hope you *consider it and _____ _____

_____ _____ .

*consider it [컨시덜] [잇] → [컨시더릿]

특정 정보 파악

17 대화를 듣고, 남자가 빌리려는 물건으로 가장 적절한 것을 고르시오.

① 종이   ② 연필
③ 볼펜   ④ 지우개
⑤ 휴대폰

17

M Excuse me. Should I _____ _____ my personal

information here?

W Yes, that's right. Don't forget to write your name on the paper.

M Okay, but I don't have a pen to _____ _____ right

now. Can you _____ _____ _____ , please?

W Sure, here you are.

M Thank you. I'll return it _____ _____ I finish using it.

직업 추론

18 대화를 듣고, 여자의 직업으로 가장 적절한 것을 고르시오.

① 학교 선생님
② 군인
③ 회사원
④ 육상 선수
⑤ 엔지니어

18

W This week _____ _____ _____ to me.

M Why? What did you do?

W I had _____ _____ _____ to do.

M Like what?

W I had to run long distances and sometimes do weapons training.

M You must be really tired.

W Yes, I am. But _____ _____ _____ is wonderful.

적절한 응답 찾기

[19-20] 대화를 듣고, 여자의 마지막 말에 이어질 남자의 응답으로 가장 적절한 것을 고르시오.

19 Man: _____

① I wish music were helpful.
② I know getting a good night's sleep is important.
③ Okay, maybe I should try doing that.
④ Sorry, but you're not helping at all.
⑤ What do you do to manage your stress?

19

M Ella, I'm so _____. What should I do?

W What is giving you so much stress?

M I have many projects to finish by this Friday. I can't sleep well either.

W How about _____ _____ some _____ _____?

M Well, I want to do something active. Nowadays, I just sit in the same place for hours.

W Then exercise will be a good way for you to _____ _____ _____.

M <u>Okay, maybe I should try doing that.</u>

적절한 응답 찾기

20 Man: _____

① I don't think that's a good idea.
② Blooming flowers look so beautiful.
③ I'd love to do whatever you want.
④ I'm happy to go to the park together with you.
⑤ Well, it's hard to grow flowers inside the house.

♥ **Sounds great.**
: 상대방의 말에 대한 동의를 나타낼 때 사용하는 표현으로, '좋은 생각이야.'라는 뜻이다.
= That sounds good.
= That's a great idea.

20 🇬🇧

M Honey, the weather has gotten very warm.

W Spring has finally come! Why don't we _____ _____ _____ _____ _____ now? It's sunny outside.

M ♥Sounds great. Some flowers might already be blooming.

W I want to decorate our garden with flowers.

M That will be beautiful.

W _____ _____ _____ _____ on the way back home.

M <u>I'd love to do whatever you want.</u>

A 들려주는 단어를 듣고 쓴 뒤, 괄호 안에 우리말 뜻을 쓰시오.

	영어	우리말		영어	우리말
1			6		
2			7		
3			8		
4			9		
5			10		

B 다음 문장을 잘 듣고 빈칸에 들어갈 단어를 채우시오.

1 I'm _____ _____ go to school now.

2 People like to have me _____ _____ _____.

3 There is _____ _____ _____ activities we'll do.

4 _____ _____ _____ _____ at the bus stop?

5 I'd like to _____ _____ _____ _____.

6 I _____ _____ _____ manage the marketing team.

7 I want a simple one _____ _____ _____ on it.

8 I want to _____ _____ _____.

9 Don't forget to _____ _____ _____ _____ the paper.

10 Aren't they _____ _____ _____ ?

1 다음을 듣고, 'this'가 가리키는 것으로 가장 적절한 것을 고르시오.

①   ②   ③

④   ⑤

2 대화를 듣고, 남자가 만든 쿠키로 가장 적절한 것을 고르시오.

①   ②   ③

④   ⑤

3 다음을 듣고, 이번 주 수요일의 날씨로 가장 적절한 것을 고르시오.

①   ②   ③

④   ⑤

4 대화를 듣고, 남자의 마지막 말의 의도로 가장 적절한 것을 고르시오.
① 동의 ② 실망 ③ 격려
④ 조언 ⑤ 칭찬

5 다음을 듣고, 여자가 새 학년 계획에 대해 언급하지 않은 것을 고르시오.
① 수학 공부하기 ② 수영 배우기
③ 야채를 먹기 ④ 좋은 일 하기
⑤ 매일 운동하기

6 대화를 듣고, 남자가 보게 될 공연의 상영 시간을 고르시오.
① 7:30 p.m. ② 8:00 p.m.
③ 8:30 p.m. ④ 9:00 p.m.
⑤ 9:30 p.m.

7 대화를 듣고, 여자의 장래 희망으로 가장 적절한 것을 고르시오.
① 감독 ② 화가 ③ 심판
④ 사진작가 ⑤ 축구선수

8 대화를 듣고, 남자의 심정으로 가장 적절한 것을 고르시오.
① calm ② lonely ③ proud
④ terrified ⑤ relieved

9 대화를 듣고, 여자가 대화 직후에 할 일로 가장 적절한 것을 고르시오.
① 전원을 연결하기
② 전화기를 교체하기
③ 컴퓨터 부품을 교체하기
④ 서비스 센터에 전화하기
⑤ 컴퓨터를 새로 구입하기

10 대화를 듣고, 무엇에 관한 내용인지 가장 적절한 것을 고르시오.
① 봉사 활동 ② 준법 정신
③ 환경 보호 ④ 절약 정신
⑤ 모금 활동

11 대화를 듣고, 두 사람이 함께 이용할 교통수단으로 가장 적절한 것을 고르시오.
① 택시   ② 버스   ③ 기차
④ 자전거   ⑤ 지하철

12 대화를 듣고, 남자가 여자를 찾아 온 이유로 가장 적절한 것을 고르시오.
① 재워 달라고
② 시계를 사려고
③ 침낭을 빌리려고
④ 함께 여행 가자고
⑤ 옷장을 정리해 달라고

13 대화를 듣고, 두 사람이 대화하는 장소로 가장 적절한 곳을 고르시오.
① 학교   ② 서점   ③ 동물원
④ 미술관   ⑤ 동물병원

14 대화를 듣고, 여자가 찾고 있는 목도리의 위치로 가장 적절한 곳을 고르시오.

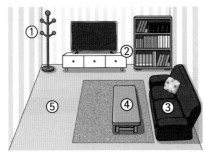

15 대화를 듣고, 여자가 남자에게 요청한 일로 가장 적절한 것을 고르시오.
① 편지 부치기
② 소포 보내기
③ 사무실에 들르기
④ 자전거 함께 타기
⑤ 여행 상품 검색하기

16 대화를 듣고, 여자가 남자에게 제안한 것으로 가장 적절한 것을 고르시오.
① 열심히 공부하기
② 한 번 더 시도하기
③ 배운 내용 암기하기
④ 스터디 그룹 가입하기
⑤ 학교에서 딴짓하지 않기

17 대화를 듣고, 남자가 지난 주말에 한 일로 가장 적절한 것을 고르시오.
① 요리하기   ② 비누 만들기
③ 방 청소하기   ④ 여동생 돌보기
⑤ 영화 보러 가기

18 대화를 듣고, 여자의 직업으로 가장 적절한 것을 고르시오.
① 여행 가이드   ② 기업 경영인
③ 방송 진행자   ④ 역사 선생님
⑤ 안전 요원

[19-20] 대화를 듣고, 여자의 마지막 말에 이어질 남자의 응답으로 가장 적절한 것을 고르시오.

19 Man: _____
① It is closed today.
② Cooking is always fun.
③ Maybe three times a week.
④ I think you are a bit overweight.
⑤ You should eat a balanced diet.

20 Man: _____
① Thank you so much. I'm glad.
② I haven't decided what I want to be.
③ Let's go to a restaurant for pizza.
④ Nothing yet. I need to buy him something quickly.
⑤ I can't believe that I graduated from school.

● 대화를 다시 듣고, 알맞은 것을 고르시오.

1 This helps you to draw curved lines.
☐ True　　　☐ False

2 Did the man bake all the cookies by himself?
☐ Yes　　　☐ No

3 What will the weather be like on Thursday?
☐ cloudy　　　☐ rainy

4 What do Taejun's parents want him to be?
☐ a scientist　　　☐ a doctor

5 The woman plans to learn how to swim.
☐ True　　　☐ False

6 Will the man watch the show at 8:00 p.m.?
☐ Yes　　　☐ No

7 Did the man watch a soccer game yesterday?
☐ Yes　　　☐ No

8 What is the man's mother's hobby?
☐ drawing flowers　　☐ collecting dishes

9 Her computer will be sent to the customer service center.
☐ True　　　☐ False

10 Did the woman throw away the empty bottle on the street?
☐ Yes　　　☐ No

11 The man wants to exchange his coat for a smaller one.
☐ True　　　☐ False

12 Jian is preparing for a field trip.
☐ True　　　☐ False

13 How many books are they going to buy?
☐ one　　　☐ two

14 The woman found her muffler on the sofa.
☐ True　　　☐ False

15 Jongwook will do what the woman asked him to do.
☐ True　　　☐ False

16 Is Minki satisfied with his grades?
☐ Yes　　　☐ No

17 What did Jihyo do last weekend?
☐ She made soap.
☐ She looked after her sisters.

18 The woman prepares trips for people.
☐ True　　　☐ False

19 Why did the woman eat nothing all day long?
☐ busy working　　☐ to lose weight

20 For whom did the woman buy flowers?
☐ her sister　　　☐ her brother

정답 및 해설 *p.21*

그림 정보 파악

1 다음을 듣고, 'this'가 가리키는 것으로 가장 적절한 것을 고르시오.

① ② ③
④ ⑤

1 🇬🇧

M This is in the shape of a _____ rectangle. This is usually _____ _____ _____, wood, or metal. You can use this to _____ length or to draw _____ _____.

그림 정보 파악

2 대화를 듣고, 남자가 만든 쿠키로 가장 적절한 것을 고르시오.

① ② ③
④ ⑤

♥ **Well done!**
: 어떤 것을 칭찬하거나 승인할 때 쓰는 표현으로, '잘했다'라는 뜻이다.
= Excellent!
= You did a good job.

2

W How delicious! Did you make all the cookies _____ _____?

M No, Grandma. This one shaped like a _____ was *made by my sister.

W _____ _____ did you bake for me?

M The square-shaped cookie.

W ♥Well done! Thank you for _____ _____ _____ _____.

*made by [메이드] [바이] → [메잇바이]

그림 정보 파악

3 다음을 듣고, 이번 주 수요일의 날씨로 가장 적절한 것을 고르시오.

① ② ③
④ ⑤

3

W Good morning. This is the weather report for this week. Monday and Tuesday will be _____ and _____. You can enjoy _____ _____. However, it will start to be _____ on Wednesday. It is _____ _____ _____ rainy on Thursday and Friday.

의도 파악

4 대화를 듣고, 남자의 마지막 말의 의도로 가장 적절한 것을 고르시오.
① 동의 ② 실망 ③ 격려
④ 조언 ⑤ 칭찬

♥ **In my opinion, ~**
: 자신의 의견을 전달할 때 쓰는 표현으로, '내 의견으로는 ~'이라는 뜻이다.
= I think/feel/believe ~

4

W Taejun, can you _____ a book on medicine?

M Sure, but I thought you are _____ _____ _____.

W I am. But my parents want me to be a doctor.

M Are you happy about that?

W Well, I don't want to _____ them.

M ♥In my opinion, you should _____ _____ _____.

언급 유무 파악

5 다음을 듣고, 여자가 새 학년 계획에 대해 언급하지 <u>않은</u> 것을 고르시오.

① 수학 공부하기　② 수영 배우기
③ 야채를 먹기　④ 좋은 일 하기
⑤ 매일 운동하기

5

W I'd like to tell you about my plans for the new school year. I'm going to _____ math _____. I'll learn _____ _____ _____ for my health. I'll also try to eat vegetables like carrots and cucumbers. Lastly, I'll do _____ _____ once a day.

숫자 정보 파악

6 대화를 듣고, 남자가 보게 될 공연의 상영 시간을 고르시오.

① 7:30 p.m.　② 8:00 p.m.
③ 8:30 p.m.　④ 9:00 p.m.
⑤ 9:30 p.m.

6

W May I help you?
M I *want to buy tickets for the 8 o'clock show.
W I'm _____ that the tickets are _____ _____.
M Do you have _____ _____?
W There are some _____ _____ for the show starting at 8:30 p.m.
M Okay. Two tickets, please.

*want to [원트] [투] → [원투]

장래 희망 파악

7 대화를 듣고, 여자의 장래 희망으로 가장 적절한 것을 고르시오.

① 감독　② 화가
③ 심판　④ 사진작가
⑤ 축구선수

7

M Did you _____ the soccer game yesterday?
W You bet! I yelled when Son Heungmin scored a _____.
M It was a really nice goal. I want to be a great _____ _____ *like him.
W I think you can.
M What do you _____ _____ _____?
W Me? A photographer. Someday, I'll _____ _____ _____ of you.

*like him [라이크] [힘] → [라이킴]

심정 추론

8 대화를 듣고, 남자의 심정으로 가장 적절한 것을 고르시오.

① calm　② lonely
③ proud　④ terrified
⑤ relieved

8 🇬🇧

W Wow, this floral plate is so beautiful.
M That's my mom's _____. Her hobby is _____ dishes.
W Can I look more closely at it?
M Go ahead. But you need to _____ _____.
W [*Crash*] I'm so sorry. It _____ _____ many pieces.
M Oh, I'm _____ _____.

할 일 파악

9 대화를 듣고, 여자가 대화 직후에 할 일로
   가장 적절한 것을 고르시오.

   ① 전원을 연결하기
   ② 전화기를 교체하기
   ③ 컴퓨터 부품을 교체하기
   ④ 서비스 센터에 전화하기
   ⑤ 컴퓨터를 새로 구입하기

9

M Yuna, why do you ＿＿＿＿＿ ＿＿＿＿＿ ＿＿＿＿＿?

W My computer won't ＿＿＿＿＿.

M You should ＿＿＿＿＿ customer service on the phone.

W I tried. But nobody answered the phone.

M Hmm... [*Pause*] Look at that! You didn't ＿＿＿＿＿ ＿＿＿＿＿
   your computer.

W I didn't? I *thought I did!

＊thought I [쏘우트] [아이] → [쏘라이]

화제·주제 파악

10 대화를 듣고, 무엇에 관한 내용인지 가장
   적절한 것을 고르시오.

   ① 봉사 활동
   ② 준법 정신
   ③ 환경 보호
   ④ 절약 정신
   ⑤ 모금 활동

♥ **Excuse me?**

: 상대방의 말을 못 들었을 경우, 혹은 제대로
들은 게 맞는지 확인하고 싶을 때 쓰는 표현으
로, '뭐라고? (다시 말해 줄래?)'라는 뜻이다.

= Pardon me?
= What did you say?

10

M Hey, ＿＿＿＿＿ ＿＿＿＿＿ ＿＿＿＿＿ the empty bottle
   on the street.

W Why? It's uncomfortable to carry.

M ♥ Excuse me? We have to ＿＿＿＿＿ the environment.

W I'm sorry. I didn't think ＿＿＿＿＿ ＿＿＿＿＿.

M You can also ＿＿＿＿＿ this glass bottle.

W I totally ＿＿＿＿＿ with you.

교통수단 파악

11 대화를 듣고, 두 사람이 함께 이용할
   교통수단으로 가장 적절한 것을 고르시오.

   ① 택시
   ② 버스
   ③ 기차
   ④ 자전거
   ⑤ 지하철

11 🇬🇧

M Sweetheart, I need to ＿＿＿＿＿ this coat for a bigger one.

W Okay. Let's go to the department store ＿＿＿＿＿ ＿＿＿＿＿.

M But it's already 7:00 p.m. I think ＿＿＿＿＿ ＿＿＿＿＿
   ＿＿＿＿＿ soon.

W You're right. We had better go there in a hurry.

M I'll ＿＿＿＿＿ ＿＿＿＿＿ ＿＿＿＿＿.

이유 추론

12 대화를 듣고, 남자가 여자를 찾아 온 이유로 가장 적절한 것을 고르시오.

① 재워 달라고
② 시계를 사려고
③ 침낭을 빌리려고
④ 함께 여행 가자고
⑤ 옷장을 정리해 달라고

12

M   Jian, do you _____ _____ _____?

W   Of course, I do. What's up?

M   I'm going on a *field trip tomorrow.

W   Sounds fun. Are you _____ _____ _____?

M   I'm still _____. So I'd like to _____ your sleeping bag.

W   If you want. It's in the closet.

*field trip [필드] [트립] → [필트립]

장소 추론

13 대화를 듣고, 두 사람이 대화하는 장소로 가장 적절한 곳을 고르시오.

① 학교   ② 서점
③ 동물원   ④ 미술관
⑤ 동물병원

13 🇬🇧

W   Look at the giraffe! Its neck is so long.

M   You're right. [*Pause*] Mom, is that a baby lion?

W   How cute! It _____ _____ a puppy.

M   Mom, I love this book. Can you buy me this one?

W   _____ _____? Don't _____ _____ _____ a math workbook, too.

M   Oh, no!

그림 정보 파악

14 대화를 듣고, 여자가 찾고 있는 목도리의 위치로 가장 적절한 곳을 고르시오.

14

M   Let's go out to *have a snowball fight.

W   Wait! I can't _____ my muffler.

M   Did you _____ the table in front of the TV?

W   Yes, but there's nothing on the table.

M   Then _____ _____ on the sofa?

W   Nope. Ah, I found it. It's _____ _____ _____.

*have a [해브] [어] → [해버]

15 대화를 듣고, 여자가 남자에게 요청한 일로
가장 적절한 것을 고르시오.

① 편지 부치기
② 소포 보내기
③ 사무실에 들르기
④ 자전거 함께 타기
⑤ 여행 상품 검색하기

15

W   Jongwook, where are you going?

M   I am _____ _____ go cycling with my friend.

W   Be careful. Oh, can you _____ _____ _____
_____ before you go?

M   Of course. What is it?

W   I want you to _____ _____ _____ at the
post office.

M   No problem. *Give it to me.

★Give it [기브] [잇] → [기빗]

16 대화를 듣고, 여자가 남자에게 제안한
것으로 가장 적절한 것을 고르시오.

① 열심히 공부하기
② 한 번 더 시도하기
③ 배운 내용 암기하기
④ 스터디 그룹 가입하기
⑤ 학교에서 딴짓하지 않기

16

W   Minki, what's wrong with you?

M   I studied really hard, but my grades didn't go up. What's your
_____?

W   I try to memorize _____ _____ _____ at
school.

M   Me, too. But for me, it's no use.

W   How about _____ _____ _____ _____?

M   Oh! That's a good idea.

17 대화를 듣고, 남자가 지난 주말에 한 일로
가장 적절한 것을 고르시오.

① 요리하기
② 비누 만들기
③ 방 청소하기
④ 여동생 돌보기
⑤ 영화 보러 가기

17

M   Jihyo, what did you do _____ _____?

W   I made soap at home with my mom.

M   At home? That _____ _____.

W   It is. We'll do it again later. What did you do?

M   My parents went to a movie, so I _____ _____
_____ my sisters.

W   What a good boy!

정답 및 해설 *p.24*

직업 추론

18 대화를 듣고, 여자의 직업으로 가장 적절한 것을 고르시오.

① 여행 가이드
② 기업 경영인
③ 방송 진행자
④ 역사 선생님
⑤ 안전 요원

♥ **You mean ~**
: 상대방의 말의 의미를 다시 확인하고 싶을 때 쓰는 표현으로, '당신의 말은 ~라는 뜻이다.
= You said that ~
= I think you mean ~

18 🇬🇧

[*Radio Music Intro*]

M Today, I'll _____ this beautiful woman.

W Thank you. I'm _____ _____ _____ you here.

M What do you do for a living?

W I help people to _____ more easily and safely.

M ♥You mean that you take them on tours.

W Yes. I take them to great places _____ _____ and explain the history of these places.

적절한 응답 찾기

[19-20] 대화를 듣고, 여자의 마지막 말에 이어질 남자의 응답으로 가장 적절한 것을 고르시오.

19 Man: _____
① It is closed today.
② Cooking is always fun.
③ Maybe three times a week.
④ I think you are a bit overweight.
⑤ You should eat a balanced diet.

19

M You _____ _____ _____. What happened?

W I didn't eat any food all day long.

M Really? Were you busy today?

W In fact, I want to _____ _____.

M Why don't you _____ _____ for your health?

W That's a good idea. _____ _____ *should I go to the gym?

M Maybe three times a week.

*should I [슈드] [아이] → [슈다이]

적절한 응답 찾기

20 Man: _____
① Thank you so much. I'm glad.
② I haven't decided what I want to be.
③ Let's go to a restaurant for pizza.
④ Nothing yet. I need to buy him something quickly.
⑤ I can't believe that I graduated from school.

20

W Look at this rose. It's so pretty, *isn't it?

M Why did you buy the flower?

W My sister will _____ _____ _____ tomorrow.

M She must be happy about that.

W I think so. Your brother and my sister are _____ _____ _____.

M That's right. Tomorrow is my brother's graduation day, too.

W _____ _____ _____ _____ for your brother?

M Nothing yet. I need to buy him something quickly.

*isn't it [이즌트] [잇] → [이즌팃]

A 들려주는 단어를 듣고 쓴 뒤, 괄호 안에 우리말 뜻을 쓰시오.

	영어	우리말			영어	우리말
1			6			
2			7			
3			8			
4			9			
5			10			

B 다음 문장을 잘 듣고 빈칸에 들어갈 단어를 채우시오.

1 It _____ _____ many pieces.

2 She must be _____ _____ _____.

3 I'm going on a(n) _____ _____ _____.

4 We have to _____ _____ _____.

5 Well, I don't _____ _____ _____ them.

6 Why don't you _____ _____ for your health?

7 I try to memorize _____ _____ _____ at school.

8 It is _____ _____ _____ _____ on Thursday and Friday.

9 I want you to _____ _____ _____ at the post office.

10 Today, I'll _____ this beautiful woman.

1 다음을 듣고, 'I'가 무엇인지 가장 적절한 것을 고르시오.

①   ②   ③

④   ⑤

2 대화를 듣고, 남자가 구입할 넥타이로 가장 적절한 것을 고르시오.

①   ②   ③

④   ⑤

3 다음을 듣고, Cebu의 오늘의 날씨로 가장 적절한 것을 고르시오.

①   ②   ③

④   ⑤

4 대화를 듣고, 여자가 한 마지막 말의 의도로 가장 적절한 것을 고르시오.
① 실망   ② 격려   ③ 칭찬
④ 거절   ⑤ 걱정

5 다음을 듣고, 여자가 엄마에 대해 언급하지 <u>않은</u> 것을 고르시오.
① 외모   ② 직업   ③ 성격
④ 봉사 활동   ⑤ 취미 생활

6 대화를 듣고, 두 사람이 만날 시각을 고르시오.
① 9:00 a.m.   ② 9:30 a.m.
③ 10:00 a.m.   ④ 10:30 a.m.
⑤ 11:00 a.m.

7 대화를 듣고, 남자의 장래 희망으로 가장 적절한 것을 고르시오.
① 화가   ② 탐험가   ③ 과학자
④ 건축가   ⑤ 고고학자

8 대화를 듣고, 남자의 심정으로 가장 적절한 것을 고르시오.
① bored   ② lonely
③ nervous   ④ pleased
⑤ disappointed

9 대화를 듣고, 남자가 대화 직후에 할 일로 가장 적절한 것을 고르시오.
① 손 씻기
② 저녁 먹기
③ 영어 공부하기
④ 일자리 구하기
⑤ 컴퓨터 게임하기

10 대화를 듣고, 무엇에 관한 내용인지 가장 적절한 것을 고르시오.
① 은행 거래   ② 용돈 저축
③ 여행 계획   ④ 선물 구입
⑤ 벼룩시장

11 대화를 듣고, 남자가 이용할 교통수단으로 가장 적절한 것을 고르시오.
① 택시　　　② 버스　　　③ 기차
④ 자전거　　⑤ 비행기

12 대화를 듣고, 남자가 여자를 도와줄 수 <u>없는</u> 이유로 가장 적절한 것을 고르시오.
① 강아지를 키워서
② 속상한 일이 생겨서
③ 밀린 과제를 해야 해서
④ 이모네 집을 방문해야 해서
⑤ 고양이 털 알레르기가 있어서

13 대화를 듣고, 두 사람의 관계로 가장 적절한 것을 고르시오.
① 선배 – 후배
② 선생님 – 학생
③ 호텔 직원 – 고객
④ 식당 종업원 – 고객
⑤ 여행 가이드 – 관광객

14 대화를 듣고, 편의점의 위치로 가장 적절한 곳을 고르시오.

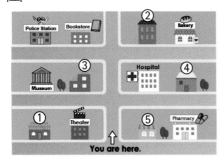

15 대화를 듣고, 남자가 여자에게 부탁한 일로 가장 적절한 것을 고르시오.
① 저녁 준비하기　　② 피자 주문하기
③ 현관문 열어주기　④ 친구네 방문하기
⑤ 전구 갈아 끼우기

16 대화를 듣고, 여자가 남자에게 제안한 것으로 가장 적절한 것을 고르시오.
① 옷 가게를 운영하기
② 일을 더 열심히 하기
③ 운동화 새로 장만하기
④ 어머님께 선물 사 드리기
⑤ 인터넷으로 운동화 구입하기

17 대화를 듣고, 두 사람이 구입할 그림을 고르시오.
① 사과 그림　　　　② 태양 그림
③ 추상화　　　　　④ 파인애플 그림
⑤ 해바라기 그림

18 대화를 듣고, 남자의 직업으로 가장 적절한 것을 고르시오.
① 요리사　　　　　② 영양사
③ 운동선수　　　　④ 헬스 트레이너
⑤ 운동기구 판매원

[19–20] 대화를 듣고, 남자의 마지막 말에 이어질 여자의 응답으로 가장 적절한 것을 고르시오.

19 Woman: _____
① I prefer winter to summer.
② Vanilla ice cream is my favorite.
③ Let's go skiing this winter vacation.
④ Your snowman looks like a real person.
⑤ Fall. I like trees with red and yellow leaves.

20 Woman: _____
① Paul, just follow your dream.
② Don't worry. It was just a dream.
③ That's strange. Nobody's here.
④ Let's go to see a horror movie.
⑤ Okay. I'll wake you up tomorrow.

Listen and Check

● 대화를 다시 듣고, 알맞은 것을 고르시오.

1 Why was this killed a lot in the past?
- ☐ because of its furry tail
- ☐ because of a myth

2 The man decides to buy a tie for his father.
- ☐ True
- ☐ False

3 It is going to rain in Hanoi.
- ☐ True
- ☐ False

4 Is the man baking pancakes on low heat?
- ☐ Yes
- ☐ No

5 What does the woman's mother do in her free time?
- ☐ play the piano
- ☐ write poems

6 Where are they flying to?
- ☐ Singapore
- ☐ Hong Kong

7 The man wants to build a nice house someday.
- ☐ True
- ☐ False

8 What is inside the box?
- ☐ books
- ☐ credit cards

9 Did he go to sleep early last night?
- ☐ Yes
- ☐ No

10 Who bought a wallet?
- ☐ the man
- ☐ the man's parents

11 There is only one option to get from France to Switzerland.
- ☐ True
- ☐ False

12 Amanda will visit her aunt this weekend.
- ☐ True
- ☐ False

13 What time does the restaurant close?
- ☐ 9:30 p.m.
- ☐ 10:00 p.m.

14 Why does the man need to go to the convenience store?
- ☐ to buy batteries
- ☐ to buy ice cream

15 The man is changing the bulb in the kitchen.
- ☐ True
- ☐ False

16 Has the man ever bought items through the Internet?
- ☐ Yes
- ☐ No

17 Why do they want to buy a painting?
- ☐ for decoration
- ☐ as a gift

18 Where are they now?
- ☐ at a store
- ☐ at a gym

19 They like both summer and winter.
- ☐ True
- ☐ False

20 Somebody was chasing the man in reality.
- ☐ True
- ☐ False

그림 정보 파악

1 다음을 듣고, 'I'가 무엇인지 가장 적절한 것을 고르시오.

① ② ③

④ ⑤

1

W I have four legs and a long, bushy tail. I usually eat fruits, frogs, birds, and rats. I look *like a dog, but I live _____ _____ _____. My furry tail is _____. So many people _____ _____ a lot in the past. I _____ _____ now. What am I?

*like a [라이크] [어] → [라이커]

그림 정보 파악

2 대화를 듣고, 남자가 구입할 넥타이로 가장 적절한 것을 고르시오.

① ② ③

④ ⑤

♥ **I'm thinking of ~**
: 자신의 의도나 현재 고려하고 있는 것을 말하기 위해 쓰는 표현으로, '~에 대해 생각 중이야'라는 뜻이다.

2

W What do you want to buy for Dad?

M ♥I'm thinking of a _____ _____.

W That looks so normal. How about this polka-dotted tie?

M It's _____ _____ _____ _____. It looks too old-fashioned.

W Hmm... Let's buy this plain one.

M You're right. _____ _____ _____ _____.

그림 정보 파악

3 다음을 듣고, Cebu의 오늘의 날씨로 가장 적절한 것을 고르시오.

① ② ③

④ ⑤

3

M Good morning. This is the weather report. Singapore will be cloudy but _____ _____ _____. However, it will be _____ _____ _____ in Cebu and Bangkok. Don't forget to _____ _____ sunscreen. The wind will _____ _____ in Hanoi.

의도 파악

4 대화를 듣고, 여자가 한 마지막 말의 의도로 가장 적절한 것을 고르시오.

① 실망   ② 격려   ③ 칭찬
④ 거절   ⑤ 걱정

4

M Honey, can you _____ _____?

W What's up? I can _____ something _____ in the kitchen.

M That's correct. I keep burning pancakes.

W Let me see. [Pause] Cook the pancakes on lower heat.

M Oh, that's the _____. Thank you.

W Don't _____ _____. You can do it.

언급 유무 파악

5 다음을 듣고, 여자가 엄마에 대해 언급하지 <u>않은</u> 것을 고르시오.

① 외모   ② 직업
③ 성격   ④ 봉사 활동
⑤ 취미 생활

5

W   I'd like to _____ my mom to you. She is tall and has _____, _____ _____. She is a lawyer and _____ _____ a law firm. Twice a month, she helps _____ _____ _____ for free. She enjoys playing the piano and watching movies.

숫자 정보 파악

6 대화를 듣고, 두 사람이 만날 시각을 고르시오.

① 9:00 a.m.
② 9:30 a.m.
③ 10:00 a.m.
④ 10:30 a.m.
⑤ 11:00 a.m.

6 🇬🇧

W   Finally, we will go to Hong Kong tomorrow!
M   You look _____ _____! You should check your _____ before you leave.
W   Of course. _____ _____ shall we meet?
M   Our _____ _____ at 12:30 p.m.
W   We should _____ _____ the airport between 9:00 a.m. and 10:00 a.m.
M   Let's meet at 9:30 in the morning.

장래 희망 파악

7 대화를 듣고, 남자의 장래 희망으로 가장 적절한 것을 고르시오.

① 화가   ② 탐험가   ③ 과학자
④ 건축가   ⑤ 고고학자

> ♥ **Why not?**
> : 상대방의 의견에 대해 승낙이나 동의를 나타낼 때 표현으로, '왜 안 되겠니?(당연하지.)'라는 뜻이다.
> = Of course.
> = I have no doubt.

7

W   The deep blue sea makes me _____ _____.
M   I agree. Nature is so peaceful and beautiful.
W   I want to _____ _____.
M   Okay. I will _____ a nice house here.
W   Are you sure?
M   ♥Why not? I'm studying to be an _____.
W   I hope your _____ _____ _____.

심정 추론

8 대화를 듣고, 남자의 심정으로 가장 적절한 것을 고르시오.

① bored
② lonely
③ nervous
④ pleased
⑤ disappointed

8 🇬🇧

M   I got a package from Grandma. Wow! It must be a _____ _____ _____.
W   Really? Can you open it?
M   _____ _____ _____. There are so many books in the box.
W   There's also a card. _____ _____ _____ please.
M   Okay. Dear Olivia. [Sigh] These are for you.

9

할 일 파악

9 대화를 듣고, 남자가 대화 직후에 할 일로 가장 적절한 것을 고르시오.

① 손 씻기
② 저녁 먹기
③ 영어 공부하기
④ 일자리 구하기
⑤ 컴퓨터 게임하기

♥ **You did a good job.**

: 어떤 것을 칭찬하거나 승인할 때 쓰는 표현으로, '잘했다.'라는 뜻이다.
= Well done!
= Excellent!

9

W	Jiwhan, _____ _____ _____ today?
M	I took an English quiz, and it was _____.
W	*Was it?
M	But I got a good grade because I studied _____ _____ at night.
W	♥You did a good job.
M	So can I play computer games now?
W	All right but only if you wash your hands _____.
M	Okay, Mom.

*Was it [워즈] [잇] → [워짓]

화제·주제 파악

10 대화를 듣고, 무엇에 관한 내용인지 가장 적절한 것을 고르시오.

① 은행 거래　② 용돈 저축
③ 여행 계획　④ 선물 구입
⑤ 벼룩시장

10 🇬🇧

M	Ta-da! I got a new wallet.
W	It's so fancy! Did your parents buy that for you?
M	Nope! I _____ ten dollars out of my allowance every month.
W	That's amazing! I should _____ how to do that _____ _____.
M	What about saving _____ _____ _____ _____ money monthly from now on?
W	That's a good idea.

교통수단 파악

11 대화를 듣고, 남자가 이용할 교통수단으로 가장 적절한 것을 고르시오.

① 택시　② 버스　③ 기차
④ 자전거　⑤ 비행기

11

M	What is the _____ _____ _____ _____ from France to Switzerland?
W	Hmm... You have two options, a plane or a train.
M	What's the _____?
W	Flying on a plane is _____. But taking a train is _____.
M	Then I should buy a _____ _____.

이유 추론

12 대화를 듣고, 남자가 여자를 도와줄 수 없는 이유로 가장 적절한 것을 고르시오.

① 강아지를 키워서
② 속상한 일이 생겨서
③ 밀린 과제를 해야 해서
④ 이모네 집을 방문해야 해서
⑤ 고양이 털 알레르기가 있어서

> 🧡 **Sorry, but I can't.**
> : 상대방의 부탁이나 요구를 거절할 때 쓰는 표현으로, '미안하지만, 나는 할 수 없어.'라는 뜻이다.
> = I'm sorry, but I can't.
> = I'm afraid that I can't.

12

W Liam, can I _____ _____ _____ a favor?

M Hello, Amanda. What do you need?

W Can you _____ _____ _____ my cat for two days?

M Is there something wrong *with you?

W No, I have to visit my aunt this weekend.

M 🧡Sorry, but I can't. I am _____ _____ cat hair.

W Ah, I didn't know that.

*with you [위드] [유] → [위듀]

관계 추론

13 대화를 듣고, 두 사람이 대화하는 관계로 가장 적절한 곳을 고르시오.

① 선배 – 후배
② 선생님 – 학생
③ 호텔 직원 – 고객
④ 식당 종업원 – 고객
⑤ 여행 가이드 – 관광객

13 🇬🇧

M Excuse me. _____ _____ _____ now?

W We _____ _____ 10:00 p.m. So you can stay here for only 30 minutes. Is that all right?

M Then I'll order some food _____ _____.

W Okay. What do you want?

M Two cheeseburgers and two orders of onion rings, please.

W _____ _____?

M That's all. Thank you.

그림 정보 파악

14 대화를 듣고, 편의점의 위치로 가장 적절한 곳을 고르시오.

14

W Juwon, this TV remote control doesn't work.

M I bought it yesterday. Check the batteries first.

W You're right. There are _____ _____ in it. I should go to the convenience store.

M It's *dark outside. Let me know where it is.

W You are so sweet! Just _____ _____ and then turn _____ _____ _____ _____ _____.

M Go straight and then turn right. And after that?

W It'll be _____ _____ _____ next to the bakery.

M Okay!

*dark outside [다크] [아웃사이드] → [달카웃사이드]

15 대화를 듣고, 남자가 여자에게 부탁한 일로 가장 적절한 것을 고르시오.

① 저녁 준비하기
② 피자 주문하기
③ 현관문 열어주기
④ 친구네 방문하기
⑤ 전구 갈아 끼우기

15

M The light in the kitchen _____ _____.

W Can you change the bulb?

M Sure. _____ _____ _____.

W Thank you. [*Doorbell rings.*] Sweetie, there's someone at the door.

M It must be the pizza _____ guy. Will you _____ _____ _____?

W I will.

제안한 것 파악

16 대화를 듣고, 여자가 남자에게 제안한 것으로 가장 적절한 것을 고르시오.

① 옷 가게를 운영하기
② 일을 더 열심히 하기
③ 운동화 새로 장만하기
④ 어머님께 선물 사 드리기
⑤ 인터넷으로 운동화 구입하기

♥ **You should + v**

: 상대방에게 어떤 물건이나 행동을 제안하거나 설득할 때 쓰는 표현으로, '너는 ～해야 해', '너는 ～ 하는 것이 좋을 거야'라는 뜻이다.
= You ought to + v
= You had better + v

16

M I have to buy sneakers, but I'm so _____ _____ these days.

W Your mom usually _____ _____ _____ _____, doesn't she?

M Yeah, but they are not my style.

W Why don't you buy sneakers _____ _____ _____?

M I've never tried that before.

W ♥You should try it. Internet shopping is usually _____.

특정 정보 파악

17 대화를 듣고, 두 사람이 구입할 그림을 고르시오.

① 사과 그림
② 태양 그림
③ 추상화
④ 파인애플 그림
⑤ 해바라기 그림

♥ **Why don't we + v?**

: 어떤 것을 함께 하고 제안할 때 쓰는 표현으로, '～는 어때?' 라는 뜻이다.
= How about -ing?
= Let's + v

17 🇬🇧

M I think the wall is _____ _____.

W ♥Why don't we _____ _____ _____ and _____ it on the wall?

M Good idea! I like this painting of apples.

W But sunflowers are _____ _____ apples for the living room.

M I agree with you.

W Okay. Let's buy this sunflower painting.

정답 및 해설 *p.29*

직업 추론

18 대화를 듣고, 남자의 직업으로 가장 적절한 것을 고르시오.

① 요리사
② 영양사
③ 운동선수
④ 헬스 트레이너
⑤ 운동기구 판매원

18

M   _____ _____ _____ _____ for dinner yesterday?

W   Two boiled _____, one tomato, and chicken breasts.

M   Perfect! Before we _____ _____, let's warm up.

W   Okay! _____ _____ _____ warmups should I do?

M   Indoor cycling for ten minutes.

W   Can I _____ this bottle _____ water?

M   Sure, you can.

적절한 응답 찾기

[19~20] 대화를 듣고, 남자의 마지막 말에 이어질 여자의 응답으로 가장 적절한 것을 고르시오.

19 Woman: _____

① I prefer winter to summer.
② Vanilla ice cream is my favorite.
③ Let's go skiing this winter vacation.
④ Your snowman looks like a real person.
⑤ Fall. I like trees with red and yellow leaves.

19

W   It's really hot. I'm _____ _____.

M   Me, too. I _____ _____ I'm melting now.

W   _____ _____. You are not a snowman.

M   Of course not. Yerim, do you like winter?

W   No, I don't. It's _____ _____ _____ _____ outside.

M   Then what's your _____ _____?

W   <u>Fall. I like trees with red and yellow leaves.</u>

적절한 응답 찾기

20 Woman: _____

① Paul, just follow your dream.
② Don't worry. It was just a dream.
③ That's strange. Nobody's here.
④ Let's go to see a horror movie.
⑤ Okay. I'll wake you up tomorrow.

♥ **Tell me about it.**

: 어떤 것에 대해서 더 알고 싶다는 호기심이나 궁금함을 나타낼 때 쓰는 표현으로, '그것에 대해 말해 줘.'라는 뜻이다.

= I'm curious about it.
= I'm interested to find out about it.

20

W   Paul, did you _____ _____ last night?

M   No. I *had a nightmare.

W   Do you mean a _____ _____? ♥ Tell me about it.

M   A ghost was chasing me, so I had to _____ _____.

W   It sounds _____.

M   I'm afraid something bad might _____ today.

W   <u>Don't worry. It was just a dream.</u>

*had a [해드] [어] → [해러]

A 들려주는 단어를 듣고 쓴 뒤, 괄호 안에 우리말 뜻을 쓰시오.

	영어	우리말			영어	우리말
1			6			
2			7			
3			8			
4			9			
5			10			

B 다음 문장을 잘 듣고 빈칸에 들어갈 단어를 채우시오.

1 Will you _____ the _____?

2 Liam, can I _____ _____ _____ _____ _____?

3 All right but only if you _____ _____ _____ _____.

4 I think the wall is _____ _____.

5 I am _____ _____ cat hair.

6 What about saving _____ _____ _____ _____ money monthly?

7 _____ _____ _____ buy sneakers through the Internet?

8 Twice a month, she helps people _____ _____ for free.

9 There are _____ _____ _____ _____.

10 We should _____ _____ the airport between 9:00 a.m. and 10:00 a.m.

1 다음을 듣고, 'this'가 가리키는 것으로 가장 적절한 것을 고르시오.

① 　② 　③

④ 　⑤

2 대화를 듣고, 남자가 구입하려는 풍선으로 가장 적절한 것을 고르시오.

① 　② 　③

④ 　⑤

3 다음을 듣고, 금요일의 날씨로 가장 적절한 것을 고르시오.

① 　② 　③

④ 　⑤

4 대화를 듣고, 여자의 마지막 말의 의도로 가장 적절한 것을 고르시오.
① 의심　② 동의　③ 칭찬
④ 비난　⑤ 조언

5 다음을 듣고, 남자가 다이어트 계획에 대해 언급하지 않은 것을 고르시오.
① 운동 계획　　② 단백질 먹기
③ 충분한 숙면　④ 목표 감량 무게
⑤ 충분한 물 섭취

6 대화를 듣고, 두 사람이 수강 신청을 할 시각을 고르시오.
① 10:00　　② 2:00　　③ 3:00
④ 4:00　　⑤ 7:00

7 대화를 듣고, 여자의 장래 희망으로 가장 적절한 것을 고르시오.
① 모델　　　　② 스타일리스트
③ 패션 디자이너　④ 일러스트레이터
⑤ 패션 잡지 편집자

8 대화를 듣고, 남자의 심정으로 가장 적절한 것을 고르시오.
① calm　　② upset　　③ bored
④ excited　⑤ pleased

9 대화를 듣고, 여자가 대화 직후에 할 일로 가장 적절한 것을 고르시오.
① 음식점 예약하기
② 서비스 평가하기
③ 인터넷 검색하기
④ 친구와 점심 먹기
⑤ 문자 메시지 보내기

10 대화를 듣고, 무엇에 관한 내용인지 가장 적절한 것을 고르시오.
① 대학 입시 상담
② 목표 대학 목록
③ 대학교 입학 통지
④ 대학교 시험 일정
⑤ 부모님 감사 인사

11 대화를 듣고, 두 사람이 함께 이용할 교통수단으로 가장 적절한 것을 고르시오.
① 배　　　　② 버스　　　　③ 택시
④ 자전거　　⑤ 지하철

12 대화를 듣고, 남자가 여자를 불러 낸 이유로 가장 적절한 것을 고르시오.
① 생일 선물을 주기 위해서
② 다퉜던 일을 사과하기 위해서
③ 여자의 물건을 돌려주기 위해서
④ 좋아하는 마음을 고백하기 위해서
⑤ 여자에게 사과할 것을 요구하기 위해서

13 대화를 듣고, 두 사람이 대화하는 장소로 가장 적절한 곳을 고르시오.
① 공원　　　　　② 온천
③ 수영장　　　　④ 수족관
⑤ 박물관

14 대화를 듣고, 여자가 가려는 장소로 가장 적절한 곳을 고르시오.

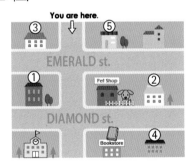

15 대화를 듣고, 남자가 여자에게 부탁한 일로 가장 적절한 것을 고르시오.
① 장소 이동하기
② 털장갑 빌려주기
③ 밖에서 기다리기
④ 친구에게 전화하기
⑤ 따뜻한 곳으로 이동하기

16 대화를 듣고, 여자가 남자에게 제안한 것으로 가장 적절한 것을 고르시오.
① 휴대폰 충전하기
② 안경 맞추러 가기
③ 충분한 휴식 취하기
④ 새 휴대폰으로 교체하기
⑤ 휴대폰 사용 시간 줄이기

17 대화를 듣고 여자가 한 일로 가장 적절한 것을 고르시오.
① 영화 시간표 확인하기
② 약속 시간 정하기
③ 운동하러 가기
④ 영화 관람하기
⑤ 숙제 같이하기

18 대화를 듣고, 여자의 직업으로 가장 적절한 것을 고르시오.
① 웨이터　　② 미식가　　③ 요리사
④ 요리 강사　　⑤ 제빵사

[19-20] 대화를 듣고, 남자의 마지막 말에 이어질 여자의 응답으로 가장 적절한 것을 고르시오.

19 Woman: _____
① I understand that.
② That's a great idea.
③ I'm sorry to hear that.
④ I don't agree with you.
⑤ I should study by myself.

20 Woman: _____
① Tell me why she feels bad.
② Don't make your friend angry.
③ You can write a letter of apology.
④ You should say sorry to your friend.
⑤ A friendship doesn't break so easily.

Listen and Check

● 대화를 다시 듣고, 알맞은 것을 고르시오.

1 People need this when they travel within their country.
☐ True   ☐ False

2 Will the man buy the balloon with letters?
☐ Yes   ☐ No

3 What will the weather be like on Tuesday?
☐ rainy   ☐ warm

4 The man is good at reading the poem.
☐ True   ☐ False

5 How much weight is the man trying to lose?
☐ six kilograms   ☐ eight kilograms

6 How many times is the class offered?
☐ two   ☐ three

7 The man supports the woman's dream.
☐ True   ☐ False

8 What makes the man feel down?
☐ a friend   ☐ a low grade

9 Was the woman happy with the service at the Italian restaurant?
☐ Yes   ☐ No

10 The woman expresses her thanks to her dad.
☐ True   ☐ False

11 What makes them take a taxi?
☐ a faster trip   ☐ the reasonable fare

12 What does the man give to the woman?
☐ flowers   ☐ chocolate

13 Do they enjoy staying in the water?
☐ Yes   ☐ No

14 The café is on Diamond Street.
☐ True   ☐ False

15 What does the woman lend to the man?
☐ her muffler   ☐ her mittens

16 Does the man like wearing eyeglasses?
☐ Yes   ☐ No

17 They will make plans to watch a movie tomorrow.
☐ True   ☐ False

18 Is it the first time for the man to have the woman's cooking?
☐ Yes   ☐ No

19 What is the woman's big worry?
☐ getting a job   ☐ finding her interest

20 The man's friend is angry because the man did not say sorry.
☐ True   ☐ False

그림 정보 파악

1 다음을 듣고, 'this'가 가리키는 것으로 가장 적절한 것을 고르시오.

① ② ③ ④ ⑤

1

M People need this to _____ _____ another country. This has a traveler's _____. This has his or her name, photograph, nationality, signature, and other information. This also has a rectangular _____. Sometimes people don't _____ _____ _____ this when they travel within their country. What is this?

그림 정보 파악

2 대화를 듣고, 남자가 구입하려는 풍선으로 가장 적절한 것을 고르시오.

① ② ③ ④ ⑤

♥ **Which do you prefer?**
: 상대방에게 선호하는 것을 물어볼 때 사용하는 표현으로, '어떤 것을 선호하나요?'라는 뜻이다. 둘 중 하나를 골라야 하는 경우, 'Which do you prefer, A or B?'라고 사용하기도 한다.
= Which do you like more?

2 🇬🇧

W Hi. What are you looking for?

M I'm looking for _____ _____ _____ _____.

W ♥Which do you prefer, ones with round shapes or heart shapes?

M I _____ _____ _____. Do you have any with big *letters on them?

W Yes, we do. This one has the word "Party" on it.

M It _____ _____ for a party. I'll buy four.

*letters on [레럴스] [온] → [레럴손]

그림 정보 파악

3 다음을 듣고, 금요일의 날씨로 가장 적절한 것을 고르시오.

① ② ③ ④ ⑤

3

M Good evening. This is the weather report for this week. It'll be sunny on Monday. The warm weather will _____ _____ Tuesday. On Wednesday, it will _____ _____ and will _____ _____ _____ in the evening. However, from Thursday to Friday, you will see _____ blue skies.

의도 파악

4 대화를 듣고, 여자의 마지막 말의 의도로 가장 적절한 것을 고르시오.
① 의심 ② 동의 ③ 칭찬
④ 비난 ⑤ 조언

4

W Max, that was _____ _____!

M What do you mean?

W How could you _____ the poem so well?

M I tried to think of the _____ of the poet.

W You're very good at _____ others' feelings!

언급 유무 파악

5 다음을 듣고, 남자가 다이어트 계획에 대해 언급하지 <u>않은</u> 것을 고르시오.

① 운동 계획
② 단백질 먹기
③ 충분한 숙면
④ 목표 감량 무게
⑤ 충분한 물 섭취

5

M I'm _____ _____ _____ six kilograms this month. I'll exercise every morning. I should drink _____ _____ of water at a minimum each day. I'll also eat more vegetables and try not to eat at night. I'll get enough sleep because a good night's sleep is _____.

숫자 정보 파악

6 대화를 듣고, 두 사람이 수강 신청을 할 시각을 고르시오.

① 10:00 ② 2:00 ③ 3:00
④ 4:00 ⑤ 7:00

♥ How about -ing?

: 상대방에게 무언가를 할 것을 권하거나 제안할 때 쓰는 표현으로, '~하는 건 어때?'라는 뜻이다.
= What about -ing?

6 🇬🇧

W What time should we _____ _____ _____ the class?
M What time *does it start?
W There are three times to choose from 10:00 a.m., 3:00 p.m., and 7:00 p.m.
M ♥How about _____ the 7:00 p.m. _____?
W I'm _____ _____ _____.
M Great!

*does it [더즈] [잇] → [더짓]

장래 희망 파악

7 대화를 듣고, 여자의 장래 희망으로 가장 적절한 것을 고르시오.

① 모델
② 스타일리스트
③ 패션 디자이너
④ 일러스트레이터
⑤ 패션 잡지 편집자

7

M Are these your new clothes? They are beautiful!
W Actually, I made them.
M Really? How amazing!
W I'm _____ _____ _____.
M You are really interested in fashion.
W I want to make _____ _____ clothing brand in the future.
M I believe you can be an _____ fashion designer.
W Thanks.

심정 추론

8 대화를 듣고, 남자의 심정으로 가장 적절한 것을 고르시오.

① calm ② upset ③ bored
④ excited ⑤ pleased

♥ Cheer up!

: 상대방이 낙담하고 있는 경우 위로를 해줄 때 사용하는 표현으로, '힘내'라는 뜻이다.

8

W James, why do you have _____ _____ _____?
M I got a _____ grade on the math exam.
W Don't worry. You can _____ _____ the next time!
M I think I have to study _____ _____.
W ♥Cheer up, James!

할 일 파악

9 대화를 듣고, 여자가 대화 직후에 할 일로 가장 적절한 것을 고르시오.

① 음식점 예약하기
② 서비스 평가하기
③ 인터넷 검색하기
④ 친구와 점심 먹기
⑤ 문자 메시지 보내기

9

M Why don't we _____ _____ _____?

W Sure, I'd like that. Where should we go?

M How about the Italian restaurant we went to before?

W I liked the food, but the _____ was _____.

M Oh, that's right. I'll search for some other restaurants on the Internet.

W I'll search, too, and then _____ _____ _____.

화제 · 주제 파악

10 대화를 듣고, 무엇에 관한 내용인지 가장 적절한 것을 고르시오.

① 대학 입시 상담
② 목표 대학 목록
③ 대학교 입학 통지
④ 대학교 시험 일정
⑤ 부모님 감사 인사

10

W I have some _____ _____ to tell you.

M What is it?

W I _____ _____ _____ from Stanford University.

M What did it say?

W It said that I was accepted to the school.

M Congratulations, dear!

W I did this _____ _____ your _____ _____, Dad.

M You're such a good-hearted daughter.

교통수단 파악

11 대화를 듣고, 두 사람이 함께 이용할 교통수단으로 가장 적절한 것을 고르시오.

① 배 ② 버스 ③ 택시
④ 자전거 ⑤ 지하철

♥ **All right.**

: 상대방의 말을 받아들일 때 사용하는 표현으로, '좋아요.', '괜찮아요.', '알겠어요.'라는 뜻이다.

= Okay.

= I'm fine with it.

11

M How should we go now?

W Wait. Let me check. We can take a bus or a taxi.

M Isn't the taxi fare _____ _____?

W It's two thousand won more expensive than a bus.

M That _____ _____.

W Then let's _____ _____ _____.

M ♥ All right.

이유 추론

12 대화를 듣고, 남자가 여자를 불러 낸 이유로 가장 적절한 것을 고르시오.

① 생일 선물을 주기 위해서
② 다퉜던 일을 사과하기 위해서
③ 여자의 물건을 돌려주기 위해서
④ 좋아하는 마음을 고백하기 위해서
⑤ 여자에게 사과할 것을 요구하기 위해서

12

W   Minho, why did you call me and ask me _____ _____ _____?

M   There's something I want to *give you and tell you.

W   _____ _____ _____?

M   Here are some flowers and a letter.

W   _____ are you _____ _____ to me?

M   I want to say I like you very much.

*give you [기브] [유] → [기뷰]

장소 추론

13 대화를 듣고, 두 사람이 대화하는 장소로 가장 적절한 곳을 고르시오.

① 공원
② 온천
③ 수영장
④ 수족관
⑤ 박물관

13

M   Now I _____ _____ _____.

W   I wanted to come here so much.

M   Is the water temperature _____?

W   It's a little hot, but I like it.

M   Let's _____ _____ _____ _____ for a few minutes.

그림 정보 파악

14 대화를 듣고, 여자가 가려는 장소로 가장 적절한 곳을 고르시오.

14

W   Excuse me. I'm new here. Do you know any cafés near here?

M   Of course, I do. There is a café very close by.

W   _____ _____ _____ _____ _____ from here?

M   Go straight to Diamond Street. Then, _____ _____.

W   Okay.

M   You will see a pet shop on your left. The café is _____ _____ the pet shop.

W   Thank you very much!

부탁한 것 파악

15 대화를 듣고, 남자가 여자에게 부탁한 일로
가장 적절한 것을 고르시오.

① 장소 이동하기
② 털장갑 빌려주기
③ 밖에서 기다리기
④ 친구에게 전화하기
⑤ 따뜻한 곳으로 이동하기

15

M Isn't it _____ _____ _____ _____
_____?

W Are you cold? They will arrive soon.

M Then do you have any hand warmers?

W No, I don't. But I have some mittens.

M Can I _____ them _____ _____ _____?

W Here you are.

M I feel much better now.

제안한 것 파악

16 대화를 듣고, 여자가 남자에게 제안한
것으로 가장 적절한 것을 고르시오.

① 휴대폰 충전하기
② 안경 맞추러 가기
③ 충분한 휴식 취하기
④ 새 휴대폰으로 교체하기
⑤ 휴대폰 사용 시간 줄이기

16

W You use your _____ _____ for several hours at a
time.

M The reason is that I can do everything with it.

W That will make your eyes _____.

M I know that.

W It's not good for your eyesight. You might have to _____
_____.

M Oh, no. I don't want to wear eyeglasses.

W You'd better _____ _____ _____ on your cell
phone then.

한 일 파악

17 대화를 듣고, 여자가 한 일로 가장 적절한
것을 고르시오.

① 영화 시간표 확인하기
② 약속 시간 정하기
③ 운동하러 가기
④ 영화 관람하기
⑤ 숙제 같이하기

17 🇬🇧

M Did you watch the movie *Aquaman*?

W Yes, I did but I still want to watch it again.

M ♥Would you like to *watch it with me _____?

W Sure! _____ _____ should we meet?

M Let me _____ the movie _____ first.

W Okay.

*watch it [워치] [잇] → [워칫]

♥ **Would you like to + v?**
: 상대방에게 무언가를 제안하거나 권유할 때
사용하는 표현으로, '~하고 싶으세요?'라는
뜻이다.

18 대화를 듣고, 여자의 직업으로 가장 적절한 것을 고르시오.

① 웨이터
② 미식가
③ 요리사
④ 요리 강사
⑤ 제빵사

18

W _____ _____ _____ _____?

M It was great.

W I'm _____ _____ hear that.

M I always thank you for the delicious dishes you make.

W It's _____ _____.

M I'll come again!

W Thank you!

[19~20] 대화를 듣고, 남자의 마지막 말에 이어질 여자의 응답으로 가장 적절한 것을 고르시오.

19 Woman: _____

① I understand that.
② That's a great idea.
③ I'm sorry to hear that.
④ I don't agree with you.
⑤ I should study by myself.

19

M Have you thought about your _____ _____?

W Yes, but I don't know what I want to do.

M What are you _____ _____?

W I don't know what I'm interested in either.

M Why don't we _____ _____ _____ the job experience program?

W <u>That's a great idea.</u>

---

20 Woman: _____

① Tell me why she feels bad.
② Don't make your friend angry.
③ You can write a letter of apology.
④ You should say sorry to your friend.
⑤ A friendship doesn't break so easily.

20

M What is a good way to _____ _____ my friend?

W Saying sorry to him or her would be good.

M I already did, but she is still _____ _____ _____.

W There's _____ good way.

M What is it?

W <u>You can write a letter of apology.</u>

A 들려주는 단어를 듣고 쓴 뒤, 괄호 안에 우리말 뜻을 쓰시오.

	영어	우리말		영어	우리말
1			6		
2			7		
3			8		
4			9		
5			10		

B 다음 문장을 잘 듣고 빈칸에 들어갈 단어를 채우시오.

1 _____ _____ we go now?

2 Can I borrow them _____ _____ _____?

3 Here are _____ _____ and _____ _____.

4 You _____ really _____ _____ fashion.

5 Would you _____ _____ _____ it with me tomorrow?

6 I got _____ _____ _____ _____ the math exam.

7 The reason is that I can _____ _____ _____ _____.

8 How _____ _____ read _____ _____ so well?

9 I'll _____ _____ some other restaurants on the Internet.

10 I'll get enough sleep because a good night's _____ _____ _____.

1 다음을 듣고, 'I'가 무엇인지 가장 적절한 것을 고르시오.

①   ②   ③

④   ⑤

2 대화를 듣고, 여자가 구입하려는 텀블러로 가장 적절한 것을 고르시오.

①   ②   ③

④   ⑤

3 다음을 듣고, New York City의 날씨로 가장 적절한 것을 고르시오.

①   ②   ③

④   ⑤

4 대화를 듣고, 남자의 마지막 말의 의도로 가장 적절한 것을 고르시오.

① 동의 ② 감사 ③ 제안
④ 불만 ⑤ 거절

5 다음을 듣고, 남자가 친구를 사귀는 방법으로 언급하지 않은 것을 고르시오.

① 영화 보기 ② 숙제 도와주기
③ 먼저 인사하기 ④ 귀 기울여 주기
⑤ 관심사 나누기

6 대화를 듣고, 여자가 치과 진료를 받을 시각을 고르시오.

① 3:00 ② 3:30 ③ 4:00
④ 4:30 ⑤ 5:00

7 대화를 듣고, 여자의 장래 희망으로 가장 적절한 것을 고르시오.

① 소설가 ② 과학자 ③ 미술 선생님
④ 종이 공예가 ⑤ 환경 운동가

8 대화를 듣고, 남자의 심정으로 가장 적절한 것을 고르시오.

① happy ② nervous ③ worried
④ jealous ⑤ relaxed

9 대화를 듣고, 여자가 대화 직후에 할 일로 가장 적절한 것을 고르시오.

① 병문안 가기
② 선물 사러 가기
③ 차 보험 처리하기
④ 친구에게 전화하기
⑤ 사고 원인 알아보기

10 대화를 듣고, 무엇에 관한 내용인지 가장 적절한 것을 고르시오.

① 풍경 ② 재능
③ 여가 활동 ④ 사진 촬영
⑤ 독서 활동

11 대화를 듣고, 두 사람이 함께 이용하고 있는 교통수단으로 가장 적절한 것을 고르시오.
① 택시   ② 버스   ③ 지하철
④ 자동차   ⑤ 오토바이

12 대화를 듣고, 남자가 약속을 취소한 이유로 가장 적절한 것을 고르시오.
① 몸 상태가 좋지 않기 때문에
② 집 청소를 도와야 하기 때문에
③ 친척들이 집에 방문하기 때문에
④ 여자와 의견 충돌이 있기 때문에
⑤ 약속을 다른 날로 바꾸고 싶기 때문에

13 대화를 듣고, 두 사람의 관계로 가장 적절한 것을 고르시오.
① 의사 – 환자   ② 점원 – 손님
③ 선생님 – 학생   ④ 미용사 – 손님
⑤ 운동선수 – 코치

14 대화를 듣고, 남자가 사려는 책의 위치로 가장 적절한 곳을 고르시오.

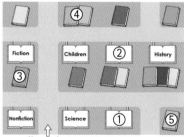

15 대화를 듣고, 남자가 여자에게 부탁한 일로 가장 적절한 것을 고르시오.
① 재료 손질하기
② 양파 구입하기
③ 같이 장 보러 가기
④ 스파게티 만들어 주기
⑤ 스파게티 소스 만들기

16 대화를 듣고, 여자가 남자에게 제안한 것으로 가장 적절한 것을 고르시오.
① 요금제 바꾸기
② 통신사 이동하기
③ 카메라 교체하기
④ 카메라 성능 좋은 휴대 전화 사기
⑤ 카메라 렌즈 구입하기

17 대화를 듣고, 남자가 빌리려는 물건으로 가장 적절한 것을 고르시오.
① USB   ② 공책   ③ 휴대 전화
④ 노트북   ⑤ 발표 자료

18 대화를 듣고, 여자의 직업으로 가장 적절한 것을 고르시오.
① 경찰   ② 청소부   ③ 간호사
④ 소방관   ⑤ 선생님

[19~20] 대화를 듣고, 남자의 마지막 말에 이어질 여자의 응답으로 가장 적절한 것을 고르시오.

19 Woman: _____
① Don't mention it.
② Sure, I'd love to do it.
③ I don't agree with you.
④ I usually eat a lot of fruit.
⑤ I'm not interested in health.

20 Woman: _____
① Easy come; easy go.
② Practice makes perfect.
③ Two heads are better than one.
④ The early bird catches the worm.
⑤ Actions speak louder than words.

Listen and Check

● 대화를 다시 듣고, 알맞은 것을 고르시오.

1 Do some people drink this to wake up?
☐ Yes   ☐ No

2 The woman wants to have her name carved on the tumbler.
☐ True   ☐ False

3 How will the weather in Washington be?
☐ sunny   ☐ rainy

4 Is the man complaining to the woman?
☐ Yes   ☐ No

5 Sharing interests is one way to make friends.
☐ True   ☐ False

6 Is the dental clinic close to the woman's school?
☐ Yes   ☐ No

7 What does the woman like to do with paper?
☐ draw pictures   ☐ do paper crafts

8 The man is looking for his missing cat.
☐ True   ☐ False

9 Why was Emily admitted to the hospital?
☐ a high fever   ☐ a car accident

10 Is the woman talented at taking pictures?
☐ Yes   ☐ No

11 They are excited about riding their bikes.
☐ True   ☐ False

12 The man is visiting his relatives today.
☐ True   ☐ False

13 The woman does not want to practice anymore.
☐ True   ☐ False

14 English textbooks are in the children's section.
☐ True   ☐ False

15 What does the man ask the woman to buy at the supermarket?
☐ spaghetti sauce   ☐ onions

16 Does the man want to buy a cell phone at a low price?
☐ Yes   ☐ No

17 The man brought his USB but not his laptop.
☐ True   ☐ False

18 Does the woman love her job?
☐ Yes   ☐ No

19 Is the woman doing something for her health?
☐ Yes   ☐ No

20 This is not the first time the man has broken a promise.
☐ True   ☐ False

그림 정보 파악

1 다음을 듣고, 'I'가 무엇인지 가장 적절한 것을 고르시오.

① ② coffee ③

④ ⑤

1

M　People like to _____ _____. They usually drink me at cafés, work, and home. They sometimes drink me to wake up or to get energy. I have caffeine. I can _____ _____ or _____. When people _____ _____ _____ _____, I become latte. I am one of the most popular drinks along with tea. What am I?

그림 정보 파악

2 대화를 듣고, 여자가 구입하려는 텀블러로 가장 적절한 것을 고르시오.

① ② ALICE ③

④ ALICE ⑤ A

♥ **I would like to + v**

: 하고 싶은 것을 말할 때 사용하는 표현으로, '〜하고 싶다'라는 뜻이다. 'I want to 〜'와 뜻은 동일하지만, 좀 더 정중하게 표현할 때 사용된다.

2

W　♥I would like to buy a tumbler.

M　We have _____ _____ _____ tumblers, one with a string and the other with no string.

W　The _____ _____ a _____ seems easier to carry.

M　That's right. Do you want to _____ _____ _____ *carved on it?

W　Yes, _____. My name is Alice.

*carved on [칼브드] [온] → [칼브돈]

그림 정보 파악

3 다음을 듣고, New York City의 날씨로 가장 적절한 것을 고르시오.

① ② ③ ☼

④ ⑤

3

M　Good evening. I'm Daniel Jackson from the weather center. We had a rainy day all over Washington, and it will _____ _____ _____. However, it will be sunny in New York City. It will be nice weather to _____ _____ _____ _____.

의도 파악

4 대화를 듣고, 남자의 마지막 말의 의도로 가장 적절한 것을 고르시오.

① 동의　② 감사　③ 제안
④ 불만　⑤ 거절

♥ **Are you sure?**

: 상대방에게 확인을 요청할 때 사용하는 표현으로, '확실한가요?'라는 뜻이다.
= Are you certain?

4 🇬🇧

W　Minseong, are you playing a game again?

M　I've already _____ _____ _____.

W　♥Are you sure?

M　Mom, why do you _____ _____ _____?

언급 유무 파악

5 다음을 듣고, 남자가 친구를 사귀는 방법으로 언급하지 <u>않은</u> 것을 고르시오.

① 영화 보기
② 숙제 도와주기
③ 먼저 인사하기
④ 귀 기울여 주기
⑤ 관심사 나누기

5

M It is not hard to _____ _____. First, you can go up to people and say hello. Second, _____ _____ _____ with them. Next, you can watch a movie or go on a trip together. Last, you should _____ carefully _____ what they say.

숫자 정보 파악

6 대화를 듣고, 여자가 치과 진료를 받을 시각을 고르시오.

① 3:00   ② 3:30   ③ 4:00
④ 4:30   ⑤ 5:00

♥ **All right.**

: 상대방의 말을 받아들일 때 사용하는 표현으로, '좋아요.', '괜찮아요.', '알겠어요.'라는 뜻이다.

= Okay.
= I'm fine with it.

6

W Do I really have to go to the _____ _____?

M Yes, you do. What time does your _____ _____ _____?

W It finishes at 3:30. And I'll _____ _____ by 4:00.

M I'll _____ _____ _____ in *front of your school.

W Okay. Then I can see you at 3:30.

M ♥ All right. I'll make an appointment with the dentist for 4:30.

*front of [프런트] [오브] → [프런터브]

장래 희망 파악

7 대화를 듣고, 여자의 장래 희망으로 가장 적절한 것을 고르시오.

① 소설가
② 과학자
③ 미술 선생님
④ 종이 공예가
⑤ 환경 운동가

7 🏴

M Irene, what did you make?

W I made the Eiffel Tower in France.

M It's awesome! How did you *make it _____ _____ _____?

W I love _____ _____ _____ so much.

M I'm sure you will be a good craftsman.

W Thanks. I really _____ _____.

*make it [메이크] [잇] → [메이킷]

심정 추론

8 대화를 듣고, 남자의 심정으로 가장 적절한 것을 고르시오.

① happy   ② nervous
③ worried   ④ jealous
⑤ relaxed

♥ **I'm so sorry to hear that.**

: 상대방의 말에 유감이나 동정을 나타낼 때 사용하는 표현으로, '유감이야.', '안됐다.'라는 뜻이다.

= That's too bad.

8

W Kyle, what's wrong?

M My cat is _____.

W ♥ I'm so sorry to hear that.

M I _____ _____ a few places, but I couldn't find her.

W How about _____ _____ _____ about it?

M Maybe I should try that.

9

할 일 파악

할 일 파악

9 대화를 듣고, 여자가 대화 직후에 할 일로 가장 적절한 것을 고르시오.

① 병문안 가기
② 선물 사러 가기
③ 차 보험 처리하기
④ 친구에게 전화하기
⑤ 사고 원인 알아보기

9

M Did you hear that Emily _____ _____ _____ the _____ ?

W Really? What happened to her?

M She _____ _____ a car accident.

W Oh, no. Is she okay now?

M I'm not sure.

W I think I should _____ her.

10

화제 · 주제 파악

10 대화를 듣고, 무엇에 관한 내용인지 가장 적절한 것을 고르시오.

① 풍경
② 재능
③ 여가 활동
④ 사진 촬영
⑤ 독서 활동

♥ **What about you?**
: 상대방의 의견을 물어볼 때 사용하는 표현으로, '네 생각은 어때?'라는 뜻이다.
= How about you?
= What do you say?
= What do you think about it?

10

W What do you do in your _____ _____ ?

M I usually read books and watch TV. ♥ What about you?

W I go out and _____ _____ _____ natural scenery.

M Cool! May I see your pictures?

W Sure, but I'm _____ _____ _____ photography.

M That's okay.

11

교통수단 파악

11 대화를 듣고, 두 사람이 함께 이용하고 있는 교통수단으로 가장 적절한 것을 고르시오.

① 택시   ② 버스   ③ 지하철
④ 자동차   ⑤ 오토바이

11

M Hey, Sunmi. Are you _____ _____ _____ for a ride today?

W Yes, I am. By the way, did you bring your helmet?

M Of course, I did. You should wear one _____ _____ _____ , too.

W That's right. Let's _____ _____ .

이유 추론

12 대화를 듣고, 남자가 약속을 취소한 이유로 가장 적절한 것을 고르시오.

① 몸 상태가 좋지 않기 때문에
② 집 청소를 도와야 하기 때문에
③ 친척들이 집에 방문하기 때문에
④ 여자와 의견 충돌이 있기 때문에
⑤ 약속을 다른 날로 바꾸고 싶기 때문에

12

W Kevin, why did you _____ _____ _____ suddenly?

M I'm so sorry. I just heard my relatives are coming to my house today.

W Well, I guess you have no choice then.

M I _____ to you.

W Accepted. Have a good time _____ _____ _____.

M Thanks. See you!

관계 추론

13 대화를 듣고, 두 사람의 관계로 가장 적절한 것을 고르시오.

① 의사 – 환자
② 점원 – 손님
③ 선생님 – 학생
④ 미용사 – 손님
⑤ 운동선수 – 코치

13 🇬🇧

M Are you _____ _____?

W Yes. Should I do more?

M Of course. You have to _____ _____ _____.

W That seems really challenging.

M I know you can do it.

W Okay, I will _____ _____.

M Perfect.

그림 정보 파악

14 대화를 듣고, 남자가 사려는 책의 위치로 가장 적절한 곳을 고르시오.

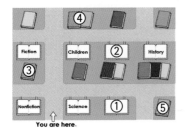

14

W How can I help you?

M I'm looking for _____ _____.

W You can get them in the _____ _____.

M Where is it?

W Go down to the children's section and _____ _____.

M Okay.

W It's between the _____ section and the children's section.

부탁한 것 파악

15 대화를 듣고, 남자가 여자에게 부탁한 일로 가장 적절한 것을 고르시오.

① 재료 손질하기
② 양파 구입하기
③ 같이 장 보러 가기
④ 스파게티 만들어 주기
⑤ 스파게티 소스 만들기

15

M Do you want to have spaghetti for lunch?

W Yes, I'd love to. That's _____ _____.

M Which sauce do you prefer, cream or tomato?

W I _____ cream sauce.

M Oh, no. I need more onions. Can you go to the supermarket and buy me some onions, please?

W Sure. _____ _____ _____ _____ _____?

M Three would be okay.

제안한 것 파악

16 대화를 듣고, 여자가 남자에게 제안한 것으로 가장 적절한 것을 고르시오.

① 요금제 바꾸기
② 통신사 이동하기
③ 카메라 교체하기
④ 카메라 성능 좋은 휴대 전화 사기
⑤ 카메라 렌즈 구입하기

16 🇬🇧

M Hi. I want to _____ _____ _____ _____.

W Here are some new models.

M Which one has the best camera?

W The one with two camera lenses. I also _____ this.

M Okay. I'll _____ it.

특정 정보 파악

17 대화를 듣고, 남자가 빌리려는 물건으로 가장 적절한 것을 고르시오.

① USB   ② 공책
③ 휴대 전화   ④ 노트북
⑤ 발표 자료

♥ **May I + v?**
: 상대방에게 허락을 구할 때 나타내는 표현으로, '~해도 될까요?'라는 뜻이다.
= Can I + v?

17

W Jordan, are you _____ _____ your presentation?

M Oh, no! I didn't _____ _____ _____.

W Do you have your USB?

M Yeah, I brought it. ♥May I _____ your laptop later?

W Sure. I'll _____ _____ to you.

직업 추론

18 대화를 듣고, 여자의 직업으로 가장 적절한 것을 고르시오.

① 경찰
② 청소부
③ 간호사
④ 소방관
⑤ 선생님

18

M Judy, what time do you finish work?

W I finish at _____ _____ _____ _____.

M Why is that?

W I sometimes work long shifts when I have to help very sick patients.

M That's right. An emergency can happen anytime.

W Yes, it can. It's tough, but I love my work.

M I'm so _____ _____ _____!

적절한 응답 찾기

[19-20] 대화를 듣고, 남자의 마지막 말에 이어질 여자의 응답으로 가장 적절한 것을 고르시오.

19 Woman: _____

① Don't mention it.
② Sure, I'd love to do it.
③ I don't agree with you.
④ I usually eat a lot of fruit.
⑤ I'm not interested in health.

19

W Eunho, what do you do to _____ _____?

M I eat vegetables and exercise every day.

W Wow! You really _____ _____ your body.

M Of course, I do. What about you?

W I do nothing, but I want to do something for my health, too.

M Do you _____ _____ _____ _____ when I exercise?

W Sure, I'd love to do it.

적절한 응답 찾기

20 Woman: _____

① Easy come; easy go.
② Practice makes perfect.
③ Two heads are better than one.
④ The early bird catches the worm.
⑤ Actions speak louder than words.

20 🇬🇧

W Charlie, you didn't _____ _____ again yesterday!

M I'm so sorry. I fell into a deep sleep.

W You always make the same _____!

M I set the alarm, but I didn't *hear it.

W That's _____ _____ _____.

M I will not _____ _____ _____ _____. Please forgive me.

W Actions speak louder than words.

*hear it [히얼] [잇] → [히어릿]

A 들려주는 단어를 듣고 쓴 뒤, 괄호 안에 우리말 뜻을 쓰시오.

	영어	우리말		영어	우리말
1			6		
2			7		
3			8		
4			9		
5			10		

B 다음 문장을 잘 듣고 빈칸에 들어갈 단어를 채우시오.

1 I will not _____ _____ wait again.

2 You have to _____ _____ _____.

3 _____ _____ _____ _____ USB?

4 I usually _____ _____ and _____ _____.

5 How _____ _____ _____ _____ _____ with paper?

6 Do you want to have your name _____ _____ _____?

7 I eat _____ and _____ every day.

8 Did you hear that Emily was _____ _____ the hospital?

9 I'll make a(n) _____ _____ the dentist for 4:30.

10 I _____ _____ a few places, but I couldn't find her.

1 다음을 듣고, 'this'가 가리키는 것으로 가장 적절한 것을 고르시오.

①   ②   ③

④   ⑤

2 대화를 듣고, 남자가 잃어버린 배낭으로 가장 적절한 것을 고르시오.

①   ②   ③

④   ⑤

3 다음을 듣고, 내일 홍콩의 날씨로 가장 적절한 것을 고르시오.

①   ②   ③

④   ⑤

4 대화를 듣고, 남자의 마지막 말의 의도로 가장 적절한 것을 고르시오.
① 실망 ② 격려 ③ 축하
④ 거절 ⑤ 동의

5 다음을 듣고, 여자가 이번 주말 계획에 대해 언급하지 <u>않은</u> 것을 고르시오.
① 방 청소하기 ② 친구네 집 방문하기
③ 영화 보기 ④ 독서하기
⑤ 개를 산책시키기

6 대화를 듣고, 남자가 놀이공원에 입장한 시각을 고르시오.
① 9:00 a.m. ② 9:30 a.m.
③ 10:00 a.m. ④ 10:30 a.m.
⑤ 11:00 a.m.

7 대화를 듣고, 여자의 장래 희망으로 가장 적절한 것을 고르시오.
① 화가 ② 승무원
③ 운전사 ④ 기술자
⑤ 전시 기획자

8 대화를 듣고, 남자의 심정으로 가장 적절한 것을 고르시오.
① lonely ② scared ③ worried
④ nervous ⑤ delighted

9 대화를 듣고, 여자가 대화 직후에 할 일로 가장 적절한 것을 고르시오.
① 빨래하기
② 옷 사러 가기
③ 식료품 구입하기
④ 세탁소에 옷 맡기기
⑤ 토마토 소스 만들기

10 대화를 듣고, 무엇에 관한 내용인지 가장 적절한 것을 고르시오.
① 취미 생활 ② 건강 검진
③ 봉사 활동 ④ 장래 희망
⑤ 전시회 안내

11 대화를 듣고, 두 사람이 함께 이용할 교통수단으로 가장 적절한 것을 고르시오.
① 버스　　　② 택시　　　③ 자전거
④ 지하철　　⑤ 비행기

12 대화를 듣고, 남자가 여자를 찾아 온 이유로 가장 적절한 것을 고르시오.
① 조퇴하려고
② 숙제 제출을 미루려고
③ 내일 결석을 알리려고
④ 시험 범위가 궁금해서
⑤ 감점 요인을 알고 싶어서

13 대화를 듣고, 두 사람이 대화하는 장소로 가장 적절한 곳을 고르시오.
① 은행　　　② 호텔　　　③ 도서관
④ 경찰서　　⑤ 박물관

14 대화를 듣고, 여자가 찾고 있는 선글라스의 위치로 가장 적절한 곳을 고르시오.

15 대화를 듣고, 여자가 남자에게 요청한 일로 가장 적절한 것을 고르시오.
① 설거지하기
② 함께 요리하기
③ 소금 추가하기
④ 대신 전화 받기
⑤ 물 가져다 주기

16 대화를 듣고, 여자가 남자에게 제안한 것으로 가장 적절한 것을 고르시오.
① 동물 키우기
② 집에 놀러 오기
③ 일찍 귀가하기
④ 선물 사다 주기
⑤ 고양이에게 밥 주기

17 대화를 듣고, 남자가 지난여름 방학에 한 일로 가장 적절한 것을 고르시오.
① 여행하기
② 일광욕하기
③ 첼로 배우기
④ 악기 공연하기
⑤ 마라톤 참여하기

18 대화를 듣고, 여자의 직업으로 가장 적절한 것을 고르시오.
① 심판　　　② 감독　　　③ 촬영 기사
④ 운동선수　⑤ 스포츠 해설가

[19-20] 대화를 듣고, 여자의 마지막 말에 이어질 남자의 응답으로 가장 적절한 것을 고르시오.

19 Man: _____
① We should take a taxi.
② Let's order some delicious food.
③ Don't worry. I'll be there soon.
④ It's all right. You did your best.
⑤ The next time, you should keep your promise.

20 Man: _____
① That's a wonderful idea!
② Hiking makes people healthy.
③ You can't pick the flowers.
④ I need to take some medicine.
⑤ No, we should finish it in two days.

Listen and Check

● 대화를 다시 듣고, 알맞은 것을 고르시오.

1 This can be broken if you do not use it carefully.

☐ True ☐ False

2 Where did the man lose his backpack?

☐ on the subway ☐ in a taxi

3 Will people need an umbrella in Taipei tomorrow?

☐ Yes ☐ No

4 Why are their neighbors so loud late at night?

☐ because of a war ☐ because of a party

5 The woman will visit her best friend this weekend.

☐ True ☐ False

6 Why did the man enter the amusement park later than the opening time?

☐ He was waiting for his friend.
☐ He missed the bus.

7 Did they already go to the Klimt exhibition?

☐ Yes ☐ No

8 Taemin won first prize in the math contest.

☐ True ☐ False

9 When did the woman buy the shirt?

☐ today ☐ yesterday

10 The woman's friend found out that he was sick.

☐ True ☐ False

11 What should they worry about?

☐ a traffic jam ☐ higher prices

12 Did the man finish his homework?

☐ Yes ☐ No

13 Why did the man visit this place?

☐ to check out a book
☐ to return a book

14 The sunglasses are not on the bench.

☐ True ☐ False

15 How does the food taste?

☐ spicy ☐ salty

16 Is the man feeding stray cats?

☐ Yes ☐ No

17 What did the woman do during summer vacation?

☐ go to the beach ☐ run a marathon

18 Jungyeon went to a baseball stadium to work.

☐ True ☐ False

19 What time did the woman arrive home yesterday?

☐ 10 p.m. ☐ 11 p.m.

20 They are hiking.

☐ True ☐ False

그림 정보 파악

1 다음을 듣고, 'this'가 가리키는 것으로 가장 적절한 것을 고르시오.

① ② ③
④ ⑤

1

M This is a _____ _____ _____. This usually sits on a table or hangs on a wall. You can also _____ a small one in your bag. When you _____ _____ this, you can see your face or check your teeth.

그림 정보 파악

2 대화를 듣고, 남자가 잃어버린 배낭으로 가장 적절한 것을 고르시오.

① ② ③
④ ⑤

♥ **What can I do for you?**
: 상대방에게 도움을 주려고 먼저 물어볼 때 쓰는 표현으로, '도와 드릴까요?'라는 뜻이다.
= How may I help you?

2

[*Telephone rings.*]

W _____ _____ _____. ♥What can I do for you?

M Hello. I lost my _____ on the subway.

W We have one with _____ _____ on it.

M No. My backpack has _____ on it.

W Sorry. We don't *have it.

*have it [해브] [잇] → [해빗]

그림 정보 파악

3 다음을 듣고, 내일 홍콩의 날씨로 가장 적절한 것을 고르시오.

① ② ③
④ ⑤

3

W Here is the weather forecast for tomorrow. You can expect a sunny day _____ in Seoul _____ in Hong Kong. However, Taipei will start to be rainy and _____. Don't _____ _____ _____ your umbrella. In Moscow, it will be _____ and _____. You can make a big snowman there.

의도 파악

4 대화를 듣고, 남자의 마지막 말의 의도로 가장 적절한 것을 고르시오.

① 실망 ② 격려 ③ 축하
④ 거절 ⑤ 동의

4 🏴

W Oh, my! _____ _____ is it now, honey?

M It's 10:30 p.m.

W What is going on at our next-door neighbors' house?

M I heard they're having a _____. But it's so _____.

W It sounds like a war _____ _____ _____.

M That's what I was going to say.

언급 유무 파악

5 다음을 듣고, 여자가 이번 주말 계획에
대해 언급하지 <u>않은</u> 것을 고르시오.

① 방 청소 하기
② 친구네 집 방문하기
③ 영화 보기
④ 독서하기
⑤ 개를 산책시키기

5

W Let me tell you about my _____ _____ this _____. I have to clean my house early in the morning because my best friend will visit my place. We will watch a movie. Second, I'll _____ _____ _____ *Harry Potter*. Lastly, I'll _____ _____ _____ in the park.

숫자 정보 파악

6 대화를 듣고, 남자가 놀이 공원에 입장한
시각을 고르시오.

① 9:00 a.m.   ② 9:30 a.m.
③ 10:00 a.m.   ④ 10:30 a.m.
⑤ 11:00 a.m.

♥ **What happened?**
: 실망스럽거나 좋지 않은 상황에 대해서 구체
적으로 물어볼 때 쓰는 표현으로, '무슨 일이
니?'라는 뜻이다.
= What's wrong?
= What is the matter (with you)?

6

W You went to the amusement _____ yesterday, right?

M Yes, I did! But I could not go in right away.

W ♥What happened? Did it _____ _____?

M No. It *opened at 10:00 a.m. _____ _____.

W Then what was the matter?

M I had to _____ _____ Jihye for 30 minutes.

*opened at [오픈드] [앳] → [오픈댓]

장래 희망 파악

7 대화를 듣고, 여자의 장래 희망으로 가장
적절한 것을 고르시오.

① 화가
② 승무원
③ 운전사
④ 기술자
⑤ 전시 기획자

7

M Soyoung, let's go to the art gallery this Friday.

W You have been _____ _____ the Klimt exhibition, right?

M Correct! I want to be a painter. Do you like painting, too?

W Yes. But it's just my _____.

M Then what do you want to be when you _____ _____?

W An engineer. I'll _____ _____ _____ _____ someday.

심정 추론

8 대화를 듣고, 남자의 심정으로 가장
적절한 것을 고르시오.

① lonely
② scared
③ worried
④ nervous
⑤ delighted

8

W Taemin, did you see the _____ on the bulletin board at school?

M Not yet. What did it say?

W Your _____ won first prize in the English _____ contest. Congratulations.

M Thanks. I'm so _____.

할 일 파악

9 대화를 듣고, 여자가 대화 직후에 할 일로 가장 적절한 것을 고르시오.

① 빨래하기
② 옷 사러 가기
③ 식료품 구입하기
④ 세탁소에 옷 맡기기
⑤ 토마토 소스 만들기

9 🇬🇧

M You _____ _____ on your shirt.

W What? Oh, no. It's _____ _____.

M I think you can wash it out.

W I'm so unlucky. I bought it yesterday.

M _____ _____ you take your shirt to the dry cleaner's now?

W That's a good idea.

화제 · 주제 파악

10 대화를 듣고, 무엇에 관한 내용인지 가장 적절한 것을 고르시오.

① 취미 생활
② 건강 검진
③ 봉사 활동
④ 장래 희망
⑤ 전시회 안내

♥ **What do you mean by that?**
: 앞서 말한 내용의 의미를 파악할 때 사용하는 표현으로, '그게 무슨 의미야?'라는 뜻이다.

10

M _____ _____ do you go to the _____?

W ♥What do you mean by that?

M A doctor discovered that my friend Hojin had a bad disease early, and that saved his life.

W What a _____!

M _____ _____ checkups are important.

W I agree. Prevention is better than a cure.

교통수단 파악

11 대화를 듣고, 두 사람이 함께 이용할 교통수단으로 가장 적절한 것을 고르시오.

① 버스   ② 택시   ③ 자전거
④ 지하철   ⑤ 비행기

11

M Let's go to Namdaemun Market to buy clothes and to eat snacks.

W Great idea. Look! Here comes the bus.

M _____ _____ _____. We should _____ _____ traffic jams at this hour.

W How about taking the _____ then?

M I _____ _____ you.

이유 추론

12 대화를 듣고, 남자가 여자를 찾아 온 이유로 가장 적절한 것을 고르시오.

① 조퇴하려고
② 숙제 제출을 미루려고
③ 내일 결석을 알리려고
④ 시험 범위가 궁금해서
⑤ 감점 요인을 알고 싶어서

12

M   Ms. Kim, may I _____ _____ you for a moment?

W   Why not? _____ _____.

M   Can I _____ _____ my homework _____?

W   Tell me the reason first.

M   I _____ the report, but I *left it at home.

W   All right. However, you will lose a few points.

*left it [레프트] [잇] → [레프팃]

장소 추론

13 대화를 듣고, 두 사람이 대화하는 장소로 가장 적절한 곳을 고르시오.

① 은행   ② 호텔   ③ 도서관
④ 경찰서   ⑤ 박물관

♥ **I got it.**

: 상대방의 말이 무슨 의미인지 이해했다고 말하고 싶을 때 쓰는 표현으로, '이해했어.'라는 뜻이다.
= I understand (it).

13 🇬🇧

W   Good afternoon. May I help you?

M   I'd like to _____ _____ this book.

W   Okay. Please _____ _____ your ID card.

M   _____ _____ can I check out a book for?

W   You have to _____ _____ by Wednesday.

M   ♥ I got it.

그림 정보 파악

14 대화를 듣고, 여자가 찾고 있는 선글라스의 위치로 가장 적절한 곳을 고르시오.

14 🇬🇧

M   Serim, what are you _____ _____?

W   I can't find my sunglasses.

M   I think I saw them on the bench.

W   No. I _____ _____ there. They're not _____ _____ _____ either.

M   There's something on the _____.

W   There they are. Thank you so much.

요청한 것 파악

15 대화를 듣고, 여자가 남자에게 요청한 일로 가장 적절한 것을 고르시오.

① 설거지하기
② 함께 요리하기
③ 소금 추가하기
④ 대신 전화 받기
⑤ 물 가져다 주기

> ♥ **I think ~**
> : 자신의 의견을 전달할 때 쓰는 표현으로, '내 생각에는 ~'이라는 뜻이다.
> = In my opinion, ~
> = In my view, ~

15

W Seungwoo, come to the kitchen and help me.

M Of course. Wow! It _____ great!

W Do you want to try some? How does it _____?

M It's great. But ♥I think it's _____ _____ _____.

W Can you pass me some water?

M Yes, _____ _____ a second.

제안한 것 파악

16 대화를 듣고, 여자가 남자에게 제안한 것으로 가장 적절한 것을 고르시오.

① 동물 키우기
② 집에 놀러 오기
③ 일찍 귀가하기
④ 선물 사다 주기
⑤ 고양이에게 밥 주기

16

W Hello. What are you doing on the street?

M Hi, Yunji. I'm _____ stray cats.

W You're so kind. I *didn't know that you love _____.

M I really do. I wish I could have one.

W _____ and _____ me. We can _____ _____ _____ my cat.

M Are you sure? I'll _____ a present for your cat.

*didn't know [디든트] [노우] → [디든노우]

한 일 파악

17 대화를 듣고, 남자가 지난여름 방학에 한 일로 가장 적절한 것을 고르시오.

① 여행하기
② 일광욕하기
③ 첼로 배우기
④ 악기 공연하기
⑤ 마라톤 참여하기

17 🇬🇧

M You've _____ _____ _____. Did you go to the beach?

W No. I ran a marathon with my friend.

M Oh, wow! Can I join you the next time?

W _____ _____ _____. What did you do during vacation?

M I learned how to play the cello.

W _____ _____! Let me hear you perform.

18 대화를 듣고, 여자의 직업으로 가장 적절한 것을 고르시오.

① 심판
② 감독
③ 촬영 기사
④ 운동선수
⑤ 스포츠 해설가

18

M Jungyeon, _____ _____ _____ _____ _____?

W I'm here to watch a _____ _____.

M Me, too. Let's sit together and talk.

W Maybe next time. I have to work now.

M What do you mean?

W _____ _____, my job is to explain the match to make people understand it easily.

[19-20] 대화를 듣고, 여자의 마지막 말에 이어질 남자의 응답으로 가장 적절한 것을 고르시오.

19 Man: _____ _____ _____

① We should take a taxi.
② Let's order some delicious food.
③ Don't worry. I'll be there soon.
④ It's all right. You did your best.
⑤ The next time, you should keep your promise.

19

M Sweetie, _____ _____ did you _____ _____ yesterday?

W I'm not sure, but it was around 11:00 p.m.

M I *asked you to come home early.

W Daddy, I'm so sorry, but I tried to hurry.

M I do not want this _____ _____ _____.

W I _____ it won't happen again, Dad.

M The next time, you should keep your promise.

*asked you [애스크드] [유] → [애스츄]

---

20 Man: _____ _____ _____

① That's a wonderful idea!
② Hiking makes people healthy.
③ You can't pick the flowers.
④ I need to take some medicine.
⑤ No, we should finish it in two days.

♥ **Cheer up!**
: 고군분투하고 있는 상대방을 격려하기 위해서 쓰는 표현으로, '기운 내!'라는 뜻이다.
= Chin up!

20

W Look! The red and yellow leaves are so beautiful!

M Yes, they are. But my legs hurt.

W ♥Cheer up! It's _____ _____ _____ _____.

M _____ _____ does it take to get to the top?

W About an hour.

M Oh, my! I can't walk any farther.

W Why don't we _____ _____ _____ for a while?

M That's a wonderful idea!

A 들려주는 단어를 듣고 쓴 뒤, 괄호 안에 우리말 뜻을 쓰시오.

	영어	우리말		영어	우리말
1			6		
2			7		
3			8		
4			9		
5			10		

B 다음 문장을 잘 듣고 빈칸에 들어갈 단어를 채우시오.

1 You can _____ it _____.

2 It sounds like a war has _____ _____.

3 Can you _____ _____ some water?

4 Jungyeon, _____ _____ _____ here?

5 You have to _____ _____ by Wednesday.

6 We should _____ _____ traffic jams at this hour.

7 Then what do you want to be when you _____ _____?

8 I do not want this _____ _____ _____.

9 I finished the report, but I _____ _____ _____ _____.

10 This usually sits on a table or _____ _____ _____ _____.

1 다음을 듣고, 'I'가 무엇인지 가장 적절한 것을 고르시오.

①   ②   ③

④   ⑤

2 대화를 듣고, 남자가 구입할 꽃으로 가장 적절한 것을 고르시오.

①   ②   ③

④   ⑤

3 다음을 듣고, 로마의 오늘의 날씨로 가장 적절한 것을 고르시오.

①   ②   ③

④   ⑤

4 대화를 듣고, 여자가 한 마지막 말의 의도로 가장 적절한 것을 고르시오.
① 동의   ② 조언   ③ 거절
④ 격려   ⑤ 실망

5 다음을 듣고, 여자가 동생에 대해 언급하지 <u>않은</u> 것을 고르시오.
① 나이   ② 장래 희망   ③ 외모
④ 취미   ⑤ 성격

6 대화를 듣고, 두 사람이 만날 시각을 고르시오.
① 6:00 p.m.   ② 6:30 p.m.
③ 7:00 p.m.   ④ 7:30 p.m.
⑤ 8:00 p.m.

7 대화를 듣고, 남자의 장래 희망으로 가장 적절한 것을 고르시오.
① 발명가   ② 지휘자
③ 로봇 제작자   ④ 우주 비행사
⑤ 피아노 연주자

8 대화를 듣고, 남자의 심정으로 가장 적절한 것을 고르시오.
① bored   ② moved   ③ excited
④ relieved   ⑤ depressed

9 대화를 듣고, 남자가 대화 직후에 할 일로 가장 적절한 것을 고르시오.
① 선물 구입하기
② 집으로 돌아가기
③ 자선냄비에 돈 넣기
④ 부모님께 선물 드리기
⑤ 크리스마스 캐럴 부르기

10 대화를 듣고, 무엇에 관한 내용인지 가장 적절한 것을 고르시오.
① 수영 경기   ② 나무 심기
③ 바다낚시   ④ 수질 오염
⑤ 준비 운동

11 대화를 듣고, 두 사람이 함께 이용할 교통수단으로 가장 적절한 것을 고르시오.
① 택시 ② 버스 ③ 기차
④ 자전거 ⑤ 비행기

12 대화를 듣고, 남자가 속상해 하는 이유로 가장 적절한 것을 고르시오.
① 동생과 다투어서
② 시험 날짜를 착각해서
③ 다른 과목을 공부해서
④ 시험 도중에 잠들어서
⑤ 이전보다 성적이 나빠서

13 대화를 듣고, 두 사람의 관계로 가장 적절한 것을 고르시오.
① 경찰관 – 학생 ② 관리자 – 점원
③ 발명가 – 기자 ④ 운전기사 – 손님
⑤ 시계 수리공 – 손님

14 대화를 듣고, 빵집의 위치로 가장 적절한 곳을 고르시오.

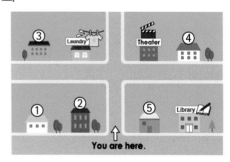

15 대화를 듣고, 남자가 여자에게 부탁한 일로 가장 적절한 것을 고르시오.
① 생활 계획표 만들기
② 미술 숙제 도와주기
③ 선거용 포스터 만들기
④ 반장 선거에 출마하기
⑤ 반 친구들과 친해지기

16 대화를 듣고, 여자가 남자에게 제안한 것으로 가장 적절한 것을 고르시오.
① 영어 일기 쓰기
② 신문 기사 읽기
③ 자신감을 가지기
④ 영문법 공부하기
⑤ 외국인과 대화하기

17 대화를 듣고, 두 사람이 보게 될 영화의 종류를 고르시오.
① 공포 영화
② 액션 영화
③ 만화 영화
④ 다큐멘터리 영화
⑤ 로맨틱 코미디 영화

18 대화를 듣고, 남자의 직업으로 가장 적절한 것을 고르시오.
① 의사 ② 작가 ③ 화가
④ 등산가 ⑤ 사진작가

[19~20] 대화를 듣고, 남자의 마지막 말에 이어질 여자의 응답으로 가장 적절한 것을 고르시오.

19 Woman: _____
① It was 7:00 p.m. when I left.
② I had to go to the restroom.
③ I don't like to watch movies.
④ I think classical music is the best.
⑤ This is my first time to see a concert.

20 Woman: _____
① Have a good time.
② Your brother is so kind.
③ I have been to Mexico once.
④ Sorry, but I'm not hungry now.
⑤ That's a great idea! What time?

Listen and Check

정답 및 해설 p.49

● 대화를 다시 듣고, 알맞은 것을 고르시오.

1 People can run faster than me.
- ☐ True
- ☐ False

2 What kind of flower does the man's friend like?
- ☐ tulips
- ☐ lilies

3 What's the weather like in Lisbon?
- ☐ rainy
- ☐ cold

4 What does the man want to do?
- ☐ buy slippers
- ☐ have a sleepover

5 Jina enjoys reading books.
- ☐ True
- ☐ False

6 They will buy a music CD after school.
- ☐ True
- ☐ False

7 What is the girl interested in?
- ☐ outer space
- ☐ robots

8 Jihyun is excited for moving to another city.
- ☐ True
- ☐ False

9 They want to buy gifts for their parents.
- ☐ True
- ☐ False

10 What are they looking at?
- ☐ the sea
- ☐ the sky

11 What is Jeonju famous for?
- ☐ street food
- ☐ beautiful nature

12 Did Jiho do well on the test?
- ☐ Yes
- ☐ No

13 A little girl was walking on the street while looking at her phone.
- ☐ True
- ☐ False

14 For what will Jun go to the bakery?
- ☐ a sandwich
- ☐ a baguette

15 Is the man running for class president in the election?
- ☐ Yes
- ☐ No

16 Sowon keeps her journal in English.
- ☐ True
- ☐ False

17 Are they talking at the movie theater?
- ☐ Yes
- ☐ No

18 What did the man draw?
- ☐ mountains
- ☐ workers

19 Chris went to a classical music concert.
- ☐ True
- ☐ False

20 Has the man visited the Mexican restaurant before?
- ☐ Yes
- ☐ No

그림 정보 파악

1 다음을 듣고, 'I'가 무엇인지 가장 적절한 것을 고르시오.

① ② ③

④ ⑤

1

W I have _____ _____ and a long tail. I usually eat _____ _____. I can run very fast. So people in the past _____ _____ when they had a _____ _____ _____ _____. What am I?

그림 정보 파악

2 대화를 듣고, 남자가 구입할 꽃으로 가장 적절한 것을 고르시오.

① ② ③

④ ⑤

2

W Welcome. _____ _____ _____ _____ _____?

M I'd like to buy a flower for my friend.

W What about this rose? Girls like roses.

M It looks pretty. But tulips are her _____ _____.

W Sorry, but we're _____ _____ _____ them. Why don't you buy this _____ _____? It's a lily.

M Okay. I'll *take it.

*take it [테이크] [잇] → [테이킷]

그림 정보 파악

3 다음을 듣고, 로마의 오늘의 날씨로 가장 적절한 것을 고르시오.

① ② ③

④ ⑤

3 🇬🇧

M Good morning! Here is today's world weather forecast. It is _____ _____ _____ cloudy in Paris. However, Rome will be sunny and warm. In Lisbon, there will be _____ _____ _____ _____. Stockholm will be very cold but will get _____ _____.

의도 파악

4 대화를 듣고, 여자가 한 마지막 말의 의도로 가장 적절한 것을 고르시오.

① 동의 ② 조언 ③ 거절
④ 격려 ⑤ 실망

♥ **Maybe ~**
: 확실하지는 않지만 약간의 가능성을 나타낼 때 쓰는 표현으로, '아마도'라는 뜻이다.
= Perhaps ~
= Possibly ~

4

M Mom, _____ _____ _____ _____ Mike's house?

W Sure. What time will you come back?

M ♥Maybe tomorrow morning.

W _____ _____. You must _____ _____ _____ _____. That's a rule.

M But I really, really want to have a sleepover.

W You'd _____ _____ to your room right now.

언급 유무 파악

5 다음을 듣고, 여자가 동생에 대해 언급하지 <u>않은</u> 것을 고르시오.

① 나이   ② 장래 희망   ③ 외모
④ 취미   ⑤ 성격

5

W Let me introduce my _____ _____ Jina. She is 10 years old and an elementary school student. She is tall but _____ _____ _____. She likes _____ _____. She wants to _____ _____ _____ in the future.

숫자 정보 파악

6 대화를 듣고, 두 사람이 만날 시각을 고르시오.

① 6:00 p.m.   ② 6:30 p.m.
③ 7:00 p.m.   ④ 7:30 p.m.
⑤ 8:00 p.m.

♥ **Sounds good.**
: 누군가의 제안에 동의할 때 쓰는 표현으로, '좋아.'라는 뜻이다.
= All right.
= No problem.

6

W Bill, can you buy a video game CD with me _____ _____?

M ♥Sounds good. Can we _____ _____ 6:30 p.m.?

W Yes! I don't have _____ _____ today.

M Oh, I'm sorry. I forgot that I have to _____ _____ with my family at 6:00 p.m.

W What? Then how about at 7:30 p.m.?

M I think that's _____. See you soon.

장래 희망 파악

7 대화를 듣고, 남자의 장래 희망으로 가장 적절한 것을 고르시오.

① 발명가   ② 지휘자
③ 로봇 제작자   ④ 우주 비행사
⑤ 피아노 연주자

7 🇬🇧

W [Clapping] Wow! That _____ _____.

M Thank you. I _____ playing the piano almost every day.

W Do you want to be a _____?

M Yes, I do. What do you want to be in the future?

W I want to be a scientist.

M A scientist? What do you like to research?

W I'm _____ _____ robots.

심정 추론

8 대화를 듣고, 남자의 심정으로 가장 적절한 것을 고르시오.

① bored   ② moved
③ excited   ④ relieved
⑤ depressed

8

M Jihyun, why the _____ _____?

W I have to _____ _____ another city next week.

M Are you sure? I can't *believe it.

W I need to transfer to _____ _____, too.

M That makes me _____ _____.

*believe it [빌리브] [잇] → [빌리빗]

9 대화를 듣고, 남자가 대화 직후에 할 일로
가장 적절한 것을 고르시오.

① 선물 구입하기
② 집으로 돌아가기
③ 자선냄비에 돈 넣기
④ 부모님께 선물 드리기
⑤ 크리스마스 캐럴 부르기

9 🇬🇧

W Christmas carols are playing everywhere!

M I like that. But it's so _____ _____.

W I know. We should be in a hurry _____ _____
_____ for our parents.

M [*A bell rings*.] Wait! I _____ _____ _____
ringing.

W Look at that. A man is ringing a bell.

M What is the red pot *next to him?

W That's a charity pot _____ _____ _____ for
the poor.

M I'll put some money into the charity pot.

*next to [넥스트] [투] → [넥스투]

---

10 대화를 듣고, 무엇에 관한 내용인지 가장
적절한 것을 고르시오.

① 수영 경기   ② 나무 심기
③ 바다낚시   ④ 수질 오염
⑤ 준비 운동

10

W Look at the deep blue sea.

M I want to _____ _____ the water now.

W Me, too. But we have to _____ _____ before
swimming.

M That's _____. Warming up reduces the _____ of
injury.

W Okay! Let's start by taking a _____ _____.

M And then let's _____ our legs.

---

11 대화를 듣고, 두 사람이 함께 이용할
교통수단으로 가장 적절한 것을 고르시오.

① 택시   ② 버스
③ 기차   ④ 자전거
⑤ 비행기

♥ **How about ~?**
: 어떤 것을 제안할 때 쓰는 표현으로, '~는 어
때?'라는 뜻이다.
= What about ~?
= Why don't we ~?

11

M I'm _____ _____! We're going to Jeonju next
week.

W I know! Jeonju is _____ _____ its street food.

M Let's take the bus to Jeonju.

W Sorry, but I _____ _____. ♥How about getting on
a train?

M That's a great idea. I like _____ _____ the train
windows.

이유 추론

12 대화를 듣고, 남자가 속상해 하는 이유로 가장 적절한 것을 고르시오.

① 동생과 다투어서
② 시험 날짜를 착각해서
③ 다른 과목을 공부해서
④ 시험 도중에 잠들어서
⑤ 이전보다 성적이 나빠서

12

W Jiho, _____ _____ _____?

M No, I'm not crying. I'm just so *mad at myself.

W Why? What's the matter?

M Well, I _____ _____ yesterday for the English test. But...

W But what?

M I didn't sleep at all last night. So I _____ _____ during the test.

W Ah! That _____ _____.

*mad at [매드] [앳] → [매댓]

관계 추론

13 대화를 듣고, 두 사람의 관계로 가장 적절한 것을 고르시오.

① 경찰관 – 학생
② 관리자 – 점원
③ 발명가 – 기자
④ 운전기사 – 손님
⑤ 시계 수리공 – 손님

13

M [A whistle blows.] Hey, you! The little girl in the school uniform.

W Excuse me? Did I do something _____?

M Do not _____ _____ _____ your phone on the street.

W Ah, I'm sorry, sir.

M It's _____ _____. You should _____ _____ _____ cars.

W Okay. I'll do that. Thank you.

그림 정보 파악

14 대화를 듣고, 빵집의 위치로 가장 적절한 곳을 고르시오.

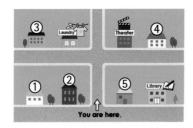

14

W Jun, can you _____ _____ _____ _____?

M Sure. What is it?

W If you buy me a baguette, I'll make you a sandwich.

M Perfect! Where is the bakery?

W _____ _____ one block and then _____ _____.

M And then?

W It'll be on your _____ _____. It's _____ _____ the library.

M Okay. I got it.

부탁한 것 파악

15 대화를 듣고, 남자가 여자에게 부탁한 일로 가장 적절한 것을 고르시오.

① 생활 계획표 만들기
② 미술 숙제 도와주기
③ 선거용 포스터 만들기
④ 반장 선거에 출마하기
⑤ 반 친구들과 친해지기

15 🇬🇧

M I'm worried about the election for _____ _____.

W Did _____ _____ to you?

M I want to _____ my classmates. But I don't know _____ _____ _____.

W Why *don't you make a poster?

M But I'm a _____ painter. Can you help me?

W Of course. Let's start right now.

*don't you [돈츠] [유] → [돈츄]

제안한 것 파악

16 대화를 듣고, 여자가 남자에게 제안한 것으로 가장 적절한 것을 고르시오.

① 영어 일기 쓰기
② 신문 기사 읽기
③ 자신감을 가지기
④ 영문법 공부하기
⑤ 외국인과 대화하기

♥ **I don't think so.**
: 어떤 일에 대해 동의하지 않거나 이의를 제기할 때 쓰는 표현으로, '난 그렇게 생각하지 않아.'라는 뜻이다.
= I don't believe so.
= I don't agree (with you).

16

M Wow, look at that. Sowon is _____ _____ a foreigner in English.

W She is so cool.

M You speak English well, too. What's the secret?

W I _____ _____ _____ in English. I write in it every day.

M It _____ _____ to me.

W ♥I don't think so. You only need to try to write at least three sentences.

특정 정보 파악

17 대화를 듣고, 두 사람이 보게 될 영화의 종류를 고르시오.

① 공포 영화
② 액션 영화
③ 만화 영화
④ 다큐멘터리 영화
⑤ 로맨틱 코미디 영화

17

M This theater is _____ _____.

W Yeah, it's Saturday. What kind of movie do you want to watch?

M I'd love to watch a _____ movie.

W Nope! I don't like scary movies. _____ _____ a romantic comedy?

M That's _____ _____ _____. Let's watch an _____ movie.

W I like that. I'll buy the tickets.

직업 추론

18 대화를 듣고, 남자의 직업으로 가장 적절한 것을 고르시오.

① 의사 ② 작가
③ 화가 ④ 등산가
⑤ 사진작가

18 🇬🇧

M Welcome to the _____ _____.

W _____ _____ _____ all these pictures?

M Yes, they are _____ _____ _____.

W I like this _____ _____ _____. The colors are so beautiful.

M Thank you. Drawing _____ makes me feel calm.

W Do you have other pictures?

M Yes, I'll show you. Follow me.

적절한 응답 찾기

[19-20] 대화를 듣고, 남자의 마지막 말에 이어질 여자의 응답으로 가장 적절한 것을 고르시오.

19 Woman: _____

① It was 7:00 p.m. when I left.
② I had to go to the restroom.
③ I don't like to watch movies.
④ I think classical music is the best.
⑤ This is my first time to see a concert.

> ♥ **What do you mean?**
> : 이해가 되지 않아 추가적인 설명이 필요할 때 쓰는 표현으로, '무슨 의미니?'라는 뜻이다.
> = What exactly is it?
> = Can you explain it?

19

W Chris, _____ _____ your summer vacation?

M It was good. I heard you *went to a classical music _____.

W Yes, I did. But I did not see _____ _____ _____.

M ♥What do you mean?

W Actually, I had to leave in the middle of the concert.

M Really? _____ _____ _____ _____?

W I had to go to the restroom.

*went to [웬트] [투] → [웬투]

적절한 응답 찾기

20 Woman: _____

① Have a good time.
② Your brother is so kind.
③ I have been to Mexico once.
④ Sorry, but I'm not hungry now.
⑤ That's a great idea! What time?

20

W Yunho, there's a Mexican restaurant _____ _____.

M It _____ _____.

W _____ _____ _____ _____ the food there?

M Yes, I had lunch with my brother there last Sunday.

W Did you? _____ _____ _____ _____ of it?

M I think it was tasty. Let's go together this Friday.

W That's a great idea! What time?

A 들려주는 단어를 듣고 쓴 뒤, 괄호 안에 우리말 뜻을 쓰시오.

	영어	우리말			영어	우리말
1				6		
2				7		
3				8		
4				9		
5				10		

B 다음 문장을 잘 듣고 빈칸에 들어갈 단어를 채우시오.

1 I'm just so _____ _____ _____.

2 She is tall but _____ _____ _____.

3 I _____ _____ _____ in English.

4 I need to _____ _____ another school, too.

5 But I really, really want to _____ _____ _____.

6 I _____ _____ the piano almost every day.

7 Do not _____ _____ _____ your phone on the street.

8 I'm worried about the _____ _____ class president.

9 We should be _____ _____ _____ to buy gifts for our parents.

10 Actually, I had to leave _____ _____ _____ _____ the concert.

1 다음을 듣고, 'this'가 가리키는 것으로 가장 적절한 것을 고르시오.

①   ②   ③

④   ⑤

2 대화를 듣고, 여자가 설명하는 책으로 가장 적절한 것을 고르시오.

①   ②   ③

④   ⑤

3 다음을 듣고, 오늘 오후의 날씨로 가장 적절한 것을 고르시오.

①   ②   ③

④   ⑤

4 대화를 듣고, 여자의 마지막 말의 의도로 가장 적절한 것을 고르시오.

① 의심 ② 거절 ③ 충고
④ 허락 ⑤ 부정

5 다음을 듣고, 남자가 연주할 수 있는 악기에 대해 언급하지 <u>않은</u> 것을 고르시오.

① 첼로 ② 플루트
③ 피아노 ④ 클라리넷
⑤ 바이올린

6 대화를 듣고, 두 사람이 만날 시각을 고르시오.

① 2시 5분 ② 2시 15분
③ 2시 20분 ④ 5시 2분
⑤ 5시 15분

7 대화를 듣고, 여자의 장래 희망으로 가장 적절한 것을 고르시오.

① 운동선수 ② 잡지 기자
③ 아나운서 ④ 방송작가
⑤ 영화배우

8 대화를 듣고, 남자의 심정으로 가장 적절한 것을 고르시오.

① shy ② sad ③ excited
④ worried ⑤ interested

9 대화를 듣고, 남자가 대화 직후에 할 일로 가장 적절한 것을 고르시오.

① 간식을 먹지 않기
② 식당을 정확히 찾기
③ 직원에게 도움을 주기
④ 친구와의 잡담을 멈추기
⑤ 영화관을 빠르게 나오기

10 다음을 듣고, 여자의 무엇에 관한 설명인지 고르시오.

① 표 예매 ② 의류 구매
③ 날씨 조사 ④ 친구관리
⑤ 여행 준비

11 대화를 듣고, 두 사람이 함께 이용할 교통수단으로 가장 적절한 것을 고르시오.
① 기차　　　② 자동차　　　③ 버스
④ 비행기　　　⑤ 지하철

12 대화를 듣고, 남자가 아이스커피를 먹지 <u>않는</u> 이유로 가장 적절한 것을 고르시오.
① 돈을 갖고 있지 않아서
② 건강에 좋지 않기 때문에
③ 치통을 가지고 있기 때문에
④ 부모님이 좋아하지 않으셔서
⑤ 차가운 음료를 좋아하지 않아서

13 대화를 듣고, 두 사람이 대화하는 장소로 가장 적절한 곳을 고르시오.
① 교실　　　② 미술관
③ 백화점　　　④ 선물 가게
⑤ 관광 안내소

14 대화를 듣고, 여자가 찾고 있는 인형의 위치로 가장 적절한 곳을 고르시오.

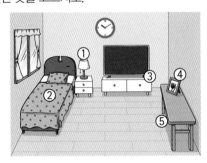

15 대화를 듣고, 여자가 남자에게 부탁한 일로 가장 적절한 것을 고르시오.
① 모임 일정을 변경하기
② 중요한 모임에 참석하기
③ 도서관에서 책을 빌려오기
④ 여동생을 유치원에 데려다 주기
⑤ 학교 행사에 초대 손님으로 참석하기

16 대화를 듣고, 여자가 남자에게 조언한 것으로 가장 적절한 것을 고르시오.
① 우산을 가져가기
② 많은 물을 마시기
③ 관광지에서 정숙하기
④ 손수건 가지고 다니기
⑤ 편안한 신발을 가져가기

17 대화를 듣고, 남자가 주문할 음식으로 가장 적절한 것을 고르시오.
① 햄버거　　　② 치즈버거
③ 스파게티　　　④ 스테이크
⑤ 샐러드

18 대화를 듣고, 남자가 언급한 아빠의 직업으로 가장 적절한 것을 고르시오.
① 기자　　　② 의학자
③ 공학자　　　④ 발명가
⑤ 아나운서

[19~20] 대화를 듣고, 남자의 마지막 말에 이어질 여자의 응답으로 가장 적절한 것을 고르시오.

19 Woman: _____
① Certainly.
② I doubt it.
③ Never mind.
④ Of course not.
⑤ Not at all.

20 Woman: _____
① So am I.
② Have a nice trip.
③ Long time, no see.
④ I am sorry to hear that.
⑤ The next time, you will do better.

● 대화를 다시 듣고, 알맞은 것을 고르시오.

1 This animal moves and hunts in groups.

☐ True ☐ False

2 Where is the woman's book?

☐ on the bed ☐ under the bed

3 Will the rain stop today?

☐ Yes ☐ No

4 The man went to bed at 2 a.m. last night.

☐ True ☐ False

5 What is the man preparing for?

☐ a concert ☐ a musical

6 Why does the woman have to go to the library?

☐ To return a book ☐ To meet a friend

7 The woman wants to interview the man.

☐ True ☐ False

8 Did the woman take her dog to a vet last weekend?

☐ Yes ☐ No

9 What does the woman tell the man to do?

☐ not to eat snacks ☐ not to speak loudly

10 The woman won't take any toothpaste on her trip.

☐ True ☐ False

11 What was the woman thinking of taking to the station?

☐ the subway ☐ a taxi

12 Does the man get a stomachache when he drinks something cold?

☐ Yes ☐ No

13 Where is the man going to buy gifts?

☐ in the modern section
☐ at the souvenir shop

14 The woman found her doll under the TV set.

☐ True ☐ False

15 The man will take his sister to the meeting.

☐ True ☐ False

16 It is very dry in Japan.

☐ True ☐ False

17 What will the man order?

☐ a cheese burger ☐ a steak

18 Did the man's father discover a new vaccine?

☐ Yes ☐ No

19 The man has no appetite in the morning.

☐ True ☐ False

20 What is the man looking forward to?

☐ the woman's birthday party
☐ his birthday party

그림 정보 파악

1 다음을 듣고, 'this'가 가리키는 것으로 가장 적절한 것을 고르시오.

① ② ③
④ ⑤

1

M This is a *kind of animal. It _____ _____ _____. Other animals are afraid of it. The _____ has long hair around his head. We call this animal the _____ _____ _____ _____. This moves and hunts in groups. What is this?

*kind of [카인드] [어브] → [카인더브]

그림 정보 파악

2 대화를 듣고, 여자가 설명하는 책으로 가 적절한 것을 고르시오.

① Toy Story EMMA
② PETER
③ Toy Story PETER
④ EMMA
⑤ Toy Story

♥ **Here it is.**
: 상대방에서 무언가를 건네줄 때 사용하는 표현으로 '여기 있습니다.', '여기요.'라는 뜻이다.
= Here you are.

2

W Dad, I can't _____ my book.

M What book _____ _____ _____ _____, Emma?

W It has the title *Toy Story* on the cover.

M Does the book have your name on it, too?

W No, it doesn't.

M Oh, ♥here it is. It is _____ _____ _____.

그림 정보 파악

3 다음을 듣고, 오늘 오후의 날씨로 가장 적절한 것을 고르시오.

① ② ③
④ ⑤

3

M Good morning. This is today's _____ _____. This morning, it's sunny and clear, but it is going to be cloudy in the afternoon. At night, _____ _____ _____ *a lot of rain with thunder and lightning. The rain will _____ _____ _____.

*a lot of [어] [랏] [어브] → [어라러브]

의도 파악

4 대화를 듣고, 여자의 마지막 말의 의도로 가장 적절한 것을 고르시오.

① 의심 ② 거절 ③ 충고
④ 허락 ⑤ 부정

4

W Jason, wake up! _____ _____ _____.

M Oh, really?

W Why are you sleepy?

M I don't know. I am _____ _____.

W What time did you go to bed last night?

M Maybe about 1:00 a.m.

W I think you should _____ _____ _____ earlier.

5 다음을 듣고, 남자가 연주할 수 있는 악기에 대해 언급하지 <u>않은</u> 것을 고르시오.

① 첼로   ② 플루트
③ 피아노   ④ 클라리넷
⑤ 바이올린

5

W   What are you doing _____ _____?

M   I am preparing for the school concert.

W   That sounds good. What _____ instruments *can you play?

M   I can play the violin, the flute, the piano, and the cello.

W   Wow, _____ _____ _____ a musical genius.

*can you [캔] [유] → [캐뉴]

6 대화를 듣고, 두 사람이 만날 시각을 고르시오.

① 2시 5분   ② 2시 15분
③ 2시 20분   ④ 5시 2분
⑤ 5시 15분

6

M   What _____ _____ _____ _____ _____?

W   I'm writing a report for my art homework. Why do you ask?

M   How about doing it with me? I can help you.

W   Thanks. That will really help me. What time can we meet?

M   What about at _____ _____ _____?

W   I have to go to the library to return this book first. How about 15 minutes _____ _____ _____?

M   Okay. Let's meet at your house then.

7 대화를 듣고, 여자의 장래 희망으로 가장 적절한 것을 고르시오.

① 운동선수   ② 잡지 기자
③ 아나운서   ④ 방송 작가
⑤ 영화배우

7

M   Hi, Jessie. What are you doing now?

W   I am _____ _____ _____ for the school newspaper.

M   You are good at writing, so I am sure _____ _____ _____ a good journalist.

W   I hope so. I want to _____ _____ for the magazine someday.

8 대화를 듣고, 남자의 심정으로 가장 적절한 것을 고르시오.

① shy   ② sad
③ excited   ④ worried
⑤ interested

8

M   Where are you going, Monica?

W   I am worried that my dog is sick. So I am going to _____ _____ _____ _____ _____.

M   I am sorry to hear that. _____ _____ to him?

W   I don't know. He was not doing well over the weekend.

M   Oh, poor dog. I hope he _____ _____ _____.

W   Thank you.

할 일 파악

9 대화를 듣고, 남자가 대화 직후에 할 일로 가장 적절한 것을 고르시오.

① 간식을 먹지 않기
② 식당을 정확히 찾기
③ 직원에게 도움을 주기
④ 친구와의 잡담을 멈추기
⑤ 영화관을 빠르게 나오기

9

W _____ me?

M Sure. What is it?

W I am a staff member at this movie theater. I think you _____ _____ _____ _____.

M I'm sorry, but I don't understand. _____ _____ _____ do?

W You can't eat snacks in this place.

M Oh, really? I didn't know that. Thanks for telling me that.

W _____ _____ _____. It's my job.

화제 · 주제 파악

10 다음을 듣고, 여자의 무엇에 관한 설명인지 고르시오.

① 표 예매
② 의류 구매
③ 날씨 조사
④ 친구 관리
⑤ 여행 준비

10 🇬🇧

M Tomorrow is your trip. Did you finish packing?

W Yes, I packed socks, clothes, and a toothbrush.

M I think you should _____ _____ _____ _____ _____.

W Oh, thanks for the advice. I will put the umbrella in my bag now. I don't need anything else.

M How about toothpaste in case your friends _____ _____ _____ _____?

W You are right. I should bring that, too.

M Now I think you are all done.

교통수단 파악

11 대화를 듣고, 두 사람이 함께 이용할 교통수단으로 가장 적절한 것을 고르시오.

① 기차
② 자동차
③ 버스
④ 비행기
⑤ 지하철

♥ **by the way**
: '그런데 말이야', '그런데'의 의미로 서로 간의 대화 중에 다른 주제의 이야기를 할 경우 사용하는 표현이다.

11

M Why are you _____ _____ _____?

W I have to go to Daejeon as soon as possible.

M Are you going to go by bus?

W No, I'll take the train. I think the train is faster.

M ♥ By the way, how will you get to the station?

W I'm _____ _____ _____ a taxi.

M I'll _____ you to the _____. I will get my car.

W Okay. Thanks.

이유 추론

12 대화를 듣고, 남자가 아이스커피를 먹지 <u>않는</u> 이유로 가장 적절한 것을 고르시오.

① 돈을 갖고 있지 않아서
② 건강에 좋지 않기 때문에
③ 치통을 가지고 있기 때문에
④ 부모님이 좋아하지 않으셔서
⑤ 차가운 음료를 좋아하지 않아서

12

M It's really hot today.

W Yeah. Let's go to the café to drink some _____ _____.

M I'd like to, but I can't.

W Why? _____ _____ _____ any money?

M No, it's not that. I get a toothache when I drink something cold.

W That's too bad. I think you should go to see a dentist.

M Thanks _____ _____ _____. I will.

장소 추론

13 대화를 듣고, 두 사람이 대화하는 장소로 가장 적절한 곳을 고르시오.

① 교실
② 미술관
③ 백화점
④ 선물 가게
⑤ 관광 안내소

13 🇬🇧

W Hi! *If you have any questions, I am here to _____ _____.

M Thanks. Where can I see the modern artists' paintings?

W Go to the _____ _____, and you will see them.

M Great. And can I buy some gifts here?

W Sure. You can buy them _____ _____ _____ _____ on the second floor.

M Thanks a lot.

*If you [이프] [유] → [이퓨]

그림 정보 파악

14 대화를 듣고, 여자가 찾고 있는 인형의 위치로 가장 적절한 곳을 고르시오.

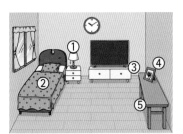

♥ **either**

: 상대방이나 자신이 미리 앞서 부정문으로 이야기를 한 후에, 다음 문장에서도 부정문을 표현하여 '역시, 또한'의 의미를 나타내려고 할 때 사용한다.

14

M Dear, what are you looking for?

W Oh, Dad. I am sad. Last night, _____ _____ _____ my little cute doll, but now it's gone.

M Calm down, honey. The doll _____ _____. It may have fallen off the bed.

W I looked under the bed and the TV, but I couldn't find it.

M How about _____ _____ _____?

W It is not there ♥either.

M How about under the table?

W Oh, you are right. I found it there. Thanks, Dad.

15

15 대화를 듣고, 여자가 남자에게 부탁한 일로 가장 적절한 것을 고르시오.

① 모임 일정을 변경하기
② 중요한 모임에 참석하기
③ 도서관에서 책을 빌려오기
④ 여동생을 유치원에 데려다 주기
⑤ 학교 행사에 초대 손님으로 참석하기

♥ **Why not?**
: '왜 안 돼?'라는 의미와 대화의 문맥에 따라 '왜 안 돼? 당연히 되지.'라는 승낙, 긍정의 의미가 있다.

W Patrick, can you _____ _____ _____ _____?
M Of course, Mom. What is it?
W Can you take your sister Jill to kindergarten for me? I _____ _____ _____ _____ an important meeting now.
M ♥Why not? Is there anything else I _____ _____ _____ _____?
W No, *that's all. Thanks.

*that's all [댓츠] [얼] → [댓철]

16

조언한 것 파악

16 대화를 듣고, 여자가 남자에게 조언한 것으로 가장 적절한 것을 고르시오.

① 우산을 가져가기
② 많은 물을 마시기
③ 관광지에서 정숙하기
④ 손수건 가지고 다니기
⑤ 편안한 신발을 가져가기

M I am going to Japan to go _____ next week.
W Good for you. Have a good trip.
M I heard that you lived in Japan. Can you give me _____ _____ about Japan?
W It is very wet in Japan. So it _____ _____ carry a handkerchief.
M Oh, thanks for the tip. I will do _____ _____ _____.

17 🇬🇧

특정 정보 파악

17 대화를 듣고, 남자가 주문할 음식으로 가장 적절한 것을 고르시오.

① 햄버거
② 치즈버거
③ 스파게티
④ 스테이크
⑤ 샐러드

M Did you decide what you will have?
W Yes, I will have a steak and salad. _____ _____ _____?
M I am not sure. I usually have spaghetti here, but I might _____ _____ _____.
W I heard that the hamburgers here are great, too.
M Oh, _____ _____ _____, I will have a cheeseburger.

정답 및 해설 *p.53*

직업 추론

18 대화를 듣고, 남자가 언급한 아빠의 직업으로 가장 적절한 것을 고르시오.

① 기자
② 의학자
③ 공학자
④ 발명가
⑤ 아나운서

18

W I watched _____ _____ _____ _____ yesterday, and I saw your father!

M Oh, right. That was my father on TV.

W Did he really discover a new vaccine to _____ the _____?

M That's right. He did that in his lab.

W That sounds really great. You must _____ _____ _____ him.

M Yes. He is my hero.

적절한 응답 찾기

[19-20] 대화를 듣고, 남자의 마지막 말에 이어질 여자의 응답으로 가장 적절한 것을 고르시오.

19 Woman: _____

① Certainly.
② I doubt it.
③ Never mind.
④ Of course not.
⑤ Not at all.

♥ **Go ahead.**
: 원래는 '앞서가다.'라는 의미에서 상대방의 말과 의도에 동조하며 '자, 어서 (해봐).'라는 의미로 쓰인다.

19

M Lily, I have _____ _____ _____ _____ you.

W ♥Go ahead. I am listening.

M Do you eat breakfast? I don't have an appetite in the morning.

W I do. You should eat breakfast for your health.

M Do you _____ _____ _____?

W <u>Certainly.</u>

적절한 응답 찾기

20 Woman: _____

① So am I.
② Have a nice trip.
③ Long time, no see.
④ I am sorry to hear that.
⑤ The next time, you will do better.

20

W I am planning _____ _____ _____ _____ for my birthday. Can you come?

M Sure. Where will you _____ the party?

W At my house, of course. My mom is going to cook some nice dishes for us.

M _____ _____ _____ _____ you have! I am looking forward to it.

W <u>So am I.</u>

A 들려주는 단어를 듣고 쓴 뒤, 괄호 안에 우리말 뜻을 쓰시오.

	영어	우리말			영어	우리말
1				6		
2				7		
3				8		
4				9		
5				10		

B 다음 문장을 잘 듣고 빈칸에 들어갈 단어를 채우시오.

1 Does the book have your _____ _____ _____?

2 I think you should _____ _____ _____ earlier.

3 I have to go to the library _____ _____ _____ _____ .

4 You _____ _____ _____ in this place.

5 How about some toothpaste _____ _____ your friends forget to bring some?

6 I'm _____ _____ taking a taxi.

7 You _____ _____ _____ at the souvenir shop.

8 Is there anything else _____ _____ _____ _____ _____?

9 I don't have a(n) _____ in the morning.

10 My mom _____ _____ _____ cook some nice dishes for us.

1 다음을 듣고, 'I'가 무엇인지 가장 적절한 것을 고르시오.

2 대화를 듣고, 남자가 깬 액자로 가장 적절한 것을 고르시오.

① ② France ③

④ ⑤ France

3 다음을 듣고, 화요일의 날씨로 가장 적절한 것을 고르시오.

① ② ③

④ ⑤

4 대화를 듣고, 남자의 마지막 말의 의도로 가장 적절한 것을 고르시오.
① 충고　　② 경고　　③ 축하
④ 격려　　⑤ 권유

5 다음을 듣고, 남자가 집을 구입할 때 체크해야 할 것으로 언급하지 <u>않은</u> 것을 고르시오.
① 다른 시간대에 방문
② 층간 소음의 정도 확인
③ 손상 부분 사진으로 기록
④ 모든 방들을 신중히 확인
⑤ 충분한 햇빛이 드는지 확인

6 대화를 듣고, 재즈 공연을 하는 시각을 고르시오.
① 5:30　　② 6:00　　③ 6:30
④ 7:00　　⑤ 7:30

7 대화를 듣고, 여자의 장래 희망으로 가장 적절한 것을 고르시오.
① 파일럿　　　　② 승무원
③ 여행 작가　　　④ 관광 가이드
⑤ 잡지 편집장

8 대화를 듣고, 남자의 심정으로 가장 적절한 것을 고르시오.
① lonely　　② scared　　③ jealous
④ surprised　　⑤ disappointed

9 대화를 듣고, 여자가 대화 직후에 할 일로 가장 적절한 것을 고르시오.
① 일하기　　　　② 전화하기
③ 퇴근하기　　　④ 낮잠 자기
⑤ 외출 준비하기

10 대화를 듣고, 무엇에 관한 내용인지 가장 적절한 것을 고르시오.
① 벼룩시장　　　② 봉사 활동
③ 헌 옷 정리　　　④ 모임 계획
⑤ 취미 생활

11 대화를 듣고, 두 사람이 함께 이용할 교통수단으로 가장 적절한 것을 고르시오.

① 배   ② 택시   ③ 자전거
④ 버스   ⑤ 헬리콥터

12 대화를 듣고, 남자가 개를 두려워하는 이유로 가장 적절한 것을 고르시오.

① 동물을 좋아하지 않기 때문에
② 개를 키워본 적이 없기 때문에
③ 개를 잃은 아픔이 있기 때문에
④ 개에 대한 안 좋은 기억 때문에
⑤ 개가 짖는 소리를 무서워하기 때문에

13 대화를 듣고, 두 사람의 관계로 가장 적절한 것을 고르시오.

① 보모 – 아이   ② 선생님 – 학생
③ 승무원 – 승객   ④ 선생님 – 학부모
⑤ 운전사 – 승객

14 대화를 듣고, Music Park의 위치로 가장 적절한 곳을 고르시오.

15 대화를 듣고, 남자가 여자에게 부탁한 일로 가장 적절한 것을 고르시오.

① 고민 들어주기
② 개 돌봐 주기
③ 함께 출장 떠나기
④ 여행 계획 작성하기
⑤ 개 호텔 예약하기

16 대화를 듣고, 여자가 남자에게 제안한 것으로 가장 적절한 것을 고르시오.

① 시력 검사하기
② 친구 놀리지 않기
③ 칠판 가까이 앉기
④ 공부할 때 안경 쓰기
⑤ 수업 도중 떠들지 않기

17 대화를 듣고, 남자가 잃어버린 물건으로 가장 적절한 것을 고르시오.

① 시계   ② 지갑   ③ 가방
④ 커플 링   ⑤ 휴대폰

18 대화를 듣고, 여자의 직업으로 가장 적절한 것을 고르시오.

① 개인 비서   ② 피부 관리사
③ 화장품 개발자   ④ 성형외과 의사
⑤ 메이크업 아티스트

[19~20] 대화를 듣고, 여자의 마지막 말에 이어질 남자의 응답으로 가장 적절한 것을 고르시오.

19 Man: _____

① Time flies so fast.
② I love it so much.
③ Well, I'm not sure.
④ Drums sound better.
⑤ I used to, but I don't anymore.

20 Man: _____

① I didn't know that.
② I like calling better.
③ I have a different idea.
④ A cell phone is necessary.
⑤ I didn't receive any messages.

Listen and Check

정답 및 해설 p.59

● 대화를 다시 듣고, 알맞은 것을 고르시오.

1 People use this to save information.
☐ True   ☐ False

2 Does the woman want to have the same frame?
☐ Yes   ☐ No

3 How will the weather be on Thursday?
☐ rainy   ☐ clear

4 The woman gave birth to a baby girl.
☐ True   ☐ False

5 Does the man talk about his neighbors?
☐ Yes   ☐ No

6 What will they do on the cruise?
☐ perform in concert   ☐ have dinner

7 The woman wants to write books about different countries.
☐ True   ☐ False

8 Does the man get better grades than David?
☐ Yes   ☐ No

9 What does the man suggest the woman do?
☐ work less   ☐ get some rest

10 They will sell items to help poor kids.
☐ True   ☐ False

11 Is it the first time for the woman to get in a helicopter?
☐ Yes   ☐ No

12 What makes the man scared of dogs?
☐ his allergic reactions
☐ his old memory

13 The man asks the woman to bring only a blanket.
☐ True   ☐ False

14 Does the man want to go to the Grand Hotel?
☐ Yes   ☐ No

15 For how long will the man stay in America?
☐ one week   ☐ one month

16 The man can't see the board clearly.
☐ True   ☐ False

17 Did he find the ring?
☐ Yes   ☐ No

18 What problem does the man want to solve?
☐ pimples   ☐ dry skin

19 They play in an orchestra.
☐ True   ☐ False

20 According to the article, what do people prefer more?
☐ calling   ☐ texting

그림 정보 파악

1 다음을 듣고, 'I'가 무엇인지 가장 적절한 것을 고르시오.

① ② ③

④ ⑤

1

M I can be small or big. I come in _____ _____. People bring me to their schools and workplaces. They need another machine to use me. They also _____ _____ _____. I can save _____ _____ _____ information. What am I?

그림 정보 파악

2 대화를 듣고, 남자가 깬 액자로 가장 적절한 것을 고르시오.

① ② ③

④ ⑤

2

W Arnold, what happened to this frame?

M I _____ _____ _____ _____. I'll buy a new one for you.

W Okay. Are you sure you will buy the _____ _____?

M A drawing of the Eiffel Tower, right?

W Yes. It also has the word "France" *on it.

*on it [온] [잇] → [오닛]

그림 정보 파악

3 다음을 듣고, 화요일의 날씨로 가장 적절한 것을 고르시오.

① ② ③

④ ⑤

3

M Good morning. This is the ABC weather forecast. It will be cloudy on Monday morning, and it will _____ _____ rain on Monday afternoon in _____ _____ of the nation. On Tuesday, it will stop raining, but the weather will _____ _____. From Wednesday to Friday, you can _____ _____ _____ again.

의도 파악

4 대화를 듣고, 남자의 마지막 말의 의도로 가장 적절한 것을 고르시오.

① 충고 ② 경고 ③ 축하
④ 격려 ⑤ 권유

💜 **Congratulations!**
: 상대방에게 축하해 줄 때 사용하는 표현으로, '축하해!'라는 뜻이다. '-s'를 반드시 붙여서 사용해야 한다.

4

[*Telephone rings.*]

W Hello.

M It's Alex. I heard you had a _____ _____.

W Yes, I did.

M I'm so _____ _____ _____. 💜 Congratulations!

W Thank you.

언급 유무 파악

5 다음을 듣고, 남자가 집을 구입할 때 체크해야 할 것으로 언급하지 <u>않은</u> 것을 고르시오.

① 다른 시간대에 방문
② 층간 소음의 정도 확인
③ 손상 부분 사진으로 기록
④ 모든 방들을 신중히 확인
⑤ 충분한 햇빛이 드는지 확인

5

M   When you buy a house, you need to be _____ _____ some things. First, you should check if the house _____ _____ _____. Next, you need to take a picture of any damage in the house. You must check every room _____ in the house. Lastly, don't forget to visit the house _____ _____ _____.

숫자 정보 파악

6 대화를 듣고, 재즈 공연을 하는 시각을 고르시오.

① 5:30   ② 6:00   ③ 6:30
④ 7:00   ⑤ 7:30

6

W   What time does the cruise tour start?

M   The tour *starts at 6:00, but we should get on the cruise ship at 5:30.

W   Okay. I'm _____ _____ have dinner on the ship!

M   Me, too! There will be a jazz concert at 7:00.

W   Wow, that's awesome!

M   We _____ _____ _____ the cruise.

W   Let's _____ _____!

*starts at [스탈츠] [엣] → [스탈쳇]

장래 희망 추론

7 대화를 듣고, 여자의 장래 희망으로 가장 적절한 것을 고르시오.

① 파일럿   ② 승무원
③ 여행 작가   ④ 관광 가이드
⑤ 잡지 편집장

♥ **be interested in ~**
: 관심사를 나타낼 때 사용하는 표현으로, '~에 관심이 있다'라는 뜻이다.
= have an interest in ~

7

M   Jasmine, are you reading a book about China?

W   Yes, ♥I'm interested in the _____ and _____ of different countries.

M   What do you want to do when you grow up?

W   I want to _____ _____ the world and write a book about it.

M   That's cool! I'm sure you'll be _____ _____ _____ _____.

W   Thanks.

심정 추론

8 대화를 듣고, 남자의 심정으로 가장 적절한 것을 고르시오.

① lonely   ② scared
③ jealous   ④ surprised
⑤ disappointed

8

W   Andy, did something bad happen?

M   I feel bad _____ _____ my friend David.

W   What makes you feel bad?

M   He and I study together, but his test results are always _____ _____ mine.

W   Oh, I see.

M   I should _____ _____ than him.

할 일 파악

9 대화를 듣고, 여자가 대화 직후에 할 일로 가장 적절한 것을 고르시오.

① 일하기
② 전화하기
③ 퇴근하기
④ 낮잠 자기
⑤ 외출 준비하기

9 🇬🇧

M Maggie, you look very tired.

W I had to work from the early morning till now.

M That _____ _____ _____.

W So I'm going to _____ _____ _____ for a while.

M You should. Get some rest.

W Please _____ _____ _____ in twenty minutes.

화제·주제 파악

10 대화를 듣고, 무엇에 관한 내용인지 가장 적절한 것을 고르시오.

① 벼룩시장
② 봉사 활동
③ 헌 옷 정리
④ 모임 계획
⑤ 취미 생활

♥ **I agree with you.**

: 상대방의 의견에 동의를 나타내는 표현으로, '당신의 의견에 동의해요.'라는 뜻이다.

= You can say that again.

= You're telling me.

= You bet.

10

W What items will you sell at a flea market?

M I will _____ _____ _____ _____.

W That sounds nice!

M I hope I can sell *all of them.

W I know. That would _____ _____ _____ a lot.

M ♥ I agree with you.

*all of [얼] [오브] → [얼로브]

교통수단 파악

11 대화를 듣고, 두 사람이 함께 이용할 교통수단으로 가장 적절한 것을 고르시오.

① 배
② 택시
③ 자전거
④ 버스
⑤ 헬리콥터

11

M This is a _____ experience.

W You're right. I can't *imagine it.

M We'll _____ _____ _____ the sky soon.

W Will there be a _____ _____?

M Yes. That will be caused by its rotor blades.

*imagine it [이메진] [잇] → [이메지닛]

이유 추론

12 대화를 듣고, 남자가 개를 두려워하는 이유로 가장 적절한 것을 고르시오.

① 동물을 좋아하지 않기 때문에
② 개를 키워본 적이 없기 때문에
③ 개를 잃은 아픔이 있기 때문에
④ 개에 대한 안 좋은 기억 때문에
⑤ 개가 짖는 소리를 무서워하기 때문에

12

W   Why are you so _____ _____ _____?
M   I have a _____ _____ about them.
W   Why? What happened?
M   A dog _____ _____ me and _____ _____
_____.
W   I see. You *have a reason for feeling that way.
M   Yes, I do.

*have a [해브] [어] → [해버]

관계 추론

13 대화를 듣고, 두 사람의 관계로 가장 적절한 것을 고르시오.

① 보모 – 아이
② 선생님 – 학생
③ 승무원 – 승객
④ 선생님 – 학부모
⑤ 운전사 – 승객

13

M   Excuse me. It's a bit cold here. Can I have a _____,
please?
W   Sure, I'll get one for you.
M   Thank you.
W   Is there _____ _____ you need, sir?
M   _____ _____ _____ _____, please.

그림 정보 파악

14 대화를 듣고, Music Park의 위치로 가장 적절한 곳을 고르시오.

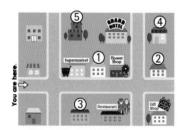

♥ **Would you say that again?**
: 상대방에게 다시 말해 줄 것을 요청하는 표현으로, '다시 한 번 말씀해 주시겠습니까?'라는 뜻이다.
= (I beg your) Pardon?
= What did you say?

14

W   Excuse me. Can you tell me _____ _____
_____ _____ Music Park?
M   Sure. _____ _____ two blocks. Then, turn left.
W   Okay.
M   And then walk down to the Grand Hotel. It's _____
_____ the hotel.
W   Sorry. ♥Would you say that again?
M   _____ _____ _____ the Grand Hotel. It's
across from it.
W   I got it. Thank you very much!

부탁한 것 파악

15 대화를 듣고, 남자가 여자에게 부탁한 일로 가장 적절한 것을 고르시오.

① 고민 들어주기
② 개 돌봐주기
③ 함께 출장 떠나기
④ 여행 계획 작성하기
⑤ 개 호텔 예약하기

♥ **Don't mention it.**
: 상대방이 감사한 마음을 표시할 때, 그에 대한 답변으로 괜찮다는 마음을 나타낼 때 사용하는 표현으로, '괜찮아요.', '별말씀을요.'라는 뜻이다.
= No problem.
= My pleasure.

15

M Jihee, would you _____ _____ _____ _____?

W Sure. What is it?

M I'm going to America on a _____ _____ for a week. But I don't have anyone to take care of my dog Mango.

W Don't worry. I can take care of her.

M Thanks a lot, Jihee. You're really a good friend.

W ♥Don't mention it.

M I'll _____ Mango to your place _____ _____ then.

제안한 것 파악

16 대화를 듣고, 여자가 남자에게 제안한 것으로 가장 적절한 것을 고르시오.

① 시력 검사하기
② 친구 놀리지 않기
③ 칠판 가까이 앉기
④ 공부할 때 안경 쓰기
⑤ 수업 도중 떠들지 않기

♥ **You'd better + v**
: 상대방에게 무언가를 조언하거나 충고를 할 때 사용하는 표현으로, '너는 ~하는 게 좋겠어'라는 뜻이다.

16

W Harry, can't you see the board _____?

M No, my eyesight is _____ _____.

W ♥You'd better wear eyeglasses when you study.

M Should I? But I will look ugly with them.

W That's not _____. You should _____ _____ your eyes first.

특정 정보 파악

17 대화를 듣고, 남자가 잃어버린 물건으로 가장 적절한 것을 고르시오.

① 시계   ② 지갑
③ 가방   ④ 커플 링
⑤ 휴대폰

17 🇬🇧

M Isabella, I am _____ _____.

W Why? What's wrong?

M I _____ _____ _____ _____.

W Oh, my God! Where did you put it?

M I put it in my _____. I think I *dropped it somewhere.

W I will help you find it.

*dropped it [드롭드] [잇] → [드롭딧]

직업 추론

18 대화를 듣고, 여자의 직업으로 가장 적절한 것을 고르시오.

① 개인 비서
② 피부 관리사
③ 화장품 개발자
④ 성형외과 의사
⑤ 메이크업 아티스트

18

W   Hi. How can I help you?

M   I came here because of my dry skin.

W   _____ _____ _____ it for a second.

M   Okay.

W   I recommend you try our _____ _____.

M   Will my skin get _____?

W   Of course. You'll _____ _____ _____ after four weeks in the program.

적절한 응답 찾기

[19-20] 대화를 듣고, 여자의 마지막 말에 이어질 남자의 응답으로 가장 적절한 것을 고르시오.

19   Man: _____
   ① Time flies so fast.
   ② I love it so much.
   ③ Well, I'm not sure.
   ④ Drums sound better.
   ⑤ I used to, but I don't anymore.

♥ **What about you?**
: 상대방의 의견을 물어볼 때 사용하는 표현으로, '네 생각은 어때?'라는 뜻이다.
= How about you?
= What do you say?
= What do you think about it?

19

M   Olivia, is this your _____?

W   Yes, it's mine.

M   Do you sometimes _____ _____ _____?

W   Yes, I _____ the orchestra at school.

M   Wow, that's so cool!

W   ♥What about you? Do you play _____ _____ instruments?

M   I used to, but I don't anymore.

적절한 응답 찾기

20   Man: _____
   ① I didn't know that.
   ② I like calling better.
   ③ I have a different idea.
   ④ A cell phone is necessary.
   ⑤ I didn't receive any messages.

20

M   Abigail, what are you reading?

W   I'm reading an article about _____ _____ _____.

M   What *does it say?

W   It says people _____ _____ _____ more than call.

M   I see.

W   _____ _____ _____ _____, texting or calling?

M   I like calling better.

*does it [더즈] [잇] → [더짓]

Vocabulary Test

정답 및 해설 *p.59*

A 들려주는 단어를 듣고 쓴 뒤, 괄호 안에 우리말 뜻을 쓰시오.

	영어	우리말		영어	우리말
1			6		
2			7		
3			8		
4			9		
5			10		

B 다음 문장을 잘 듣고 빈칸에 들어갈 단어를 채우시오.

1 Where did you _____ _____?

2 Sure, I'll _____ _____ for you.

3 That would _____ _____ _____ a lot.

4 Why are you _____ _____ _____ dogs?

5 You should _____ _____ your eyes first.

6 I'm going to _____ _____ _____ for a while.

7 I'm going to America on a business trip _____ _____ _____.

8 I'm interested _____ the _____ and _____ of different countries.

9 First, you should check if the house gets _____ _____.

10 You'll feel a difference after _____ _____ in the program.

1 다음을 듣고, 'this'가 가리키는 것으로 가장 적절한 것을 고르시오.

①   ②   ③

④   ⑤

2 대화를 듣고, 남자가 구입한 것으로 가장 적절한 것을 고르시오.

①   ②   ③

④   ⑤

3 다음을 듣고, 내일 아침의 날씨로 가장 적절한 것을 고르시오.

①   ②   ③

④   ⑤

4 대화를 듣고, 남자의 마지막 말의 의도로 가장 적절한 것을 고르시오.
① 거절　　　② 동의　　　③ 조언
④ 실망　　　⑤ 칭찬

5 다음을 듣고, 여자가 신년 계획에 대해 언급하지 <u>않은</u> 것을 고르시오.
① 일찍 일어나기
② 엄마와 매일 운동하기
③ 중국어 배우기
④ 할리우드 영화 보기
⑤ 동생과 잘 지내기

6 대화를 듣고, 남자가 도서관에 도착한 시각을 고르시오.
① 5:13 p.m.　　② 5:30 p.m.　　③ 6:13 p.m.
④ 6:30 p.m.　　⑤ 7:13 p.m.

7 대화를 듣고, 여자의 장래 희망으로 가장 적절한 것을 고르시오.
① 모델　　　　　　② 외교관
③ 연예인　　　　　④ 웨딩 플래너
⑤ 패션 스타일리스트

8 대화를 듣고, 남자의 심정으로 가장 적절한 것을 고르시오.
① lonely　　② proud　　③ happy
④ frightened　　⑤ disappointed

9 대화를 듣고, 여자가 대화 직후에 할 일로 가장 적절한 것을 고르시오.
① 수학 공부하기　　② 샌드위치 먹기
③ 손 씻으러 가기　　④ 성적표 보여주기
⑤ 아빠와 요리하기

10 대화를 듣고, 무엇에 관한 내용인지 가장 적절한 것을 고르시오.
① 건강 검진　　　② 모금 활동
③ 환경 보호　　　④ 자원 봉사
⑤ 지구 온난화

11 대화를 듣고, 두 사람이 함께 이용할 교통수단으로 가장 적절한 것을 고르시오.
① 걷기   ② 버스   ③ 자전거
④ 지하철   ⑤ 택시

12 대화를 듣고, 남자가 여자를 찾아 온 이유로 가장 적절한 것을 고르시오.
① 음향기기를 빌리기 위해서
② 현재 시간을 확인하기 위해서
③ 라디오 음량을 줄이기 위해서
④ 시험에 관한 조언을 얻기 위해서
⑤ 과제물 제출 날짜를 늦추기 위해서

13 대화를 듣고, 두 사람이 대화하는 장소로 가장 적절한 곳을 고르시오.
① 학교   ② 병원   ③ 약국
④ 편의점   ⑤ 도서관

14 대화를 듣고, 여자가 찾고 있는 카메라의 위치로 가장 적절한 곳을 고르시오.

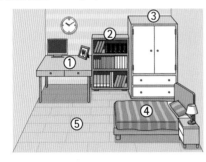

15 대화를 듣고, 여자가 남자에게 요청한 일로 가장 적절한 것을 고르시오.
① 외출하기
② 책 빌려주기
③ 놀이공원 가기
④ 좋은 책 소개하기
⑤ 서점에 함께 가기

16 대화를 듣고, 여자가 남자에게 제안한 것으로 가장 적절한 것을 고르시오.
① 선물 가게 들르기
② 햄버거 먹기
③ 회전목마 타기
④ 기념사진 찍기
⑤ 롤러코스터 타기

17 대화를 듣고, 남자가 지난 주말에 한 일로 가장 적절한 것을 고르시오.
① 등산하기   ② 자전거 타기
③ 방 청소하기   ④ 풍경화 그리기
⑤ 친구와 외출하기

18 대화를 듣고, 여자의 직업으로 가장 적절한 것을 고르시오.
① 화가   ② 작가   ③ 의사
④ 배우   ⑤ 감독

[19–20] 대화를 듣고, 여자의 마지막 말에 이어질 남자의 응답으로 가장 적절한 것을 고르시오.

19 Man: _____
① That's my dream car.
② Here is your order. Enjoy!
③ No problem. Take your time.
④ I'm sorry, but we are not ready yet.
⑤ Nice choice! This is the best-selling item on the menu.

20 Man: _____
① Let's clean the window.
② I don't like playing outside.
③ Korean summers are too hot.
④ Oh, no! The snowman is melting.
⑤ That's okay. We can dress warmly.

Listen and Check

대화를 다시 듣고, 알맞은 것을 고르시오.

1 This helps you to erase something on paper.

☐ True ☐ False

2 For whom does the boy want to buy a hat?

☐ his sister ☐ his mother

3 When will the rain stop?

☐ tomorrow morning
☐ tomorrow afternoon

4 They will learn how to swim together this Sunday.

☐ True ☐ False

5 Did the woman decide to learn Chinese?

☐ Yes ☐ No

6 The woman arrived at the library earlier than Jaejoon.

☐ True ☐ False

7 What does the woman recommend to the man?

☐ a white shirt ☐ a black shirt

8 Why was the baseball game canceled?

☐ because of a traffic jam
☐ because of a storm warning

9 The woman got a good grade in math.

☐ True ☐ False

10 Why will they raise money?

☐ to help people in the Philippines
☐ to join a club

11 Where are they going?

☐ to a gallery ☐ to a cousin's wedding

12 Does the man have a test tomorrow?

☐ Yes ☐ No

13 What does the doctor tell the man to do?

☐ drink some water ☐ take a pill

14 What is the woman looking for?

☐ a mobile phone ☐ a camera

15 George is watching the movie *Harry Potter*.

☐ True ☐ False

16 They prefer the roller coaster to the merry-go-round.

☐ True ☐ False

17 What did Jimin do last weekend?

☐ went to a mountain
☐ cleaned her room

18 Did the woman give her autograph?

☐ Yes ☐ No

19 How much must the woman pay for the food?

☐ 20 dollars ☐ 25 dollars

20 What's the weather like?

☐ snowy ☐ rainy

130

그림 정보 파악

1 다음을 듣고, 'this'가 가리키는 것으로 가장 적절한 것을 고르시오.

① ② ③
④ ⑤

1

M This is usually soft and _____ _____ _____.
This helps you to _____ _____ what you
_____ _____ paper. You may *find this in your
pencil case. What is this?

*find this [파인드] [디스] → [파인디스]

그림 정보 파악

2 대화를 듣고, 남자가 구입한 것으로 가장 적절한 것을 고르시오.

① ② ③
④ ⑤

2

W Welcome. May I help you?

M I want to _____ _____ _____ for my sister.

W How about this hat? A big star is *drawn on it.

M She doesn't like star shapes. Do you _____
_____ _____?

W Then let me show you this one with a _____ _____
_____.

M Perfect! I'll _____ _____.

*drawn on it [드로운] [온] [잇] → [드로우노닛]

그림 정보 파악

3 다음을 듣고, 내일 아침의 날씨로 가장 적절한 것을 고르시오.

① ② ③
④ ⑤

3 🇬🇧

W Good morning. This is the weather _____ for today and
tomorrow. It'll be warm and sunny this afternoon. However,
it'll start to rain this evening, and _____ _____
_____ _____ tomorrow morning. After the
rain stops tomorrow afternoon, you can see _____
_____.

의도 파악

4 대화를 듣고, 남자의 마지막 말의 의도로 가장 적절한 것을 고르시오.

① 거절   ② 동의   ③ 조언
④ 실망   ⑤ 칭찬

4

W Greg, what did you do last weekend?

M I did _____ _____ at a _____ _____.
What did you do?

W I went to the sea to go swimming.

M Wow! I want to learn _____ _____ _____.

W Why don't you go with me this Sunday?

M I'd like to, but I have something to do. _____ _____
_____.

언급 유무 파악

5 다음을 듣고, 여자가 신년 계획에 대해
언급하지 <u>않은</u> 것을 고르시오.

① 일찍 일어나기
② 엄마와 매일 운동하기
③ 중국어 배우기
④ 할리우드 영화 보기
⑤ 동생과 잘 지내기

5

W Happy New Year, everyone! I'd like to tell you about
my _____ for this year. I plan to get up early and
_____ _____ my Mom every day. I have also
decided to learn Chinese and watch Chinese movies. Lastly,
I will _____ _____ _____ _____ my
brother.

숫자 정보 파악

6 대화를 듣고, 남자가 도서관에 도착한
시각을 고르시오.

① 5:13 p.m.
② 5:30 p.m.
③ 6:13 p.m.
④ 6:30 p.m.
⑤ 7:13 p.m.

6

[*Telephone rings.*]

W Hello. Jaejoon, I'm sorry I'm late. I missed the bus. Where are
you?

M I'm already in the _____.

W Really? _____ _____ did you _____?

M I think I arrived at _____ _____.

W Oh, I'm sorry, but I'll be there at six thirty.

M That's okay. _____ _____ on your way here.

장래 희망 추론

7 대화를 듣고, 여자의 장래 희망으로 가장
적절한 것을 고르시오.

① 모델
② 외교관
③ 연예인
④ 웨딩 플래너
⑤ 패션 스타일리스트

7

M I have a date. But I can't decide _____ _____
_____.

W Hmm... How about a white shirt and blue jeans with this
jacket?

M Wow! That looks great. I think you are _____.

W Thanks. I dream of _____ _____ _____
_____ celebrities in the future.

심정 추론

8 대화를 듣고, 남자의 심정으로 가장
적절한 것을 고르시오.

① lonely
② proud
③ happy
④ frightened
⑤ disappointed

8

W Jaewon, what's the _____ _____ _____?
You look sad.

M I bought a ticket for tomorrow's baseball game.

W Oh, you are _____! Everyone wants to see the baseball
game.

M I know. But _____ _____ _____ because of
the storm warning.

W Really? Then you can't go there?

M I _____ _____.

9

9 대화를 듣고, 여자가 대화 직후에 할 일로
가장 적절한 것을 고르시오.

① 수학 공부하기
② 샌드위치 먹기
③ 손 씻으러 가기
④ 성적표 보여주기
⑤ 아빠와 요리하기

9

M Hello, sweetie. _____ _____ _____?

W It was great. I got a _____ _____ in math.

M Good job. You _____ _____ yesterday.

W Yes, I did. Dad, I'm so hungry. Can you make me a sandwich?

M _____ _____? I'll make you one. Wash your
hands first.

W Okay, Dad. Thank you!

---

10 대화를 듣고, 무엇에 관한 내용인지 가장
적절한 것을 고르시오.

① 건강 검진
② 모금 활동
③ 환경 보호
④ 자원 봉사
⑤ 지구 온난화

♥ **That's too bad.**
: 상대방의 의견에 유감이나 동정을 말하고 싶
을 때 쓰는 표현으로, '안됐다.'라는 뜻이다.
= What a pity.
= I'm sorry to hear that.

10 🇬🇧

M Jiyoon, did you hear that a tsunami hit the Philippines?

W Yes, I did. ♥That's too bad.

M Why don't we _____ _____ to help the people
there?

W What a good idea! We can also ask our classmates to

_____ _____.

M Right. We should _____ _____ _____.

W That's a _____ _____.

---

11 대화를 듣고, 두 사람이 함께 이용할
교통수단으로 가장 적절한 것을 고르시오.

① 걷기
② 버스
③ 자전거
④ 지하철
⑤ 택시

11

M Miyeon, are you ready to go to your cousin's wedding?

W Of course. Is it _____ _____ _____?

M No. We can take a cab. It takes 5 minutes.

W Then let's _____ _____ _____. I want to
walk.

M _____ _____!

이유 추론

12 대화를 듣고, 남자가 여자를 찾아 온 이유로 가장 적절한 것을 고르시오.

① 음향기기를 빌리기 위해서
② 현재 시간을 확인하기 위해서
③ 라디오 음량을 줄이기 위해서
④ 시험에 관한 조언을 얻기 위해서
⑤ 과제물 제출 날짜를 늦추기 위해서

💙 **Do you mind if I ~?**

: 상대방에게 허락을 구할 때 쓰는 표현으로, '~하면 신경 쓰이니?'라는 뜻이다.

= May/Can I ~?
= Is it okay if I ~?

12

[*Knocking on the door*]

W   Come in.

M   Hey, 💙do you mind *if I ask you to _____ _____ _____ _____ on the radio?

W   Absolutely not. Is it _____ _____?

M   Just a little bit. I actually have a final exam tomorrow.

W   Oh, I _____ _____ _____. I am sorry I bothered you.

M   Thank you for your understanding.

*if I ask you [이프] [아이] [에스크] [유] → [이파에스큐]

장소 추론

13 대화를 듣고, 두 사람이 대화하는 장소로 가장 적절한 곳을 고르시오.

① 학교
② 병원
③ 약국
④ 편의점
⑤ 도서관

13 🇬🇧

W   Good morning. _____ _____ _____ _____ today?

M   I feel _____ _____ than before.

W   That sounds good. Let me see. _____ _____ _____ and say, "Ah."

M   Ah.

W   Your _____ looks okay now. But remember to drink a lot of water.

M   Okay, I will.

그림 정보 파악

14 대화를 듣고, 여자가 찾고 있는 카메라의 위치로 가장 적절한 곳을 고르시오.

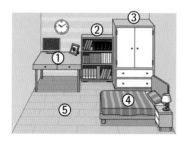

14

M   Dajeong, why are you _____ a _____?

W   Dad, can you help me? I think I lost my camera.

M   Calm down. _____ _____ _____ first.

W   I've already checked my bed and closet.

M   Did you _____ _____ the desk?

W   I think so. Ah, I *found it. It's on the floor.

*found it [파운드] [잇] → [파운딧]

요청한 것 파악

15 대화를 듣고, 여자가 남자에게 요청한 일로 가장 적절한 것을 고르시오.

① 외출하기
② 책 빌려주기
③ 놀이공원 가기
④ 좋은 책 소개하기
⑤ 서점에 함께 가기

> ♥ **I bet.**
> : 상대방에게 자신의 강한 확신을 나타내는 표현으로, '당연하지.'라는 뜻이다.
> = I'm sure.
> = I have no doubt.

15

W   George, what are you reading?

M   I'm reading the book *Harry Potter* _____ by J. K. Rowling.

W   A _____ _____? I heard that it is very popular.

M   ♥I bet. Have you *read it before?

W   Not yet. Can I _____ _____ after you _____ _____ it?

M   Yes, you can.

*read it [레드] [잇] → [레딧]

제안한 것 파악

16 대화를 듣고, 여자가 남자에게 제안한 것으로 가장 적절한 것을 고르시오.

① 가게 들르기
② 햄버거 먹기
③ 회전목마 타기
④ 기념사진 찍기
⑤ 롤러코스터 타기

16

M   Jayeon, look at the roller coaster. It's so fast.

W   It looks _____. It looks like people are _____ _____ _____ _____.

M   I _____ _____ you. Let's ride the merry-go-round _____.

W   That's a great idea. Before that, let's go to the gift shop.

M   Why? What do you need?

W   I just want to buy something as a _____.

한 일 파악

17 대화를 듣고, 남자가 지난 주말에 한 일로 가장 적절한 것을 고르시오.

① 등산하기
② 자전거 타기
③ 방 청소하기
④ 풍경화 그리기
⑤ 친구와 외출하기

17 🇬🇧

M   Jimin, what did you do _____ _____?

W   My friend and I went to Halla Mountain. We saw some _____ _____ there.

M   That _____ _____! I like hiking. I'll visit there someday.

W   You should. What did you do?

M   I _____ my room all day. It was a _____.

W   Good job.

직업 추론

18 대화를 듣고, 여자의 직업으로 가장 적절한 것을 고르시오.

① 화가　② 작가　③ 의사
④ 배우　⑤ 감독

♥ **I got it.**

: 상대방의 말이 무슨 의미인지 이해했다고 말하고 싶을 때 쓰는 표현으로, '이해했어.'라는 뜻이다.

= I understand.

18

M　I'm so glad to see you here. Your work is _____.

W　Thank you so much.

M　I love _____ _____ _____ the characters in your book.

W　I'm glad you like it. Where should I _____ _____ you?

M　On the _____ _____ of your book, please.

W　Okay. ♥I got it.

적절한 응답 찾기

[19~20] 대화를 듣고, 여자의 마지막 말에 이어질 남자의 응답으로 가장 적절한 것을 고르시오.

19 Man: _____

① That's my dream car.
② Here is your order. Enjoy!
③ No problem. Take your time.
④ I'm sorry, but we are not ready yet.
⑤ Nice choice! This is the best-selling item on the menu.

19 🇬🇧

M　May I _____ _____ _____ _____?

W　I'd like two cheeseburgers and one order of fried potatoes.

M　Okay. _____ _____?

W　One orange juice and two hot chocolates, please.

M　That'll be 25 dollars.

W　Oh, no! I left my purse in my car. Would you _____ _____ _____?

M　No problem. Take your time.

적절한 응답 찾기

20 Man: _____

① Let's clean the window.
② I don't like playing outside.
③ Korean summers are too hot.
④ Oh, no! The snowman is melting.
⑤ That's okay. We can dress warmly.

20

W　Get up and _____ _____ the window. It's snowing.

M　Wow! Mom, it's so pretty.

W　The whole world has turned white.

M　Mom, why don't we _____ _____?

W　What for?

M　Let's make a snowman and have a _____ _____.

W　But it's _____ _____ _____, isn't it?

M　That's okay. We can dress warmly.

A 들려주는 단어를 듣고 쓴 뒤, 괄호 안에 우리말 뜻을 쓰시오.

	영어	우리말		영어	우리말
1			6		
2			7		
3			8		
4			9		
5			10		

B 다음 문장을 잘 듣고 빈칸에 들어갈 단어를 채우시오.

1   I think I _____ _____ 5:30.

2   A big star _____ _____ _____ it.

3   The _____ world has _____ _____.

4   I feel _____ _____ than before.

5   I _____ _____ the sea to go swimming.

6   _____ _____ _____ because of the storm warning.

7   I will _____ _____ _____ _____ my brother.

8   Why don't we _____ _____ to help them?

9   It _____ _____ people are falling to the ground.

10   Do you mind if I ask you to _____ the _____ _____ on the radio?

1 다음을 듣고, 'this'가 가리키는 것으로 가장 적절한 것을 고르시오.

2 대화를 듣고, 남자가 구입하려고 하는 필통으로 가장 적절한 것을 고르시오.

3 다음을 듣고, 수요일의 날씨로 가장 적절한 것을 고르시오.

4 대화를 듣고, 남자의 마지막 말의 의도로 가장 적절한 것을 고르시오.
① 부탁 ② 제안 ③ 거절
④ 감사 ⑤ 동의

5 다음을 듣고, 여자가 요리 수업에 대해 언급하지 <u>않은</u> 것을 고르시오.
① 신청 방법 ② 쿠키 목록
③ 수업 요일 ④ 수업 장소
⑤ 수업 인원

6 대화를 듣고, 두 사람이 만날 시각을 고르시오.
① 1:00 ② 2:00 ③ 3:00
④ 4:00 ⑤ 5:00

7 대화를 듣고, 여자의 장래 희망으로 가장 적절한 것을 고르시오.
① 감독 ② 연기자
③ 프로듀서 ④ 드라마 작가
⑤ 문화 평론가

8 대화를 듣고, 남자의 심정으로 가장 적절한 것을 고르시오.
① angry ② upset
③ bored ④ delighted
⑤ disappointed

9 대화를 듣고, 여자가 대화 직후에 할 일로 가장 적절한 것을 고르시오.
① 잘못을 지적하기
② 시험지 확인하기
③ 부모님께 연락하기
④ 친구에게 전화하기
⑤ 선생님께 말씀드리기

10 대화를 듣고, 무엇에 관한 내용인지 가장 적절한 것을 고르시오.
① 진로 상담 ② 직업 면접
③ 편집 방법 ④ 부서 이동
⑤ 직업 박람회

11 대화를 듣고, 두 사람이 함께 이용할 교통수단으로 가장 적절한 것을 고르시오.
① 버스   ② 택시   ③ 지하철
④ 자전거   ⑤ 자동차

12 대화를 듣고, 남자가 여자에게 화가 난 이유로 가장 적절한 것을 고르시오.
① 남자와의 약속을 어겨서
② 남자에게 거짓말을 하여서
③ 부름에 대답을 하지 않아서
④ 장소를 깨끗이 치우지 않아서
⑤ 자신의 잘못을 인정하지 않아서

13 대화를 듣고, 두 사람이 대화하는 장소로 가장 적절한 곳을 고르시오.
① 카페   ② 운동장   ③ 안경점
④ 문구점   ⑤ 옷 가게

14 대화를 듣고, 여자가 가려고 하는 장소로 가장 적절한 곳을 고르시오.

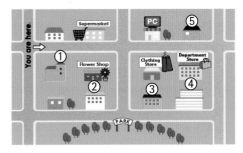

15 대화를 듣고, 남자가 여자에게 요청한 일로 가장 적절한 것을 고르시오.
① 물건 환불하기
② 물건 교환하기
③ 가격 재확인하기
④ 물건 추천해 주기
⑤ 신상 물건 예약하기

16 대화를 듣고, 여자가 남자에게 제안한 것으로 가장 적절한 것을 고르시오.
① 요리 해주기
② 카드 만들기
③ 사과 편지 쓰기
④ 파티 열어 주기
⑤ 선물 사러 가기

17 대화를 듣고, 남자가 지난 주말에 한 일로 가장 적절한 것을 고르시오.
① 가족 여행   ② 관광 투어
③ 요리 연습   ④ 우정 여행
⑤ 사진관 방문

18 대화를 듣고, 여자의 직업으로 가장 적절한 것을 고르시오.
① 경찰   ② 선생님   ③ 상담사
④ 경영진   ⑤ 치과 의사

[19-20] 대화를 듣고, 여자의 마지막 말에 이어질 남자의 응답으로 가장 적절한 것을 고르시오.

19 Man: _____
① I want to sleep more.
② I can still bear it.
③ That's such a foolish idea.
④ I sleep for about three hours.
⑤ Sleeping enough really matters.

20 Man: _____
① I don't agree with you.
② It takes a long time to charge it.
③ I want to exchange it for a new one.
④ I think I use it every thirty minutes.
⑤ It's true that smartphones are useful.

Listen and Check

정답 및 해설 p.69

● 대화를 다시 듣고, 알맞은 것을 고르시오.

1 People usually use this to protect their skin.
☐ True ☐ False

2 Does the man want to buy pencils?
☐ Yes ☐ No

3 How will the weather be on Tuesday morning?
☐ sunny ☐ rainy

4 The woman asks the man to watch the magic show together.
☐ True ☐ False

5 Are there cooking classes every Wednesday?
☐ Yes ☐ No

6 What time does the break finish at Alice Flowers?
☐ at 1:00 ☐ at 3:00

7 The woman has little interest in writing drama scripts.
☐ True ☐ False

8 Does the man feel happy about his friend's news?
☐ Yes ☐ No

9 The man will tell the teacher about Chloe cheating.
☐ True ☐ False

10 When will the man start working?
☐ this week ☐ next week

11 They are going on a picnic at the park.
☐ True ☐ False

12 What does the man want the woman to do?
☐ share a house
☐ keep some places clean

13 The woman knows her corrected eyesight.
☐ True ☐ False

14 Is the department store close to the aquarium?
☐ Yes ☐ No

15 Why does the man want to exchange the earphones?
☐ They are in poor condition.
☐ They are the wrong model.

16 The man is going to make a Christmas card for his girlfriend.
☐ True ☐ False

17 The man enjoyed his trip to Busan with his family.
☐ True ☐ False

18 When will the man go to the clinic?
☐ now ☐ tomorrow

19 The woman knows why the man doesn't sleep enough.
☐ True ☐ False

20 The woman thinks positively about using smartphones.
☐ True ☐ False

그림 정보 파악

1 다음을 듣고, 'this'가 가리키는 것으로 가장 적절한 것을 고르시오.

① ② ③

④ ⑤

1

M People use this to _____ their skin _____ the sun. They use this _____ _____. There are _____ _____, like cream-based and gel-based ones. What is this?

그림 정보 파악

2 대화를 듣고, 남자가 구입하려고 하는 필통으로 가장 적절한 것을 고르시오.

① ② ③

④ ⑤

2

W What can I do for you?

M I'm looking for a pencil case for my younger sister.

W These _____ _____ _____ images of a rabbit and a teddy bear are very _____.

M I will get the one with the _____ _____ the teddy bear and the word "Teddy" on it.

W Great _____. Your sister will like it.

그림 정보 파악

3 다음을 듣고, 수요일의 날씨로 가장 적절한 것을 고르시오.

① ② ③

④ ⑤

3 🇬🇧

M I'm Brian Tyler from the weather center. This is the weather report for this week. It will _____ _____ _____ _____, but the rain will stop in the afternoon. From Tuesday to Thursday, _____ _____ _____ _____ _____. On Friday, it will rain again.

의도 파악

4 대화를 듣고, 남자의 마지막 말의 의도로 가장 적절한 것을 고르시오.

① 부탁 ② 제안 ③ 거절
④ 감사 ⑤ 동의

4

W Aaron, do you have any plans for this evening?

M I have a _____ _____ _____ _____. Why?

W There is a magic show at the Lala Concert Hall at 8:00 p.m.

M Really? _____ _____ _____.

W Why don't we go there together?

M I'm sorry, but I can't.

언급 유무 파악

5 다음을 듣고, 여자가 요리 수업에 대해 언급하지 <u>않은</u> 것을 고르시오.

① 신청 방법
② 쿠키 목록
③ 수업 요일
④ 수업 장소
⑤ 수업 인원

5

W Hi, everyone. We are going to have new cooking classes at Merry Bakery. The classes will be from 11:00 a.m. to 1:00 p.m. _____ _____ _____ _____. You can _____ _____ _____ the _____ at the bakery in the first week of March. Please note that the number of participants in each class is _____ _____ five.

숫자 정보 파악

6 대화를 듣고, 두 사람이 만날 시각을 고르시오.

① 1:00
② 2:00
③ 3:00
④ 4:00
⑤ 5:00

6

W Albert, _____ _____ _____ _____ to buy plants tomorrow?

M We're going to Alice Flowers.

W I know that _____. It's closed from 1:00 p.m. to 3:00 p.m.

M Oh, I didn't know that. I was thinking about _____ _____ _____ _____ at 2:00.

W Then how about _____ _____ 4:00?

M That sounds great.

장래 희망 파악

7 대화를 듣고, 여자의 장래 희망으로 가장 적절한 것을 고르시오.

① 감독 ② 연기자
③ 프로듀서 ④ 드라마 작가
⑤ 문화 평론가

♥ **How + 형용사!**
: 감탄을 나타낼 때 사용하는 표현으로, '~하구나!'라는 뜻이다. 사람의 성품을 나타내는 형용사와 해당 사람을 함께 표현할 경우, 'how + 형용사 + of + 목적격' 형태로 한다.

7

M Ivy, what are you _____?

W It's a _____ _____.

M ♥How awesome! Can I see it?

W Why not? I hope to write a drama that gets _____ _____ _____ someday.

M I believe you will become _____ _____ _____.

W Thank you for saying that.

심정 추론

8 대화를 듣고, 남자의 심정으로 가장 적절한 것을 고르시오.

① angry ② upset
③ bored ④ delighted
⑤ disappointed

8 🇬🇧

W Hi, Carlo. How are you today?

M I _____ _____ _____.

W Is something wrong?

M My old *friend is _____ _____ _____ _____.

W You must be so sad.

M Yes, I am. He is _____ _____ _____.

*friend is [프렌드] [이즈] → [프렌디즈]

할 일 파악

9 대화를 듣고, 여자가 대화 직후에 할 일로 가장 적절한 것을 고르시오.

① 잘못을 지적하기
② 시험지 확인하기
③ 부모님께 연락하기
④ 친구에게 전화하기
⑤ 선생님께 말씀드리기

9

M Kayla, what's the _____?

W I saw Chloe _____ _____ _____ _____ _____.

M That's not _____.

W What *should I do?

M What about _____ the teacher _____ _____?

W I think I should do that.

*should I [슈드] [아이] → [슈다이]

화제 · 주제 파악

10 대화를 듣고, 무엇에 관한 내용인지 가장 적절한 것을 고르시오.

① 진로 상담
② 직업 면접
③ 편집 방법
④ 부서 이동
⑤ 직업 박람회

10 🇬🇧

W Mr. Park, do you have any editing _____?

M Yes, I do. After graduation, I _____ _____ _____ _____ for two years.

W Can you start working next week?

M Of course. I'd love to!

W Good. I'm _____ _____ _____ some great work from you.

M Thank you. I'll do my best.

교통수단 파악

11 대화를 듣고, 두 사람이 함께 이용할 교통수단으로 가장 적절한 것을 고르시오.

① 버스
② 택시
③ 지하철
④ 자전거
⑤ 자동차

11

M _____ should we go for the picnic?

W How about Green Park?

M It will _____ _____ thirty minutes to get there on foot. Do you have a bicycle?

W No, I don't. It's just _____ _____ _____ _____ _____ by subway.

M Okay. Then let's take that.

이유 추론

12 대화를 듣고, 남자가 여자에게 화가 난 이유로 가장 적절한 것을 고르시오.

① 남자와의 약속을 어겨서
② 남자에게 거짓말을 하여서
③ 부름에 대답을 하지 않아서
④ 장소를 깨끗이 치우지 않아서
⑤ 자신의 잘못을 인정하지 않아서

12

W Dad, did you call me?

M Yes, I did. _____ _____ _____ the living room and the kitchen.

W I'll _____ _____ _____ later.

M I hope you keep the place clean.

W Okay. I'll try to do that.

M _____ _____ _____ the people you are sharing the house with.

장소 추론

13 대화를 듣고, 두 사람이 대화하는 장소로 가장 적절한 곳을 고르시오.

① 카페
② 운동장
③ 안경점
④ 문구점
⑤ 옷 가게

13

M Good afternoon. What are you looking for?

W I would like to _____ contact lenses.

M _____ _____ _____ contact lenses do you want, clear or colored ones?

W _____ _____, please.

M What is your _____ _____?

W I think I should _____ _____ _____ _____.

그림 정보 파악

14 대화를 듣고, 여자가 가려고 하는 장소로 가장 적절한 곳을 고르시오.

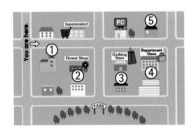

14

W Excuse me. Is the Blue Aquarium _____ _____?

M Yes, it is.

W _____ _____ _____ _____ _____?

M Go straight two blocks. Then, turn right.

W Okay.

M Then you will see a department store _____ _____ _____. The Blue Aquarium is _____ _____ the department store.

15 대화를 듣고, 남자가 여자에게 요청한 일로
가장 적절한 것을 고르시오.

① 물건 환불하기
② 물건 교환하기
③ 가격 재확인하기
④ 물건 추천해 주기
⑤ 신상 물건 예약하기

15

M　Hi. I bought these earphones here yesterday.

W　Is there a _____ _____ the earphones?

M　No, there isn't. I just bought the wrong model.

W　All right. I can _____ _____ _____ _____
_____ for you.

M　Thank you very much.

---

16 대화를 듣고, 여자가 남자에게 제안한
것으로 가장 적절한 것을 고르시오.

① 요리 해주기
② 카드 만들기
③ 사과 편지 쓰기
④ 파티 열어 주기
⑤ 선물 사러 가기

> ♥ **That's a good idea.**
>
> : 상대방의 말에 대한 동의를 나타낼 때 사용
> 하는 표현으로, '좋은 생각이야.'라는 뜻이다.
> = Sounds great.
> = That sounds good.

16　🇬🇧

W　What are you planning to *give your girlfriend this Christmas?

M　Well, I am _____ _____ _____ _____.

W　Why don't you buy a small gift for her?

M　Sadly, I don't have _____ _____.

W　How about making a _____ _____ yourself?

M　♥That's a good idea!

*give your [기브] [유얼] → [기뷰얼]

---

17 대화를 듣고, 남자가 지난 주말에 한 일로
가장 적절한 것을 고르시오.

① 가족 여행
② 관광 투어
③ 요리 연습
④ 우정 여행
⑤ 사진관 방문

17

M　Lauren, _____ _____ _____ _____?

W　It was great. I went on _____ _____ _____.
What about you?

M　I went to Busan with some friends.

W　What did you do there?

M　We took many pictures and went swimming at the beach.

W　You _____ _____ _____ _____.

직업 추론

18 대화를 듣고, 여자의 직업으로 가장 적절한 것을 고르시오.

① 경찰
② 선생님
③ 상담사
④ 경영진
⑤ 치과 의사

♥ **What's up?**

: 상대방의 의도를 묻거나 안부를 물을 때 사용하는 표현으로, '무슨 일이야?', '어떻게 지내?'라는 뜻이다.

안부를 묻는 경우의 표현은 다음과 같다.

= How are you?
= How is it going?
= How have you been?

18

[*Telephone rings.*]

W   Hello.

M   Diana, this is Eric.

W   ♥What's up?

M   I have a _____ _____ now.

W   Oh, _____ _____ _____ _____ tomorrow. Let me *check it.

M   _____ _____. Thanks.

*check it [체크] [잇] → [체킷]

적절한 응답 찾기

[19-20] 대화를 듣고, 여자의 마지막 말에 이어질 남자의 응답으로 가장 적절한 것을 고르시오.

19   Man: _____
① I want to sleep more.
② I can still bear it.
③ That's such a foolish idea.
④ I sleep for about three hours.
⑤ Sleeping enough really matters.

19

M   Reese, do I _____ _____?

W   What do you mean? About your looks?

M   No, about the condition of my body.

W   Why are you asking such a question? Are you sick?

M   I _____ _____ _____ these days.

W   _____ _____ _____ do you sleep each day?

M   I sleep for about three hours.

적절한 응답 찾기

20   Man: _____
① I don't agree with you.
② It takes a long time to charge it.
③ I want to exchange it for a new one.
④ I think I use it every thirty minutes.
⑤ It's true that smartphones are useful.

20

M   What do you think of using a smartphone?

W   Well, I like mine because it's very _____.

M   Children get smartphones _____ _____.

W   Times change. Of course, they should know how to control themselves.

M   That's right.

W   _____ _____ _____ _____ _____ your smartphone?

M   I think I use it every thirty minutes.

A 들려주는 단어를 듣고 쓴 뒤, 괄호 안에 우리말 뜻을 쓰시오.

	영어	우리말			영어	우리말
1				6		
2				7		
3				8		
4				9		
5				10		

B 다음 문장을 잘 듣고 빈칸에 들어갈 단어를 채우시오.

1 I'll _____ _____ _____ later.

2 Why are you _____ _____ _____ _____ ?

3 I have a _____ _____ after school.

4 What about _____ _____ _____ _____ ?

5 How often do you _____ _____ _____ ?

6 I was thinking about _____ _____ _____ meet at 2:00.

7 I'm _____ _____ a pencil case for my younger sister.

8 After graduation, I _____ _____ _____ _____ for two years.

9 We took _____ _____ and _____ _____ at the beach.

10 You can _____ _____ _____ the classes at the bakery in the first week of March.

1 다음을 듣고, 'this'가 가리키는 것으로 가장 적절한 것을 고르시오.

①   ②   ③

④   ⑤

2 대화를 듣고, 여자가 기르고 있는 반려동물로 가장 적절한 것을 고르시오.

①   ②   ③

④   ⑤

3 다음을 듣고, Beijing의 날씨로 가장 적절한 것을 고르시오.

①   ②   ③

④   ⑤

4 대화를 듣고, 남자의 마지막 말의 의도로 가장 적절한 것을 고르시오.
① 고민 ② 승낙 ③ 충고
④ 거절 ⑤ 안내

5 다음을 듣고, 남자가 친구에 대해 언급하지 <u>않은</u> 것을 고르시오.
① 고향 ② 나이 ③ 취미
④ 습관 ⑤ 이름

6 대화를 듣고, 현재의 시각을 고르시오.
① 5시 30분 ② 5시 15분
③ 5시 40분 ④ 6시 10분
⑤ 6시 30분

7 대화를 듣고, 여자가 원하는 후식으로 가장 적절한 것을 고르시오.
① 차 ② 커피
③ 물 ④ 도넛
⑤ 치즈 케이크

8 대화를 듣고, 남자의 심정으로 가장 적절한 것을 고르시오.
① shy ② excited
③ curious ④ interested
⑤ surprised

9 대화를 듣고, 남자가 대화 직후에 할 일로 가장 적절한 것을 고르시오.
① 주유소에 가기
② 집을 수리하기
③ 철물점에 가기
④ 페달을 수리하기
⑤ 친구의 수리를 도와주기

10 대화를 듣고, 여자의 무엇에 관한 내용인지 가장 적절한 것을 고르시오.
① 식사 습관 ② 집의 전통
③ 좋아하는 음식 ④ 선호하는 나라
⑤ 가고 싶은 여행지

11 대화를 듣고, 남자가 이용할 교통수단으로 가장 적절한 것을 고르시오.
① 기차   ② 버스   ③ 선박
④ 비행기   ⑤ 자동차

12 대화를 듣고, 남자가 서점에 간 이유로 가장 적절한 것을 고르시오.
① 책을 구매하려고
② 친구를 만나려고
③ 저자를 만나려고
④ 책을 교환하려고
⑤ 기분을 전환하려고

13 대화를 듣고, 두 사람이 대화하는 장소로 가장 적절한 곳을 고르시오.
① 병원   ② 은행
③ 우체국   ④ 신발 가게
⑤ 쇼핑센터

14 대화를 듣고, 여자가 찾고 있는 국자의 위치로 가장 적절한 곳을 고르시오.

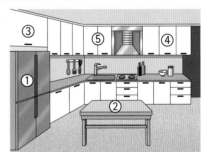

15 대화를 듣고, 남자가 여자에게 부탁한 일로 가장 적절한 것을 고르시오.
① 상점에서 물건 사기
② 구매 물건 목록 작성하기
③ 야채를 깨끗하게 손질하기
④ 저녁 식사 테이블을 정리하기
⑤ 물건을 휴대폰으로 주문하기

16 대화를 듣고, 여자가 남자에게 제안한 것으로 가장 적절한 것을 고르시오.
① 옷을 여러 벌 입기
② 뜨거운 음료 마시기
③ 마음을 편하게 하기
④ 수건으로 땀을 닦기
⑤ 병원에 가서 진찰 받기

17 대화를 듣고, 남자의 엄마가 남자에게 요청한 일로 가장 적절한 것을 고르시오.
① 방을 청소하기
② 도서관에 가기
③ 엄마에게 전화하기
④ 휴대폰을 고치러 가기
⑤ 책을 사러 서점에 가기

18 대화를 듣고, 남자의 장래 희망으로 가장 적절한 것을 고르시오.
① 여행가   ② 조종사   ③ 사진작가
④ 지리학자   ⑤ 엔지니어

[19~20] 대화를 듣고, 남자의 마지막 말에 이어질 여자의 응답으로 가장 적절한 것을 고르시오.

19 Woman: _____
① Never mind.
② Then I should ask her.
③ She is not here now.
④ You had better forget it.
⑤ I told you it is right there.

20 Woman: _____
① No. It is not fair.
② Don't mention it.
③ I am good at leading.
④ You did the right thing.
⑤ Don't worry. I'll help you.

Listen and Check

● 대화를 다시 듣고, 알맞은 것을 고르시오.

1 This helps us forget important days.
☐ True   ☐ False

2 What pet does the woman's mom love?
☐ a cat   ☐ a hamster

3 Will Hong Kong have a rainy day like Tokyo?
☐ Yes   ☐ No

4 The hill is very far from the woman's house.
☐ True   ☐ False

5 Where does Mijin live now?
☐ Daejeon   ☐ Mokpo

6 What time does the lecture start?
☐ at 5:15   ☐ at 5:30

7 The woman just wants a cup of tea.
☐ True   ☐ False

8 Does the woman suggest going out to the park?
☐ Yes   ☐ No

9 What does the woman tell the man to do?
☐ buy a bicycle
☐ go to the hardware shop

10 The woman loves to eat pizza.
☐ True   ☐ False

11 What kind of vehicle will the man take?
☐ a bus   ☐ a train

12 Does the man want a refund at the bookstore?
☐ Yes   ☐ No

13 Where is the ATM in the shopping center?
☐ on the first floor   ☐ on the second floor

14 The scoop is in the cupboard near the refrigerator.
☐ True   ☐ False

15 Can the man remember everything that the woman wants?
☐ Yes   ☐ No

16 The woman thinks a hot drink will help the man relax.
☐ True   ☐ False

17 The man's mom wants the man to organize the living room.
☐ True   ☐ False

18 Does the woman advise him to be a photographer?
☐ Yes   ☐ No

19 The man remembers that Cathy was near the drawer.
☐ True   ☐ False

20 Who chose the man as the club president?
☐ the members of the club
☐ the teachers of the school

그림 정보 파악

1 다음을 듣고, 'this'가 가리키는 것으로 가장 적절한 것을 고르시오.

① ② ③ October 10
④ ⑤

1

M We can _____ _____ on the wall. There are many kinds and sizes of this. _____ _____ _____ days and dates. We can find every holiday in the year on it. This helps us remember _____ _____ and schedule our activities. What is this?

그림 정보 파악

2 대화를 듣고, 여자가 기르고 있는 반려동물로 가장 적절한 것을 고르시오.

① ② ③
④ ⑤

♥ **such as ~**
: 앞에 특정한 명사를 가리켜 그 명사의 예를 열거할 경우 사용되며, '~와 같은'의 의미이다.

2

W Oh, *look at the puppies _____ _____. I want to have one.

M _____ _____ _____ ask your mom for one?

W She doesn't like pets ♥ such as dogs, hamsters, and birds.

M But I know that you have a pet. Her name is Lucky, right?

W Yes. My mom loves her. She was a cute little kitten

_____ _____ _____ _____ _____.

*look at [룩] [앳] → [루캣]

그림 정보 파악

3 다음을 듣고, Beijing의 날씨로 가장 적절한 것을 고르시오.

① ② ③
④ ⑤

3

W Here is the _____ _____ for Asia. Tokyo will be sunny _____ _____ _____. However, in Seoul, it will be rainy with strong winds. And it will be very windy and cloudy in Beijing. But the _____ _____ _____ is very low. So people in Beijing don't have to carry umbrellas. Lastly, Hong Kong will have a _____ _____ like Tokyo.

의도 파악

4 대화를 듣고, 남자의 마지막 말의 의도로 가장 적절한 것을 고르시오.

① 고민 ② 승낙 ③ 충고
④ 거절 ⑤ 안내

4

M What _____ _____ _____ _____ this Saturday?

W I'm going to _____ _____ to the hill with one of my friends. It is not _____ _____ _____ _____. Will you join us?

M I'd like to, but I have a lot of homework to do on that day. I promise I will go with you the next time.

언급 유무 파악

5 다음을 듣고, 남자가 친구에 대해 언급하지 <u>않은</u> 것을 고르시오.

① 고향　② 나이　③ 취미
④ 습관　⑤ 이름

5

M I would like to _____ my friend to you. Her name is Mijin, and she is from Mokpo. She is 13 years old. She was _____ _____, and her family moved to Daejeon. Her hobbies are listening to music and _____ _____. I am very happy to be friends with a _____ _____ _____ _____.

숫자 정보 파악

6 대화를 듣고, 현재의 시각을 고르시오.

① 5시 30분
② 5시 15분
③ 5시 40분
④ 6시 10분
⑤ 6시 30분

6 🇬🇧

M Oh, I'm so sorry _____ _____ _____.

W That's all right. But we have to _____ a bit.

M What time _____ _____ _____ _____?

W It starts at five thirty. There are only fifteen minutes _____.

M All right. Let's *take a taxi, and we will get there in ten minutes.

W Okay.

*take a [테이크] [어] → [테이커]

특정 정보 파악

7 대화를 듣고, 여자가 원하는 후식으로 가장 적절한 것을 고르시오.

① 차
② 커피
③ 물
④ 도넛
⑤ 치즈 케이크

7

M Did you _____ your _____?

W Yes, I did. The shrimp soup was _____ _____.

M I'm happy to hear you enjoyed your dinner. What would you like for dessert? We have tea, coffee, doughnuts, and cheesecake.

W I am _____. So just a glass of _____ _____, please.

심정 추론

8 대화를 듣고, 남자의 심정으로 가장 적절한 것을 고르시오.

① shy
② excited
③ curious
④ interested
⑤ surprised

8

W It's a sunny Sunday afternoon. Let's go out to the park.

M That's a good idea. I'll buy _____ _____ _____ _____.

W Okay. I'll buy something to eat at the _____.

M [*Thunder booms.*] Oh, wait. Did you hear that? What was that sound?

W It _____ _____ _____.

M Oh, look at those _____ _____ _____!

할 일 파악

9 대화를 듣고, 남자가 대화 직후에 할 일로 가장 적절한 것을 고르시오.

① 주유소에 가기
② 집을 수리하기
③ 철물점에 가기
④ 페달을 수리하기
⑤ 친구의 수리를 도와주기

9 🇬🇧

W Is that your bicycle?

M Yes. But I haven't used it _____ _____ _____. I am worried that it's not working well.

W Shall we _____ it together? I think the chain and pedals _____ _____.

M Yes, you're right. You are like a bicycle genius!

W Thank you. Anyway, you need to go to the hardware shop to buy some grease.

M Okay. I _____ _____ _____ soon.

화제·주제 파악

10 대화를 듣고, 여자의 무엇에 관한 내용인지 가장 적절한 것을 고르시오.

① 식사 습관
② 집의 전통
③ 좋아하는 음식
④ 선호하는 나라
⑤ 가고 싶은 여행지

10

W Hi. How has it been going?

M Great. Yesterday, I went to an Italian restaurant with my family. _____ _____ _____ _____ _____ there.

W Oh, do you like Italian food?

M Yes. My favorite dish is pizza. Do you like pizza, too?

W I don't _____ _____ _____ _____.

M Then what kind of food do you like to eat?

W I like to have anything _____ _____ _____ it is Korean food.

교통수단 파악

11 대화를 듣고, 남자가 이용할 교통수단으로 가장 적절한 것을 고르시오.

① 기차　　② 버스　　③ 선박
④ 비행기　⑤ 자동차

11

W Christmas is just _____ _____ _____ from now.

M Yes. I'm _____ _____ see my family.

W So how are you going home? By train or bus?

M I _____ _____ _____ _____ by car, but driving would be very boring and the traffic would be heavy.

W You are right. Then how about taking a bus?

M I mentioned the _____, so I *won't do that. I should see if I can buy a ticket for a train.

W What a good _____!

*won't do [오운트] [두] → [오운두]

이유 추론

12 대화를 듣고, 남자가 서점에 간 이유로 가장 적절한 것을 고르시오.

① 책을 구매하려고
② 친구를 만나려고
③ 저자를 만나려고
④ 책을 교환하려고
⑤ 기분을 전환하려고

♥ **I see.**

: '알겠어.'라는 의미로 상대방의 이야기를 이해했을 때 사용하는 표현이다.
= I understand.

12

M Hello. I bought this book yesterday. Here is my _____.

W Yes, I remember you. You bought it _____ _____ _____.

M That's _____. But my son said that he had _____ read the book _____.

W Oh, ♥I see.

M So can I _____ _____ _____ another one?

W Of course. Please choose another one and then let me know.

장소 추론

13 대화를 듣고, 두 사람이 대화하는 장소로 가장 적절한 곳을 고르시오.

① 병원
② 은행
③ 우체국
④ 신발 가게
⑤ 쇼핑센터

13

W _____ _____. Where can I find the women's coats?

M They're _____ _____ _____ _____.

W What about shoes and accessories?

M They are also on the third floor.

W Is there an ATM in this _____?

M Yes. there's one on the first floor.

W Thank you so much.

M You're _____.

그림 정보 파악

14 대화를 듣고, 여자가 찾고 있는 국자의 위치로 가장 적절한 곳을 고르시오.

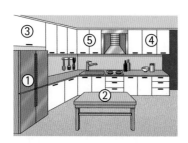

14

W Honey, did you see the scoop on the table? I can't find it.

M I think you *put it in the refrigerator _____ _____.

W No, it's not there.

M What about in the cupboard _____ _____ _____?

W _____ _____ _____. No, it's not there either.

M Then look in all the other cupboards. Okay?

W Yes. I found it! It is in the cupboard _____ _____ _____.

*put it [풀] [잇] → [푸릿]

15 대화를 듣고, 남자가 여자에게 부탁한 일로 가장 적절한 것을 고르시오.

① 상점에서 물건 사기
② 구매 물건 목록 작성하기
③ 야채를 깨끗하게 손질하기
④ 저녁 식사 테이블을 정리하기
⑤ 물건을 휴대폰으로 주문하기

15

W   Can you ＿＿＿＿ ＿＿＿＿ ＿＿＿＿ ＿＿＿＿ ?

M   Sure. What is it, Mom?

W   Can you go to the store for me? I have to prepare dinner now.

M   No problem. ＿＿＿＿ ＿＿＿＿ ＿＿＿＿ ＿＿＿＿ ?

W   I need noodles, vegetables, and, oh, I need juice and fruit, too.

M   I can't remember *all of those. Can you ＿＿＿＿ ＿＿＿＿ ＿＿＿＿ for me?

W   All right. Wait a moment.

*all of [올] [오브] → [얼러브]

---

16 대화를 듣고, 여자가 남자에게 제안한 것으로 가장 적절한 것을 고르시오.

① 옷을 여러 벌 입기
② 뜨거운 음료 마시기
③ 마음을 편하게 하기
④ 수건으로 땀을 닦기
⑤ 병원에 가서 진찰 받기

16

W   Are you okay? You are ＿＿＿＿ .

M   I don't feel well. I have a headache and ＿＿＿＿ ＿＿＿＿ ＿＿＿＿ .

W   You must have a cold. First, you need something hot to drink.

M   Will that help?

W   Of course. A hot drink will ＿＿＿＿ ＿＿＿＿ ＿＿＿＿ .

M   Thanks. Would you make one for me?

W   Sure. I'll ＿＿＿＿ ＿＿＿＿ ＿＿＿＿ .

---

17 대화를 듣고, 남자의 엄마가 남자에게 요청한 일로 가장 적절한 것을 고르시오.

① 방을 청소하기
② 도서관에 가기
③ 엄마에게 전화하기
④ 휴대폰을 고치러 가기
⑤ 책을 사러 서점에 가기

17

M   Sally, what are you going to do on Saturday?

W   I'm going to the library. ＿＿＿＿ ＿＿＿＿ ＿＿＿＿ ＿＿＿＿ ?

M   I don't have any plans yet. But my mom asked me to ＿＿＿＿ ＿＿＿＿ my room.

W   After that, why don't you study ＿＿＿＿ ＿＿＿＿ me at the library?

M   Oh, that is a good idea. ＿＿＿＿ ＿＿＿＿ clean my room first then.

장래 희망 추론

18 대화를 듣고, 남자의 장래 희망으로 가장 적절한 것을 고르시오.

① 여행가
② 조종사
③ 사진작가
④ 지리학자
⑤ 엔지니어

18

W Steve, did you really take this picture?

M Yes, I took it in Germany.

W It looks fantastic. Do you like _____ _____ ?

M Well, I especially like doing that on tours. I want _____ _____ _____ in the world.

W Then I think you should become a traveler.

M That sounds like a good idea. I hope my dream _____ _____ .

W I hope it does, too.

적절한 응답 찾기

[19~20] 대화를 듣고, 남자의 마지막 말에 이어질 여자의 응답으로 가장 적절한 것을 고르시오.

19 Woman: _____

① Never mind.
② Then I should ask her.
③ She is not here now.
④ You had better forget it.
⑤ I told you it is right there.

19 🇬🇧

W Jim, did you see _____ _____ _____ ?

M Yes, I saw it in the _____ .

W Well, I can't find it there. Was there _____ near the drawer?

M Yes. I _____ Cathy _____ _____ .

W Then I should ask her.

적절한 응답 찾기

20 Woman: _____

① No. It is not fair.
② Don't mention it.
③ I am good at leading.
④ You did the right thing.
⑤ Don't worry. I'll help you.

💛 **I can't believe it.**
: 상대방의 이야기를 실제로 믿을 수 없거나 놀람, 감탄, 충격의 느낌을 전달할 때 사용되는 표현이다.

20

W Benjamin, I have some good _____ for you. You were chosen as the president *of our club this year.

M Wow, 💛I can't believe it, Ms. Smith. Did you _____ me as the president?

W No. The members of the club recommended you.

M I didn't do anything for them. And I _____ _____ _____ _____ leading the members.

W Don't worry. I'll help you.

*of our [어브] [아우얼] → [어바우얼]

A 들려주는 단어를 듣고 쓴 뒤, 괄호 안에 우리말 뜻을 쓰시오.

	영어	우리말		영어	우리말
1			6		
2			7		
3			8		
4			9		
5			10		

B 다음 문장을 잘 듣고 빈칸에 들어갈 단어를 채우시오.

1 This _____ _____ _____ important days and schedule our activities.

2 I promise I _____ _____ _____ _____ the next time.

3 I am very happy _____ _____ _____ with a nice girl like her.

4 I am happy _____ _____ _____ enjoyed your dinner.

5 I'll _____ _____ _____ _____ at the supermarket.

6 I like to have anything _____ _____ _____ it is Korean food.

7 I mentioned the traffic, so I _____ _____ _____.

8 I can't remember _____ _____ _____.

9 I hope my dream _____ _____.

10 You were _____ _____ the president of our club this year.

1 다음을 듣고, 'I'가 무엇인지 가장 적절한 것을 고르시오.

①    ②   ③

④   ⑤

2 대화를 듣고, 여자가 잃어버린 지우개로 가장 적절한 것을 고르시오.

①   ②   ③

④   ⑤

3 다음을 듣고, Sydney의 날씨로 가장 적절한 것을 고르시오.

4 대화를 듣고, 남자의 마지막 말의 의도로 가장 적절한 것을 고르시오.
① 감사   ② 거절   ③ 위로
④ 격려   ⑤ 충고

5 다음을 듣고, 남자의 가족 여행에 관해 언급되지 <u>않은</u> 것을 고르시오.
① 여행하는 시기   ② 여행 목적지
③ 방문할 관광지   ④ 돌아오는 날짜
⑤ 관광지의 역사

6 대화를 듣고, 여자가 공항에 도착할 시각을 고르시오.
① 4:00   ② 4:30   ③ 5:00
④ 5:30   ⑤ 6:00

7 대화를 듣고, 여자의 장래 희망으로 가장 적절한 것을 고르시오.
① 기자   ② 작곡가
③ 음향 감독   ④ 아나운서
⑤ 방송 연출가

8 대화를 듣고, 남자의 심정으로 가장 적절한 것을 고르시오.
① upset   ② pleased
③ disappointed   ④ relieved
⑤ scared

9 대화를 듣고, 여자가 대화 직후에 할 일로 가장 적절한 것을 고르시오.
① 페인트칠하기
② 바닥 청소하기
③ 무대 장치 꾸미기
④ 페인트 롤러 찾기
⑤ 선생님께 여쭤보기

10 대화를 듣고, 무엇에 관한 내용인지 가장 적절한 것을 고르시오.
① 미래 계획   ② 은행 상품
③ 통장 개설   ④ 저축 방법
⑤ 은행 업무

11 대화를 듣고, 두 사람이 함께 이용할 교통수단으로 가장 적절한 것을 고르시오.

① 버스   ② 택시   ③ 자동차
④ 자전거   ⑤ 비행기

12 대화를 듣고 남자가 모임을 피하는 이유로 가장 적절한 것을 고르시오.

① 모임 자체를 싫어하기 때문에
② 모이는 시간에 애매하기 때문에
③ 모임에 다퉜던 친구가 있기 때문에
④ 모임에 오는 참여자가 많기 때문에
⑤ 바쁜 일정으로 참여가 어렵기 때문에

13 대화를 듣고, 두 사람의 관계로 가장 적절한 것을 고르시오.

① 점원 – 손님   ② 배달원 – 고객
③ 운전자 – 승객   ④ 디자이너 – 모델
⑤ 라디오 DJ – 청취자

14 대화를 듣고, 여자가 찾는 물건의 위치로 가장 적절한 곳을 고르시오.

15 대화를 듣고, 남자가 여자에게 부탁한 일로 가장 적절한 것을 고르시오.

① 대신 전화해 주기
② 버스표 예매하기
③ 함께 드라이브하기
④ 터미널에 태워다 주기
⑤ 버스 시간표 변경하기

16 대화를 듣고, 여자가 남자에게 제안한 것으로 가장 적절한 것을 고르시오.

① 날씨 확인하기
② 함께 산행하기
③ 실내에 머무르기
④ 여행 일정 세우기
⑤ 해변으로 놀러 가기

17 대화를 듣고, 남자가 가져갈 물건으로 가장 적절한 것을 고르시오.

① 종이   ② 연필   ③ 색연필
④ 필통   ⑤ 만년필

18 대화를 듣고, 여자의 직업으로 가장 적절한 것을 고르시오.

① 작가   ② 공무원
③ 사진작가   ④ 자세 교정사
⑤ 출입국 관리인

[19–20] 대화를 듣고, 여자의 마지막 말에 이어질 남자의 응답으로 가장 적절한 것을 고르시오.

19 Man: _____

① I won't be late.
② I'm afraid I can't.
③ I'll be back next Friday.
④ I can see you then.
⑤ I'm so excited about it.

20 Man: _____

① Of course, I like it.
② Performing in a play isn't so easy.
③ I'm glad to meet you again.
④ You can do better the next time.
⑤ Remember to bring your script.

Listen and Check

정답 및 해설 *p.79*

대화를 다시 듣고, 알맞은 것을 고르시오.

1 The machine is small enough to carry around.
☐ True   ☐ False

2 Does the eraser have a plain white cover?
☐ Yes   ☐ No

3 How will the weather in Brisbane be?
☐ rainy   ☐ sunny

4 Kelly has trouble getting up early in the morning.
☐ True   ☐ False

5 Where did the man see the Colosseum before the trip?
☐ in a book   ☐ in a movie

6 Will the woman arrive at 4:00?
☐ Yes   ☐ No

7 The woman is interested in world issues.
☐ True   ☐ False

8 Did the man expect the surprise party?
☐ Yes   ☐ No

9 What will the man do for the festival?
☐ paint the wall   ☐ set up the stage

10 The man tells the woman how he saves his money.
☐ True   ☐ False

11 Does the man accept the woman's suggestion?
☐ Yes   ☐ No

12 The man wants to say sorry to his friend.
☐ True   ☐ False

13 What does the woman ask the man to do?
☐ write her signature   ☐ pay a delivery fee

14 Where did the woman find her pencil case?
☐ on the bookshelf   ☐ on the desk

15 What time is it now?
☐ 3:40   ☐ 4:00

16 The man will change his plans because of the weather.
☐ True   ☐ False

17 Will the man exchange the notebook for another one?
☐ Yes   ☐ No

18 What does the man ask the woman to do?
☐ issue a passport   ☐ take a photo

19 They will go on a trip together.
☐ True   ☐ False

20 Is the woman happy with her performance on the stage?
☐ Yes   ☐ No

그림 정보 파악

1 다음을 듣고, 'I'가 무엇인지 가장 적절한 것을 고르시오.

① ② ③ ④ ⑤

1

M I am a machine. People use me to _____ _____ and to send messages. They also use me to play games. They can _____ _____ _____ _____. They put me inside their pockets and their bags. They need to _____ _____ to use me. What am I?

그림 정보 파악

2 대화를 듣고, 여자가 잃어버린 지우개로 가장 적절한 것을 고르시오.

① ② ③ ④ ⑤

💗 **What does it look like?**

: 사물의 생김새를 물어볼 때 사용하는 표현으로, '어떻게 생겼어?'라는 뜻이다. 사람의 생김새를 물을 때에는 it 대신 사람을 나타내는 단어를 넣어서 사용할 수 있다.

2 🇬🇧

W I think I lost my eraser. I can't *find it.

M 💗What does it look like?

W It is rectangular _____ _____ and _____ _____ _____ on it.

M Anything else?

W I _____ _____ _____ on the cover.

*find it [파인드] [잇] → [파인딧]

그림 정보 파악

3 다음을 듣고, Sydney의 날씨로 가장 적절한 것을 고르시오.

① ② ③ ④ ⑤

3

M Good morning. Here's the weather forecast for today. There _____ _____ _____ _____ in Melbourne, but you can still enjoy the beauty of nature. In Brisbane, it will be _____ _____ _____. It will be clear but _____ _____ _____. In Sydney, it will be windy and cold.

의도 파악

4 대화를 듣고, 남자의 마지막 말의 의도로 가장 적절한 것을 고르시오.

① 감사 ② 거절 ③ 위로
④ 격려 ⑤ 충고

4 🇬🇧

M What is wrong, Kelly? You look so tired today.

W You're right. I have _____ _____ these days.

M Do you use your smartphone _____ _____ bed?

W Yes, I do.

M Maybe you should _____ _____ _____.

언급 유무 파악

5 다음을 듣고, 남자의 가족 여행에 관해 언급되지 <u>않은</u> 것을 고르시오.

① 여행하는 시기
② 여행 목적지
③ 방문할 관광지
④ 돌아오는 날짜
⑤ 관광지의 역사

5

M My family will _____ _____ _____ to Rome next month. _____ _____ _____ _____, we will visit the Colosseum. I saw this place in a movie. This place was _____ _____. The next day, we will try some Italian dishes. On the last day, we will go to _____ in the city.

숫자 정보 파악

6 대화를 듣고, 여자가 공항에 도착할 시각을 고르시오.

① 4:00
② 4:30
③ 5:00
④ 5:30
⑤ 6:00

6

[Telephone rings.]

W Jonathan, are you at the airport? I was supposed to leave an _____ _____.

M I know. I am surprised you called me. What happened?

W There is a delay. The plane will _____ _____ _____ _____.

M Then _____ _____ will you arrive here?

W I will be there at 5:00.

M Okay. I'll _____ _____ _____.

W All right. See you later.

장래 희망 파악

7 대화를 듣고, 여자의 장래 희망으로 가장 적절한 것을 고르시오.

① 기자
② 작곡가
③ 음향 감독
④ 아나운서
⑤ 방송 연출가

7

M Eva, what are you reading?

W I'm _____ _____ _____.

M A newspaper? Isn't it boring to read?

W I want to tell people about _____ _____ and everything on TV in the future.

M I believe you will be a great reporter.

W Thanks. I'll _____ _____ _____.

심정 추론

8 대화를 듣고, 남자의 심정으로 가장 적절한 것을 고르시오.

① upset
② pleased
③ disappointed
④ relieved
⑤ scared

8

W Danny, you seem to be feeling good today.

M Yes. My friends threw me a _____ _____ for my birthday.

W That is nice. Were you expecting it?

M No, I thought my friends _____ _____ _____ my birthday.

W No way. So how was the party?

M It was _____ _____!

할 일 파악

9 대화를 듣고, 여자가 대화 직후에 할 일로
가장 적절한 것을 고르시오.

① 페인트칠하기
② 바닥 청소하기
③ 무대 장치 꾸미기
④ 페인트 롤러 찾기
⑤ 선생님께 여쭤보기

9

M	What should we do for the school _____?
W	We need to _____ the _____.
M	I'll set up the stage then.
W	Okay. I'll paint the walls with _____ colors.
M	Do you have a roller to paint with?
W	No. I think I should _____ _____ _____.

화제·주제 파악

10 대화를 듣고, 무엇에 관한 내용인지 가장
적절한 것을 고르시오.

① 미래 계획
② 은행 상품
③ 통장 개설
④ 저축 방법
⑤ 은행 업무

10 🇬🇧

W	I don't know how to _____ _____.
M	It's not difficult at all.
W	How do you _____ your money?
M	I make different _____ for different goals.
W	That _____ _____!
M	It really is.

교통수단 파악

11 대화를 듣고, 두 사람이 함께 이용할
교통수단으로 가장 적절한 것을 고르시오.

① 버스　　② 택시　　③ 자동차
④ 자전거　　⑤ 비행기

11

M	Would you like to _____ _____ _____ _____ in Sunny Park?
W	I'd love to, but it'll take too much time to _____ _____ _____ _____.
M	How about _____ our bikes?
W	*That's a good idea!

*That's a [뎃츠] [어] → [뎃처]

이유 추론

12 대화를 듣고, 남자가 모임을 피하는 이유로 가장 적절한 것을 고르시오.

① 모임 자체를 싫어하기 때문에
② 모이는 시간에 애매하기 때문에
③ 모임에 다퉜던 친구가 있기 때문에
④ 모임에 오는 참여자가 많기 때문에
⑤ 바쁜 일정으로 참여가 어렵기 때문에

♥ **Why don't you ~?**

: 상대방에게 무언가를 할 것을 권하거나 제안할 때 쓰는 표현으로, '~하는 게 어때?'라는 뜻이다.
= What about ~?
= How about ~?

12

W   Austin, are you _____ the meeting?

M   I'm sorry, but I can't be there.

W   Why do you keep _____ us?

M   I had a _____ _____ Brian.

W   ♥Why don't you _____ _____ _____ him?

M   We still need some time.

관계 추론

13 대화를 듣고, 두 사람의 관계로 가장 적절한 것을 고르시오.

① 점원 – 손님
② 배달부 – 고객
③ 운전자 – 승객
④ 디자이너 – 모델
⑤ 라디오 DJ – 청취자

13

[*Telephone rings.*]

M   Hello.

W   Hi. Is this Mr. Kim Minsu?

M   Yes. _____ is this?

W   I'm _____ _____ _____ to your address. Are you at home, sir?

M   Yes, I am at home now.

W   Please note that you have to _____ _____ _____.

그림 정보 파악

14 대화를 듣고, 여자가 찾는 물건의 위치로 가장 적절한 곳을 고르시오.

14

W   William, have you _____ _____ _____ _____?

M   Yes. I saw it in the living room.

W   Where in the living room did you see it?

M   I remember it was _____ _____ _____.

W   Okay. I'll go and check.

M   Did you find it?

W   Yes, I found it there. It was _____ _____ _____ _____.

부탁한 것 파악

15 대화를 듣고, 남자가 여자에게 부탁한 일로 가장 적절한 것을 고르시오.

① 대신 전화해 주기
② 버스표 예매하기
③ 함께 드라이브하기
④ 터미널에 태워다 주기
⑤ 버스 시간표 변경하기

15 🇬🇧

M Sofia, are you busy right now?

W Not really. What's up?

M Can you _____ _____ _____ the bus terminal, please?

W Sure. What time does your bus leave?

M It *leaves at 4:00.

W We should hurry. We only _____ _____ _____.

M I know. Let's _____ _____.

*leaves at [리브스] [엣] → [리브셋]

제안한 것 파악

16 대화를 듣고, 여자가 남자에게 제안한 것으로 가장 적절한 것을 고르시오.

① 날씨 확인하기
② 함께 산행하기
③ 실내에 머무르기
④ 여행 일정 세우기
⑤ 해변으로 놀러 가기

16

W Philip, what are you thinking _____ _____ _____?

M I wonder if I should go to the mountains or the beach this Sunday.

W There will be _____ _____ that day. How about _____ _____?

M Really? Maybe I should _____ _____ _____.

W Yes. It's better for you to stay inside.

특정 정보 파악

17 대화를 듣고, 남자가 가져갈 물건으로 가장 적절한 것을 고르시오.

① 종이 ② 연필 ③ 색연필
④ 필통 ⑤ 만년필

17

M Hi. I came to _____ this notebook.

W Is there something wrong with it?

M Some pages _____ _____ when I *opened it.

W I'm so sorry about that.

M I want to exchange it _____ _____ _____ _____ pencils.

opened it [오픈드] [잇] → [오픈딧]

18 대화를 듣고, 여자의 직업으로 가장 적절한 것을 고르시오.

① 작가
② 공무원
③ 사진작가
④ 자세 교정사
⑤ 출입국 관리인

♥ **Exactly!**

: 상대방의 말에 대한 강한 수긍을 나타낼 때 사용하는 표현으로, '바로 그거에요.'라는 뜻이다.

= That's it!
= You got it!
= There you go!

18

W   Hi. What can I do for you?

M   I need a photo for my _____.

W   Okay. Please sit there.

M   *Should I just _____ _____ _____?

W   Please _____ _____ _____ a bit to the right.

M   Like this?

W   ♥Exactly!

*Should I [슈드] [아이] → [슈다이]

[19~20] 대화를 듣고, 여자의 마지막 말에 이어질 남자의 응답으로 가장 적절한 것을 고르시오.

19 Man: _____

① I won't be late.
② I'm afraid I can't.
③ I'll be back next Friday.
④ I can see you then.
⑤ I'm so excited about it.

19

M   Esther, were you waiting for me?

W   Yes, there's _____ _____ _____ _____ _____ _____.

M   What is it?

W   What are your plans for this Saturday?

M   I'm _____ _____ _____ _____ _____.

W   When are you coming back?

M   I'll be back next Friday.

20 Man: _____

① Of course, I like it.
② Performing in a play isn't so easy.
③ I'm glad to meet you again.
④ You can do better the next time.
⑤ Remember to bring your script.

♥ **What's the matter?**

: 상대방에 대한 걱정을 나타낼 때 사용하는 표현으로, '무슨 일이야?'라는 뜻이다.

= What's wrong?
= Did anything go wrong?

20

M   Carrie, how are you today?

W   I _____ _____ _____.

M   ♥What's the matter?

W   I _____ _____ _____ on the stage.

M   I'm sorry to hear that.

W   That was really _____.

M   You can do better the next time.

A 들려주는 단어를 듣고 쓴 뒤, 괄호 안에 우리말 뜻을 쓰시오.

	영어	우리말		영어	우리말
1			6		
2			7		
3			8		
4			9		
5			10		

B 다음 문장을 잘 듣고 빈칸에 들어갈 단어를 채우시오.

1 I saw this ＿＿＿＿＿ ＿＿＿＿＿ ＿＿＿＿＿ ＿＿＿＿＿.

2 I forgot my lines ＿＿＿＿＿ ＿＿＿＿＿ ＿＿＿＿＿.

3 The plane will leave ＿＿＿＿＿ ＿＿＿＿＿ ＿＿＿＿＿.

4 ＿＿＿＿＿ ＿＿＿＿＿ ＿＿＿＿＿ your bus leave?

5 Do you have a roller ＿＿＿＿＿ ＿＿＿＿＿ ＿＿＿＿＿?

6 I want to ＿＿＿＿＿ ＿＿＿＿＿ for a set of pencils.

7 I thought my friends had ＿＿＿＿＿ ＿＿＿＿＿ my birthday.

8 Why don't you ＿＿＿＿＿ ＿＿＿＿＿ ＿＿＿＿＿ him?

9 It will take too much time to travel ＿＿＿＿＿ ＿＿＿＿＿ ＿＿＿＿＿.

10 People use me ＿＿＿＿＿ ＿＿＿＿＿ ＿＿＿＿＿ and to send messages.

1 다음을 듣고, 'this'가 가리키는 것으로 가장 적절한 것을 고르시오.

① ② ③

④ ⑤

2 대화를 듣고, 여자가 찾고 있는 지갑으로 가장 적절한 것을 고르시오.

① ② ③

④ ⑤

3 다음을 듣고, 목요일 오전의 날씨로 가장 적절한 것을 고르시오.

① ② ③

④ ⑤

4 대화를 듣고, 남자의 마지막 말의 의도로 가장 적절한 것을 고르시오.
① 거절 ② 동의 ③ 제안
④ 축하 ⑤ 부탁

5 다음을 듣고, 남자가 독서 모임에 대해 언급하지 <u>않은</u> 것을 고르시오.
① 멤버 수
② 전화 번호
③ 모임 요일
④ 독서 모임 회장
⑤ 독서 모임 활동

6 대화를 듣고, 두 사람이 만날 시각을 고르시오.
① 3:30 ② 4:00 ③ 4:30
④ 5:00 ⑤ 5:30

7 대화를 듣고, 여자의 장래 희망으로 가장 적절한 것을 고르시오.
① 사진작가 ② 전문 기술자
③ 미술 선생님 ④ 자동차 딜러
⑤ 자동차 디자이너

8 대화를 듣고, 남자의 심정으로 가장 적절한 것을 고르시오.
① sad ② relaxed ③ excited
④ annoyed ⑤ disappointed

9 대화를 듣고, 여자가 남자에게 알려준 정보로 가장 적절한 것을 고르시오.
① 백화점 세일 정보
② 남자 시계 가격
③ 여자 시계 가격
④ 자신의 생일 날짜
⑤ 시계 수리 방법

10 대화를 듣고, 무엇에 관한 내용인지 가장 적절한 것을 고르시오.
① 수학여행 ② 추억 회상
③ 학교 축제 ④ 학부모 초대
⑤ 제주도 홍보

11 대화를 듣고, 두 사람이 함께 이용할 교통수단으로 가장 적절한 것을 고르시오.
① 버스 　　② 택시 　　③ 지하철
④ 자전거 　　⑤ 자동차

12 대화를 듣고, 남자가 여자를 초대한 이유로 가장 적절한 것을 고르시오.
① 친구들과 다 함께 놀기 위해서
② 대회 우승을 기념하기 위해서
③ 피아노 연주를 들려주기 위해서
④ 남자의 생일을 축하하기 위해서
⑤ 피아노 교습소를 소개하기 위해서

13 대화를 듣고, 두 사람이 대화하는 장소로 가장 적절한 곳을 고르시오.
① 호텔 　　② 학교 　　③ 공원
④ 영화관 　　⑤ 독서실

14 대화를 듣고, 여자가 가려고 하는 장소로 가장 적절한 곳을 고르시오.

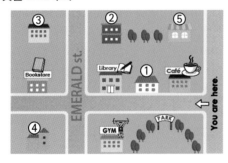

15 대화를 듣고, 남자가 여자에게 요청한 일로 가장 적절한 것을 고르시오.
① 호흡법 가르쳐 주기
② 뛰는 연습 같이하기
③ 저녁 운동 같이하기
④ 휴식 방법 물어보기
⑤ 마라톤 참가 신청하기

16 대화를 듣고, 여자가 남자에게 부탁한 일로 가장 적절한 것을 고르시오.
① 설거지하기
② 재활용하기
③ 쓰레기 버리기
④ 화장실 청소하기
⑤ 책꽂이 정리하기

17 대화를 듣고, 두 사람이 내일 할 일로 가장 적절한 것을 고르시오.
① 소풍 가기
② 도시락 만들기
③ 돗자리 사러 가기
④ 공원에서 운동하기
⑤ 개 산책시키기

18 대화를 듣고, 여자의 직업으로 가장 적절한 것을 고르시오.
① 코치 　　② 약사 　　③ 의사
④ 선생님 　　⑤ 간호사

[19-20] 대화를 듣고, 남자의 마지막 말에 이어질 여자의 응답으로 가장 적절한 것을 고르시오.

19 Woman: _____
① Baking cookies is fun.
② They taste really good.
③ Sorry, but I'm afraid I can't.
④ It's okay. I can do it alone.
⑤ No problem. I can give you some.

20 Woman: _____
① I'm going with my family.
② I'm going to take the train.
③ So we are both going to Seoul.
④ There are many things to do in Seoul.
⑤ It will take about three hours to get there.

Listen and Check

정답 및 해설 *p.84*

● 대화를 다시 듣고, 알맞은 것을 고르시오.

1 Some students use this to take notes in school.

☐ True　　　☐ False

11 Will the man drive the woman to her house?

☐ Yes　　　☐ No

2 Will they look for the purse together?

☐ Yes　　　☐ No

12 What is the man planning to do with his friends?

☐ have a party　　　☐ play the piano

3 How will the weather be on Friday?

☐ sunny　　　☐ rainy

13 The woman wants the man to get some rest.

☐ True　　　☐ False

4 The woman suggests the man throw a party for Kate.

☐ True　　　☐ False

14 Is the hair salon on Emerald Street?

☐ Yes　　　☐ No

5 One activity the book club does is writing poems.

☐ True　　　☐ False

15 What problem does the man have when he runs?

☐ running fast　　　☐ breath control

6 Why are they meeting earlier than 5:00 p.m.?

☐ to get good seats　☐ to buy tickets

16 The man will throw away the garbage after he cleans his room.

☐ True　　　☐ False

7 The man is amazed by the woman's drawing of a sports car.

☐ True　　　☐ False

17 Does the woman want to walk the dogs at the park?

☐ Yes　　　☐ No

8 Does the man want to apologize to Jessica?

☐ Yes　　　☐ No

18 How often does the man need to go to the hospital?

☐ every day　　　☐ every week

9 The man is going to buy a watch today.

☐ True　　　☐ False

19 The woman is baking cookies for her family.

☐ True　　　☐ False

10 On what day is the woman leaving for Jeju Island?

☐ Wednesday　　　☐ Friday

20 Are they going to Seoul on the same day?

☐ Yes　　　☐ No

그림 정보 파악

1 다음을 듣고, 'this'가 가리키는 것으로 가장 적절한 것을 고르시오.

① ② ③
④ ⑤

1

M Students usually _____ _____ _____ school. They use this when they take notes in class. This sometimes has a small eraser _____ _____. Students can erase what they write with this when they _____ _____ _____. What is this?

그림 정보 파악

2 대화를 듣고, 여자가 찾고 있는 지갑으로 가장 적절한 것을 고르시오.

① ② ③ Choco
④ MiMi ⑤

2

M Minjin, what are you looking for?

W I think I _____ _____ _____. I can't find it.

M What does it look like?

W It has an image of a _____ _____ _____.

M Is there anything else you can tell me about the purse?

W It has the _____ Mimi under the kitten.

M Okay. Let's _____ _____ _____.

그림 정보 파악

3 다음을 듣고, 목요일 오전 날씨로 가장 적절한 것을 고르시오.

① ② ③
④ ⑤

3

W Good evening. I'm Mary Nelson. This is the _____ _____ for this week. It'll be sunny on Monday. On Tuesday and Wednesday, it will be cloudy and windy. On Thursday morning, it'll be rainy. However, _____ _____ _____, the rain will stop. On Friday, the _____ _____ _____ _____, and it will be sunny again.

의도 파악

4 대화를 듣고, 남자의 마지막 말의 의도로 가장 적절한 것을 고르시오.

① 거절 ② 동의 ③ 제안
④ 축하 ⑤ 부탁

4 🏴

W John, did you _____ _____ _____?

M No. What is going on?

W Kate is _____ _____ _____ _____.

M I didn't know that. When is she leaving?

W She's leaving this Friday.

M How about _____ _____ _____ for her before she leaves?

언급 유무 파악

5 다음을 듣고, 남자가 독서 모임에 대해 언급하지 <u>않은</u> 것을 고르시오.

① 멤버 수
② 전화 번호
③ 모임 요일
④ 독서 모임 회장
⑤ 독서 모임 활동

5 🇬🇧

M Hi, everyone. Let me introduce _____ _____ _____. There are twelve members in the club. We read different *genres of books and meet to talk about them every Thursday. We also do _____ _____ writing poems and having a book festival. If you're _____ _____ _____, call us at 180-1234.

*genres of [잔르스] [오브] → [잔르소브]

숫자 정보 파악

6 대화를 듣고, 두 사람이 만날 시각을 고르시오.

① 3:30   ② 4:00   ③ 4:30
④ 5:00   ⑤ 5:30

6

W Kyungmin, are we still _____ _____ _____ game this Saturday?

M Of course. When _____ _____ _____?

W The game starts at 5:00 p.m. Why don't we meet at 4:30?

M The line for tickets will be long. So we'd better meet earlier. What about 4:00?

W Okay. See you at the ticket _____ _____.

장래 희망 파악

7 대화를 듣고, 여자의 장래 희망으로 가장 적절한 것을 고르시오.

① 사진작가
② 전문 기술자
③ 미술 선생님
④ 자동차 딜러
⑤ 자동차 디자이너

7

M Wow, is *this a picture of _____ _____ _____?

W Yes, it is. I drew it.

M It looks _____. You are so good at art!

W Thanks. I want to _____ _____ _____ _____ and show them to people someday.

M Oh, I didn't know that. I'm sure you will be a great car _____.

W I hope so.

*this a [디스] [어] → [디서]

심정 추론

8 대화를 듣고, 남자의 심정으로 가장 적절한 것을 고르시오.

① sad   ② relaxed
③ excited   ④ annoyed
⑤ disappointed

8

W What's the matter, Mark?

M I had an _____ _____ Jessica.

W Why did you have an argument with her?

M She took my notebook _____ _____ _____ _____ to me.

W Oh, no. Did she _____ _____ _____?

M Yes, she did. But I still feel bad.

특정 정보 파악

9 대화를 듣고, 여자가 남자에게 알려준 정보로 가장 적절한 것을 고르시오.
① 백화점 세일 정보
② 남자 시계 가격
③ 여자 시계 가격
④ 자신의 생일 날짜
⑤ 시계 수리 방법

9

M Hi, Jenny. That watch _____ _____ _____ _____. Where did you get it?

W Thanks. My parents bought it for me for my birthday at the department store.

M I'd like a man's watch just like it.

W The department store is _____ _____ _____ now. You can get one _____ _____ _____ _____.

M Really? I'll have to go there and get one now!

W Let's go together. There's something I have to buy, too.

화제·주제 파악

10 대화를 듣고, 무엇에 관한 내용인지 가장 적절한 것을 고르시오.
① 수학여행
② 추억 회상
③ 학교 축제
④ 학부모 초대
⑤ 제주도 홍보

10

W Dad, *here's a letter from the school.

M What _____ _____ _____?

W It's about the _____ _____ _____ to Jeju Island.

M Let me see. So you're going there this Wednesday and coming back on Friday.

W That's right. I'm staying there for two nights.

M Okay. I hope you make some _____ _____.

*here's a [히얼스] [어] → [히얼서]

교통수단 파악

11 대화를 듣고, 두 사람이 함께 이용할 교통수단으로 가장 적절한 것을 고르시오.
① 버스   ② 택시   ③ 지하철
④ 자전거   ⑤ 자동차

11 🇬🇧

M Lucy, what happened to your arm?

W I _____ _____ _____ _____ and hurt my arm.

M Oh, no. You should be careful when you walk down stairs. How will you go home?

W Well, I think I have to _____ _____ _____ today.

M Okay. Let's take one _____. I'll go and get one.

12 대화를 듣고, 남자가 여자를 초대한 이유로 가장 적절한 것을 고르시오.

① 친구들과 다 함께 놀기 위해서
② 대회 우승을 기념하기 위해서
③ 피아노 연주를 들려주기 위해서
④ 남자의 생일을 축하하기 위해서
⑤ 피아노 교습소를 소개하기 위해서

♥ **Congratulations!**
: 상대방에게 축하해 줄 때 사용하는 표현으로, '축하해'라는 뜻이다. '-s'를 반드시 붙여서 사용해야 한다.

12

W Sumin, you look happy. Did something good happen?

M I _____ _____ _____ in the piano contest! I still can't *believe it.

W ♥Congratulations, Sumin! I know _____ _____ _____.

M Thanks. I'm planning to invite some friends to my house so that we can _____ _____ _____. Are you free this Saturday?

W Yes, I am. How many people are going?

M Four, including you.

*believe it [빌리브] [잇] → [빌리빗]

장소 추론

13 대화를 듣고, 두 사람이 대화하는 장소로 가장 적절한 곳을 고르시오.

① 호텔
② 학교
③ 공원
④ 영화관
⑤ 독서실

---

13 🇬🇧

M Julia, why did you _____ _____ _____ this place?

W Isn't it beautiful? Look at those _____ and _____!

M I know, but I have no time to enjoy those things now.

W Listen, Charlie. You need to _____ _____ _____ sometimes.

M Okay, I got it.

W Great! *Let's sit on that wooden _____ for a moment.

*Let's sit [렛츠] [싯] → [렛싯]

그림 정보 파악

14 대화를 듣고, 여자가 가려고 하는 장소로 가장 적절한 곳을 고르시오.

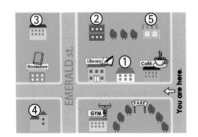

14

W Jason, do you know any _____ _____ _____ _____?

M Of course. There's Beauty Hair Salon.

W How can I _____ _____ _____ _____?

M Go straight to Emerald Street. Then, turn right.

W Okay.

M Then, you will see a bookstore on your left. Beauty Hair Salon is _____ _____ the bookstore.

W Thanks!

요청한 것 파악

15 대화를 듣고, 남자가 여자에게 요청한 일로 가장 적절한 것을 고르시오.

① 호흡법 가르쳐 주기
② 뛰는 연습 같이하기
③ 저녁 운동 같이하기
④ 휴식 방법 물어보기
⑤ 마라톤 참가 신청하기

15

M Jiho, are you _____ _____ the marathon?

W Yes, I am. I run 2 kilometers every day. I'm preparing _____ _____ _____.

M Wow, you're doing great! Could you teach me _____ _____ _____ while running?

W Sure. I'll show you how I control my breathing. It's not _____ at all. How about meeting this evening?

M That sounds nice!

부탁한 것 파악

16 대화를 듣고, 여자가 남자에게 부탁한 일로 가장 적절한 것을 고르시오.

① 설거지하기
② 재활용하기
③ 쓰레기 버리기
④ 화장실 청소하기
⑤ 책꽂이 정리하기

16

W Matthew, we need to _____ _____ _____ today.

M Okay, Mom. What should I do?

W I want you to _____ _____ _____.

M All right. Anything else?

W Oh, before that, could you help me throw away the garbage?

M No problem. I'll _____ _____ _____ then.

할 일 파악

17 대화를 듣고, 두 사람이 내일 할 일로 가장 적절한 것을 고르시오.

① 소풍 가기
② 도시락 만들기
③ 돗자리 사러 가기
④ 공원에서 운동하기
⑤ 개 산책시키기

♥ **I'd love to.**
: 상대방의 제안을 수락할 때 사용하는 표현으로, '~ 하고 싶다.', '좋다.'라는 뜻이다. 때때로 제안을 받아들이고 싶지만, 거절을 해야 할 때는 'I'd love to, but ~'을 사용하기도 하며 '고맙지만 사양할게.'라는 뜻을 가진다.

17 🇬🇧

M Stella, do you have any plans for tomorrow?

W Nothing much. Why?

M In that case, would you like to _____ _____ _____ at the park together?

W ♥I'd love to! Is there _____ _____ _____ _____ to the park?

M Can you _____ _____ _____ _____?

W Sure, I can bring one. See you tomorrow then!

18 대화를 듣고, 여자의 직업으로 가장 적절한 것을 고르시오.

① 코치
② 약사
③ 의사
④ 선생님
⑤ 간호사

18

W   Let me _____ _____ _____. Does it hurt very much?

M   Yes, it does. I started to _____ _____ last night.

W   How did you get hurt?

M   I had a car accident yesterday afternoon.

W   I see. You should come here every week. I'll _____ _____ _____ for you.

M   Okay, I will. Thank you very much.

[19~20] 대화를 듣고, 남자의 마지막 말에 이어질 여자의 응답으로 가장 적절한 것을 고르시오.

19 Woman: _____

① Baking cookies is fun.
② They taste really good.
③ Sorry, but I'm afraid I can't.
④ It's okay. I can do it alone.
⑤ No problem. I can give you some.

♥ **What + a(n) + 형용사 + 명사 + (주어 + 동사)!**
: 감탄을 나타낼 때 사용하는 표현으로, '~이 구나!'라는 뜻이다.

19

M   Cindy, are you baking something? Something _____ _____.

W   I'm _____ _____ for my friends.

M   ♥What a good friend you are! I'm happy that you _____ _____ your friends.

W   Thank you, Dad.

M   Do you _____ _____ _____, Cindy?

W   <u>It's okay. I can do it alone.</u>

20 Woman: _____

① I'm going with my family.
② I'm going to take the train.
③ So we are both going to Seoul.
④ There are many things to do in Seoul.
⑤ It will take about three hours to get there.

20

M   Clara, I heard you are going to visit Seoul.

W   Yes, I'm _____ _____ _____.

M   I'm going to Seoul, too. What day are you leaving?

W   I'm _____ _____ _____.

M   I'm going this Friday, too! How are you going to _____ _____?

W   <u>I'm going to take the train.</u>

A 들려주는 단어를 듣고 쓴 뒤, 괄호 안에 우리말 뜻을 쓰시오.

	영어	우리말			영어	우리말
1				6		
2				7		
3				8		
4				9		
5				10		

B 다음 문장을 잘 듣고 빈칸에 들어갈 단어를 채우시오.

1 What a _____ _____ you are!

2 I had an _____ _____ Jessica.

3 You can get one _____ _____ _____ price.

4 I want you _____ _____ your room.

5 I heard you _____ _____ _____ _____ Seoul.

6 I had a _____ _____ yesterday afternoon.

7 I think I have to _____ _____ _____ today.

8 Let's sit on that wooden bench _____ _____ _____.

9 Could you _____ _____ how to breathe while running?

10 Would you like _____ _____ _____ _____ at the park together?

1 다음을 듣고, 'I'가 무엇인지 가장 적절한 것을 고르시오.

2 대화를 듣고, 남자가 구입한 물건으로 가장 적절한 것을 고르시오.

3 다음을 듣고, Seattle의 오늘 날씨로 가장 적절한 것을 고르시오.

4 대화를 듣고, 여자가 한 마지막 말의 의도로 가장 적절한 것을 고르시오.
① 질투   ② 슬픔   ③ 걱정
④ 감사   ⑤ 동정

5 다음을 듣고, 여자가 방과 후에 한 일로 언급하지 <u>않은</u> 것을 고르시오.
① 샤워하기   ② 교실 청소
③ 편의점 가기   ④ 음악회 가기
⑤ 가족과 식사하기

6 대화를 듣고, 두 사람이 출발할 시각을 고르시오.
① 4시   ② 5시   ③ 6시
④ 7시   ⑤ 8시

7 대화를 듣고, 남자의 장래 희망으로 가장 적절한 것을 고르시오.
① 역사 선생님   ② 등반가
③ 여행 가이드   ④ 박물관 직원
⑤ 국립공원 안내원

8 대화를 듣고, 남자의 심정으로 가장 적절한 것을 고르시오.
① depressed   ② satisfied
③ relieved   ④ happy
⑤ nervous

9 대화를 듣고, 남자가 대화 직후에 할 일로 가장 적절한 것을 고르시오.
① 이사할 곳 찾기
② Amy에게 전화하기
③ 공원에 직접 가보기
④ 인터넷 검색하기
⑤ 집을 정리하기

10 대화를 듣고, 무엇에 관한 내용인지 가장 적절한 것을 고르시오.
① 방학 과제   ② 학교 시험
③ 실험 주제   ④ 학교 시설
⑤ 컴퓨터 고장

11 대화를 듣고, 남자가 이용할 교통수단으로 가장 적절한 것을 고르시오.
　① 버스　　　　② 도보　　　　③ 자전거
　④ 지하철　　　⑤ 자동차

12 대화를 듣고, 남자가 화가 난 이유로 가장 적절한 것을 고르시오.
　① 직원들이 불친절해서
　② 손님이 불만이 말해서
　③ 식당의 서비스가 느려서
　④ 주문한 음식이 맛이 없어서
　⑤ 가게 사장이 보이지 않아서

13 대화를 듣고, 두 사람의 관계로 가장 적절한 것을 고르시오.
　① 딸 – 아빠　　　② 엄마 – 아들
　③ 직원 – 손님　　④ 은행원 – 손님
　⑤ 선생님 – 학생

14 대화를 듣고, 남자의 기숙사 방의 위치로 가장 알맞은 곳을 고르시오.

15 대화를 듣고, 남자가 여자에게 부탁한 일로 가장 적절한 것을 고르시오.
　① 전화하기
　② 커피 준비하기
　③ 의자 나르기
　④ 인쇄물 복사하기
　⑤ 방문객 맞이하기

16 대화를 듣고, 여자가 남자에게 제안한 것으로 가장 적절한 것을 고르시오.
　① 행사에 함께 가기
　② 학교에서 공부하기
　③ 가족 행사 참석하기
　④ 자선 행사 주최하기
　⑤ 불쌍한 아이들 돕기

17 대화를 듣고, 두 사람이 구입할 물건을 고르시오.
　① 지도　　　　　② 역사책
　③ 트렁크　　　　④ 배낭
　⑤ 휴대용 충전기

18 대화를 여자의 직업으로 가장 적절한 것을 고르시오.
　① 배우　　　　　② 가수
　③ 연극 감독　　　④ 극장 직원
　⑤ 아나운서

[19–20] 대화를 듣고, 남자의 마지막 말에 이어질 여자의 응답으로 가장 적절한 것을 고르시오.

19 Woman: _____
　① Cheer up.
　② Good for you.
　③ The more, the better.
　④ Thank you for the advice.
　⑤ I appreciate your hard work.

20 Woman: _____
　① I beg your pardon?
　② Thanks for the good tips.
　③ You will do better the next time.
　④ Sorry. I called the wrong number.
　⑤ Don't worry. We will take care of it.

Listen and Check

정답 및 해설 p.89

● 대화를 다시 듣고, 알맞은 것을 고르시오.

1 I enjoy moving around during the day.
☐ True　　　☐ False

2 What did the man buy for his mother?
☐ a handkerchief　　☐ sunglasses

3 It will be cloudy in the morning in New York.
☐ True　　　☐ False

4 The woman's purse is in the subway office.
☐ True　　　☐ False

5 What did the woman buy at the convenience store?
☐ pens　　　☐ pencils

6 How long does it usually take to get to the theater?
☐ about one hour　　☐ about two hours

7 The man's dream is to travel to every country.
☐ True　　　☐ False

8 Did the man feel down because of the game?
☐ Yes　　　☐ No

9 What does the woman tell the man to do?
☐ text Amy　　☐ call Amy

10 The woman knows many things about computers.
☐ True　　　☐ False

11 The man is going downtown to have lunch with his friend.
☐ True　　　☐ False

12 Was the man mad about the service in the restaurant?
☐ Yes　　　☐ No

13 What does the man ask the woman to do?
☐ give him some money
☐ buy him some pens

14 The man's room is next to the elevator.
☐ True　　　☐ False

15 Did the woman make some copies for the man?
☐ Yes　　　☐ No

16 The woman doesn't feel like going to the charity event.
☐ True　　　☐ False

17 Where is Chen moving back?
☐ China　　　☐ Japan

18 Did the man accept the woman's offer?
☐ Yes　　　☐ No

19 The man got up early to exercise.
☐ True　　　☐ False

20 The woman left a message for Rachael.
☐ True　　　☐ False

그림 정보 파악

1 다음을 듣고, 'I'가 무엇인지 가장 적절한 것을 고르시오.

① ② ③ ④ ⑤

1

W   I can fly _____ _____ my wings, but people say I am not a bird. When people see me, most of them are _____ _____ me. I love living in caves, and I enjoy _____ _____ _____ _____. I also hate dirty air, so you may not see me in cities. What am I?

그림 정보 파악

2 대화를 듣고, 남자가 구입한 물건으로 가장 적절한 것을 고르시오.

① ② ③ ④ ⑤

2

W   Did you buy a gift _____ _____ _____?

M   Yes, I did.

W   Didn't you say you were going to buy her sunglasses?

M   I was going to, but they were _____ _____ _____. I'll show you what I bought. Wait a minute.

W   _____ _____ _____ it's a skirt.

M   No, it's a handkerchief.

그림 정보 파악

3 다음을 듣고, Seattle의 오늘 날씨로 가장 적절한 것을 고르시오.

① ② ③ ④ ⑤

3

M   Good morning! This is Jim Smith with the _____ weather _____. Yesterday, 1 to 3 inches of snow fell in Chicago. Today, it will be sunny in the morning in New York. But in the afternoon, it will be _____. In Seattle, there will be a lot of rain and thunderstorms. So don't _____ _____ _____ your umbrella.

의도 파악

4 대화를 듣고, 여자가 한 마지막 말의 의도로 가장 적절한 것을 고르시오.

① 질투   ② 슬픔   ③ 걱정
④ 감사   ⑤ 동정

4

[*Telephone rings.*]

M   Daegu Metro office. How can I help you?

W   _____ _____ _____ _____ on the subway.

M   I am sorry to hear that. What does it _____ _____?

W   It is black, and my ID card, two credit cards, and a little money are in it.

M   Fortunately, _____ _____ _____ _____. Can you come in the afternoon and ★get it?

W   Oh, really? You are a lifesaver.

★get it [겟] [잇] → [게릿]

5 다음을 듣고, 여자가 방과 후에 한 일로 언급하지 <u>않은</u> 것을 고르시오.

① 샤워하기
② 교실 청소
③ 편의점 가기
④ 음악회 가기
⑤ 가족과 식사하기

5

W After school _____ _____, I cleaned my classroom with my friends. On the way home, I _____ _____ a convenience store to buy some pens. I _____ _____ _____ and did my homework at home. After that, I went to a classical music concert with my family and had a great time.

숫자 정보 파악

6 대화를 듣고, 두 사람이 출발할 시각을 고르시오.

① 4시   ② 5시   ③ 6시
④ 7시   ⑤ 8시

♥ **Shall we ~?**

: '우리 ~할까요?'라는 표현으로 격식을 갖추어 권유할 때 쓰인다.
= Why don't we ~?
= Let's ~

6

W When does the musical start?
M _____ _____ _____ eight o'clock. What time is it?
W It's 6:00.
M ♥Shall we leave now?
W Now? I think it's _____ _____. It takes about an hour to get there.
M I know, but it's Friday. There will be heavy traffic today.
W _____ _____ _____. Let's go now then.

장래 희망 파악

7 대화를 듣고, 남자의 장래 희망으로 가장 적절한 것을 고르시오.

① 역사 선생님
② 등반가
③ 여행 가이드
④ 박물관 직원
⑤ 국립공원 안내원

7

W Jacob, what is your _____ _____?
M I like Korean history. That is why I like to go to the National Museum of Korea.
W Do you want to be a history teacher _____ _____ _____ _____?
M No, I like traveling, too. I actually want to be a tour guide for foreigners.
W That _____ _____.

심정 추론

8 대화를 듣고, 남자의 심정으로 가장 적절한 것을 고르시오.

① depressed   ② satisfied
③ relieved   ④ happy
⑤ nervous

8

M After all, we lost the game _____ _____ _____. It was all my fault.
W You did your best. Don't feel so sad.
M No, I made lots of _____ _____.
W People make mistakes. I think you'll _____ _____ in the next game.
M Thanks, but I cannot help feeling down.

할 일 파악

9 대화를 듣고, 남자가 대화 직후에 할 일로 가장 적절한 것을 고르시오.

① 이사할 곳 찾기
② Amy에게 전화하기
③ 공원에 직접 가보기
④ 인터넷 검색하기
⑤ 집을 정리하기

9

W What are you doing this weekend, Michael?

M I need to _____ _____ a new place to live.

W Oh, are there any neighborhoods you have in mind?

M I want to move _____ _____ Central Park.

W I heard Amy lives near that park. Why don't you *give her a call right now and ask her _____ _____ _____?

M That's a good idea.

*give her [기브] [헐] → [기벌]

화제·주제 파악

10 대화를 듣고, 무엇에 관한 내용인지 가장 적절한 것을 고르시오.

① 방학 과제
② 학교 시험
③ 실험 주제
④ 학교 시설
⑤ 컴퓨터 고장

♥ **give somebody a hand**
: 직역하면 '누군가에게 손을 주다'라는 뜻이다. '누군가에게 도움을 주다'라는 의미로 사용된다.

10 🇬🇧

W Oh, no! _____ _____ _____ _____?

M What's wrong, Claire?

W I was writing my research paper on the computer, but _____ _____ _____ _____, and I can't turn it back on again.

M You said you have to finish your paper _____ _____.

W That's right. Jim, you know a lot about computers, right? Can you ♥give me a hand?

교통수단 파악

11 대화를 듣고, 남자가 이용할 교통수단으로 가장 적절한 것을 고르시오.

① 버스　　② 도보　　③ 자전거
④ 지하철　　⑤ 자동차

11

M Mom, can you _____ _____ _____?

W Sorry, but I'm busy right now. Why do you want to go downtown?

M I'm going to meet my friend _____ _____.

W Why don't you take the subway or a bus?

M Okay. I'll take the subway. I think it will be _____.

이유 추론

12 대화를 듣고, 남자가 화가 난 이유로 가장 적절한 것을 고르시오.

① 직원들이 불친절해서
② 손님이 불만이 말해서
③ 식당의 서비스가 느려서
④ 주문한 음식이 맛이 없어서
⑤ 가게 사장이 보이지 않아서

♥ **That's not all.**
: 말하려는 내용이 한 가지가 아닐 때 쓰이며, '그게 전부가 아니야.'의 의미이다.

12 🇬🇧

W Sir, is there something wrong?

M I'm very upset. The food came here _____ _____ _____ _____ _____ _____.

W I'm sorry that this happened to you.

M ♥That's not all. I also waited thirty minutes to get the bill!

W I'm sorry again. We are very busy today.

M _____ _____ _____. I want your manager here _____ _____.

관계 추론

13 대화를 듣고, 두 사람의 관계로 가장 적절한 것을 고르시오.

① 딸 – 아빠
② 엄마 – 아들
③ 직원 – 손님
④ 은행원 – 손님
⑤ 선생님 – 학생

13

M Can we talk for a minute?

W Sure. _____ _____ _____?

M Would you give me some money? I need to buy some notebooks.

W I gave you your allowance yesterday.

M I know, but I *spent it all on a gift for my friend.

W I think you _____ _____ _____ your money more _____. Here you are.

M Thank you.

*spent it all [스펜트] [잇] [얼] → [스펜티럴]

그림 정보 파악

14 대화를 듣고, 남자의 기숙사 방의 위치로 가장 알맞은 곳을 고르시오.

14

M Hello. My name is Jayden.

W Hi. I'm Pam. Nice to meet you.

M Do you live in the dorm, too?

W Yes. I live on the second floor. Is your room _____ _____ _____ _____?

M Yes. My room is _____ _____ _____ _____ the third floor _____ _____ the elevator. It's across from the staff room. You can come by my room anytime.

W Thanks. I will.

부탁한 것 파악

15 대화를 듣고, 남자가 여자에게 부탁한 일로 가장 적절한 것을 고르시오.

① 전화하기
② 커피 준비하기
③ 의자 나르기
④ 인쇄물 복사하기
⑤ 방문객 맞이하기

♥ **Let me ~**
: 원래는 '내가 ~하도록 허락해 줘'의 의미이지만 '내가 ~하겠어', '내가 ~할게'로 사용된다.
= I will ~

15

W You look very busy.

M Yes. The meeting starts in ten minutes.

W ♥Let me give you a hand. Do you need me to _____ _____ _____ the chairs?

M It is okay. I can do that. Can you call James and tell him that I am here?

W Of course. You have to make _____ _____ _____ _____, right?

M Actually, I did that yesterday.

제안한 것 파악

16 대화를 듣고, 여자가 남자에게 제안한 것으로 가장 적절한 것을 고르시오.

① 행사에 함께 가기
② 학교에서 공부하기
③ 가족 행사 참석하기
④ 자선 행사 주최하기
⑤ 불쌍한 아이들 돕기

♥ **feel like -ing**
: '~하고 싶은 느낌이다', '~하고 싶다'의 의미로 소망 또는 바람을 나타낸다.
= be dying to + v
= look forward to -ing

16

M Ashley, what are you reading?

W I am _____ _____ sports. So I am reading an article about sports news.

M I see. Did you hear that the local baseball team will _____ _____ _____ _____ to *help poor children?

W No, I didn't. Where will it be held?

M Near our school. We can have fun at the event and _____ _____ _____ _____ _____.

W I ♥feel like going there. Will you go with me?

M I want to, but I have to attend a family reunion.

*help poor [헬프] [퓨어] → [헬퓨어]

특정 정보 파악

17 대화를 듣고, 두 사람이 구입할 물건을 고르시오.

① 지도
② 역사책
③ 트렁크
④ 배낭
⑤ 휴대용 충전기

---

17 🇬🇧

M Anna, let's buy a present for Chen. He's _____ _____ _____ China this Monday.

W Good idea. I will miss him.

M Then how about a book on the _____ of China?

W That is _____. Why don't we buy him a backpack?

M That would be good. I think he needs a new one.

W Yeah. I am _____ he will like it.

직업 추론

18 대화를 여자의 직업으로 가장 적절한 것을
고르시오.

① 배우   ② 가수
③ 연극 감독   ④ 극장 직원
⑤ 아나운서

18

M What did you think of my performance?

W It was great, and your _____ _____ _____.

M Really? I'm happy to hear that.

W Are you a professional actor?

M No. I'm a singer. But I *would like to be an actor.

W How about _____ _____ _____ in my new
play? I need someone to play the hero.

M How wonderful! I _____ _____ _____.

*would like [우드] [라이크] → [울라이크]

적절한 응답 찾기

[19~20] 대화를 듣고, 남자의 마지막 말에
이어질 여자의 응답으로 가장 적절한 것을
고르시오.

19 Woman: _____

① Cheer up.
② Good for you.
③ The more, the better.
④ Thank you for the advice.
⑤ I appreciate your hard work.

19

W Good morning, Aiden. _____ _____ _____
_____ so early?

M I exercised this morning. And you? Are you _____, too?

W No. I have to finish my report. I was too tired to do it last night.

M I see. You had _____ _____ _____ every
day for your health.

W <u>Thank you for the advice.</u>

적절한 응답 찾기

20 Woman: _____

① I beg your pardon?
② Thanks for the good tips.
③ You will do better the next time.
④ Sorry. I called the wrong number.
⑤ Don't worry. We will take care of
it.

20 🇬🇧

[*Telephone rings.*]

M Hello.

W Hello. This is Victoria, Rachael's friend. _____
_____ _____ _____ _____?

M Rachael? I don't know anyone here _____ _____
_____.

W That's strange. Isn't this 6666-0509?

M No, it isn't. It's 6666-0905.

W <u>Sorry. I called the wrong number.</u>

A 들려주는 단어를 듣고 쓴 뒤, 괄호 안에 우리말 뜻을 쓰시오.

	영어	우리말		영어	우리말
1			6		
2			7		
3			8		
4			9		
5			10		

B 다음 문장을 잘 듣고 빈칸에 들어갈 단어를 채우시오.

1 Today, it will _____ _____ in the morning in New York.

2 Can you _____ in the afternoon and _____ _____?

3 I went to a _____ _____ _____ with my family.

4 I actually want to be a tour guide _____ _____.

5 Thanks, but I _____ _____ _____ _____.

6 I need to _____ _____ a new place to live.

7 You said you _____ _____ _____ your paper by tomorrow.

8 You can _____ _____ my room anytime.

9 I am reading _____ _____ _____ sports news.

10 I was _____ _____ _____ do it last night.

1 다음을 듣고, 'this'가 가리키는 것으로 가장 적절한 것을 고르시오.

①   ②   ③

④   ⑤

2 대화를 듣고, 여자가 선물로 구입한 것으로 가장 적절한 것을 고르시오.

①   ②   ③

④   ⑤

3 다음을 듣고, 내일 오후의 날씨로 가장 적절한 것을 고르시오.

①   ②   ③

④   ⑤

4 대화를 듣고, 남자의 마지막 말의 의도로 가장 적절한 것을 고르시오.
① 승낙   ② 거절
③ 비난   ④ 질책
⑤ 충고

5 다음을 듣고, 두 남자가 지난 일요일에 한 일로 언급하지 <u>않은</u> 것을 고르시오.
① 서점에 가기
② 병원에 가서 치료하기
③ 친구의 집을 방문하기
④ 친구의 쾌유를 빌기
⑤ 친구 어머니의 음식을 대접받기

6 대화를 듣고, 두 사람이 집을 나서는 시각을 고르시오.
① 2시 40분   ② 3시 5분
③ 3시 10분   ④ 3시 13분
⑤ 3시 30분

7 대화를 듣고, 여자의 장래 희망으로 가장 적절한 것을 고르시오.
① 교수   ② 가수   ③ 댄서
④ 작곡가   ⑤ 상담가

8 대화를 듣고, 남자의 심정으로 가장 적절한 것을 고르시오.
① sad   ② upset   ③ happy
④ pleased   ⑤ curious

9 대화를 듣고, 남자가 대화 직후 할 일로 가장 적절한 것을 고르시오.
① 플라스틱 병 버리기
② 도서관에서 책 대출하기
③ 우유 마시기
④ 시청에 방문하기
⑤ 빈 병 씻기

10 대화를 듣고, 무엇에 관한 내용인지 가장 적절한 것을 고르시오.
① 수업 계획   ② 선박 여행
③ 지도 구입   ④ 여행 계획
⑤ 숙박 예약

11 대화를 듣고, 여자가 이용할 교통수단으로 가장 적절한 것을 고르시오.

① 택시 　　② 버스 　　③ 지하철
④ 자전거 　　⑤ 오토바이

12 대화를 듣고, 여자가 영어 듣기 시험에서 집중을 할 수 없었던 이유로 가장 적절한 것을 고르시오.

① 늦잠을 자서
② 공부를 하지 않아서
③ 우울한 일이 있어서
④ 밤에 야식을 먹어서
⑤ 늦게까지 공부를 해서

13 대화를 듣고, 두 사람이 대화하는 장소로 가장 적절한 곳을 고르시오.

① 거실 　　② 침실 　　③ 주방
④ 화장실 　　⑤ 다용도실

14 대화를 듣고, 여자가 찾는 빵집의 위치로 가장 적절한 곳을 고르시오.

15 대화를 듣고, 남자가 여자에게 부탁한 일로 가장 적절한 것을 고르시오.

① 외출을 준비하기
② 침실을 정리하기
③ 즉시 전화를 받기
④ 서류를 동료에게 전달하기
⑤ 학교 숙제를 잊지 말고 하기

16 대화를 듣고, 여자가 남자에게 제안한 것으로 가장 적절한 것을 고르시오.

① 거실을 청소하기
② 집 안에 머무르기
③ 집 안을 환기시키기
④ 엄마의 허락을 받기
⑤ 엄마의 심부름을 하기

17 대화를 듣고, 두 사람이 저녁을 먹을 곳으로 가장 적절한 곳을 고르시오.

① 중국 음식점 　　② 친구네 집
③ 이태리 음식점 　　④ 공원
⑤ 일본 음식점

18 대화를 듣고, 여자가 주말에 한 일로 가장 적절한 것을 고르시오.

① 마을을 구경하기 　　② 캐나다를 여행하기
③ 친척집을 방문하기 　　④ 과학 숙제를 끝내기
⑤ 사촌을 관광시켜 주기

[19-20] 대화를 듣고, 여자의 마지막 말에 이어질 남자의 응답으로 가장 적절한 것을 고르시오.

19 Man: _____

① Good for you.
② Maybe next time.
③ They feel very comfortable.
④ What do you think?
⑤ I don't feel very well.

20 Man: _____

① I am a freshman.
② I will try my best.
③ Don't say that.
④ I am good at sports.
⑤ I got a good grade on my test.

Listen and Check

● 대화를 다시 듣고, 알맞은 것을 고르시오.

1 People do not use this to take pictures anymore.

☐ True　　　　☐ False

2 Who will the woman give the gift to?

☐ her friends　　☐ her parents

3 Was it very warm yesterday?

☐ Yes　　　　☐ No

4 The woman asks the man to go to school with her.

☐ True　　　　☐ False

5 Where did the man's friend take him?

☐ to a bookstore　　☐ to the hospital

6 What time does Tom's class finish?

☐ at 3:10　　　☐ at 3:30

7 The woman wants to be a world-famous singer-songwriter.

☐ True　　　　☐ False

8 The woman was on a diet and lost 5 kilograms.

☐ True　　　　☐ False

9 The woman asked the man to buy some bread.

☐ True　　　　☐ False

10 They will go to the beach near the seafood market.

☐ True　　　　☐ False

11 What will the woman take to the ballpark?

☐ a bus　　　　☐ the subway

12 Was the woman too tired to focus on the English test?

☐ Yes　　　　☐ No

13 What will the man do before helping the woman?

☐ He will cook dinner.

☐ He will wash his hands.

14 The bakery is opposite the supermarket.

☐ True　　　　☐ False

15 Is the woman going to give the papers to her father?

☐ Yes　　　　☐ No

16 They need their mom's permission to go out.

☐ True　　　　☐ False

17 They will have lunch at the new Italian restaurant.

☐ True　　　　☐ False

18 How many more days does the man give the woman to finish the report?

☐ 2 days　　　　☐ 3 days

19 The man is trying on shoes in the woman's store.

☐ True　　　　☐ False

20 What club is the man trying to join?

☐ the badminton club

☐ the tennis club

190

그림 정보 파악

1 다음을 듣고, 'this'가 가리키는 것으로 가장 적절한 것을 고르시오.

① ② ③
④ ⑤

1 🇬🇧

M Usually, we can _____ _____ _____ this. And we used to think this was _____ _____ the greatest _____ in the world. But not so many people use this anymore because the smartphone can also take pictures. However, professional photographers still use this _____ _____ _____. What is this?

그림 정보 파악

2 대화를 듣고, 여자가 선물로 구입한 것으로 가장 적절한 것을 고르시오.

① ② ③
④ ⑤

2

W Tomorrow, we're _____ _____ home at last.
M Yeah. I miss my family and friends.
W _____ _____ _____ _____. By the way, did you buy any gifts for your family?
M _____ _____. I haven't bought anything. How about you?
W I already bought a miniature of a palace. I will give it to my parents.

그림 정보 파악

3 다음을 듣고, 내일 오후의 날씨로 가장 적절한 것을 고르시오.

① ② ③
④ ⑤

3

W Hello, everyone. This is channel 7, where we are all about weather. Yesterday was very cold, _____ _____? Today, it will be warm. We think it will be a good time to _____ _____ to play. However, we will have rain tomorrow morning, and the rain will _____ _____ _____ in the afternoon. _____ _____ _____ the cold weather tomorrow. See you next time.

의도 파악

4 대화를 듣고, 남자의 마지막 말의 의도로 가장 적절한 것을 고르시오.
① 승낙 ② 거절 ③ 비난
④ 질책 ⑤ 충고

4

W I didn't do my math homework. I had _____ _____ _____ _____ _____.
M You have enough time now, don't you? Why don't you do it now?
W You're right. But I can't concentrate at home.
M What about going to the _____ then?
W Could you _____ _____ with me?
M _____ _____?

언급 유무 파악

5 다음을 듣고, 두 남자가 지난 일요일에 한 일로 언급하지 <u>않은</u> 것을 고르시오.

① 서점에 가기
② 병원에 가서 치료하기
③ 친구의 집을 방문하기
④ 친구의 쾌유를 빌기
⑤ 친구 어머니의 음식을 대접받기

5

M My friend _____ _____ to the bookstore last Sunday. Then, he got a phone call from our _____ _____ Dave. He broke his leg and was staying at home. So we visited his house and _____ him up to help him _____ _____. His mother cooked us a nice dinner.

숫자 정보 파악

6 대화를 듣고, 두 사람이 집을 나서는 시각을 고르시오.

① 2시 40분
② 3시 5분
③ 3시 10분
④ 3시 13분
⑤ 3시 30분

6 🇬🇧

M Let's go to pick up Tom, darling.
W We don't need to start now. His class _____ _____ 3:30.
M Does it? I thought his class finishes at 3:00.
W The class _____ _____.
M I didn't know that.
W We can _____ twenty minutes before his class is _____.
M I see.

장래 희망 파악

7 대화를 듣고, 여자의 장래 희망으로 가장 적절한 것을 고르시오.

① 교수
② 가수
③ 댄서
④ 작곡가
⑤ 상담가

7

W I heard you are _____ _____ _____.
M Yes, I am. _____, I want to be a singer-songwriter.
W I think you'll *become a good singer.
M Thank you. What do _____ _____ _____ _____? Did you say that you want to be a dancer?
W Yes, I want to be a world-famous dancer.

*become a [비컴] [어] → [비커머]

심정 추론

8 대화를 듣고, 남자의 심정으로 가장 적절한 것을 고르시오.

① sad   ② upset
③ happy   ④ pleased
⑤ curious

8

M You look really happy now. What's up?
W Do I? Ha-ha. Maybe I have a good _____ for that.
M Tell me the reason, please.
W I was on a diet and finally _____ six kilograms.
M Wow, congratulations. How did you lose weight?
W Well, I decided not to eat foods _____ _____ snacks and sodas.

할 일 파악

9 대화를 듣고, 남자가 대화 직후 할 일로 가장 적절한 것을 고르시오.

① 플라스틱 병 버리기
② 도서관에서 책 대출하기
③ 우유 마시기
④ 시청에 방문하기
⑤ 빈 병 씻기

♥ **It's no big deal.**
: '큰일이 아냐.', '별거 아냐.'의 의미로 상대방이 고마워하거나 미안해하거나 또는 무언가를 부탁할 때 대답하는 표현이다.

9

W Are you going out now?

M Yes, Mom. I am going to the library to do some research _____ _____ _____ of our city.

W Okay, but could you _____ _____ these plastic bottles on your way out?

M Sure. ♥ It's no big deal.

W Oh, can you also get some milk at the grocery store on your _____ _____ _____?

M Yes, I can.

화제·주제 파악

10 대화를 듣고, 무엇에 관한 내용인지 가장 적절한 것을 고르시오.

① 수업 계획
② 선박 여행
③ 지도 구입
④ 여행 계획
⑤ 숙박 예약

10 🇬🇧

M _____ _____ Busan do you want to go first?

W Hmm... How about the seafood market near the port?

M That would be nice. Let me see the map. The market is _____ _____ _____ the port.

W You are right. We can _____ the _____ morning at the market. I am looking forward to going there.

M _____ _____ _____.

교통수단 파악

11 대화를 듣고, 여자가 이용할 교통수단으로 가장 적절한 것을 고르시오.

① 택시 ② 버스 ③ 지하철
④ 자전거 ⑤ 오토바이

11

W Excuse me. How can I _____ _____ the ballpark?

M You can take the subway or a bus.

W Do you know _____ _____ _____ _____?

M Taking a bus will be faster. The bus stop is _____ _____ _____ from here.

W Thank you very much.

이유 추론

12 대화를 듣고, 여자가 영어 듣기 시험에서 집중을 할 수 없었던 이유로 가장 적절한 것을 고르시오.

① 늦잠을 자서
② 공부를 하지 않아서
③ 우울한 일이 있어서
④ 밤에 야식을 먹어서
⑤ 늦게까지 공부를 해서

12

M What's wrong, Mia? You look down.

W I didn't _____ _____ the English listening test.

M What happened? You studied hard for the test.

W Well, maybe _____ _____ _____ until late last night.

M _____ _____ _____ _____ _____ before the test next time.

W I will. Thanks.

장소 추론

13 대화를 듣고, 두 사람이 대화하는 장소로 가장 적절한 곳을 고르시오.

① 거실
② 침실
③ 주방
④ 화장실
⑤ 다용도실

13

W Adam, lunch is almost ready.

M _____ _____ _____ _____ today?

W Tomato soup and sandwiches. I just need to _____ the soup a bit more.

M They smell so good.

W Can you _____ _____ _____ the table?

M Yes, Mom. Let me wash my hands first.

그림 정보 파악

14 대화를 듣고, 여자가 찾는 빵집의 위치로 가장 적절한 곳을 고르시오.

14 🇬🇧

M I think you are _____. Can I help you?

W Oh, thanks. I am new here. Where is Prince Bakery?

M _____ _____ two blocks and then turn right. You can see a big supermarket.

W And?

M The bakery is _____ _____ _____ the supermarket.

W Thanks a lot.

M You are _____.

15 대화를 듣고, 남자가 여자에게 부탁한 일로 가장 적절한 것을 고르시오.

① 외출을 준비하기
② 침실을 정리하기
③ 즉시 전화를 받기
④ 서류를 동료에게 전달하기
⑤ 학교 숙제를 잊지 말고 하기

15

[*Telephone rings*.]

W   Hello.

M   Oh, Cathy, you are home. I need your help. Can you _____ _____ _____ my desk, please?

W   Yes, Dad. I am at your desk now.

M   I _____ _____ _____ some important papers to work. I think I put them on my desk. Can you see them?

W   Yes. I found them.

M   My co-worker will *visit our house. Her name is Ms. Johnson. Would you _____ _____ _____ _____ ?

W   Sure. I will.

*visit our [비지트] [아우얼] → [비짓아월]

---

16 대화를 듣고, 여자가 남자에게 제안한 것으로 가장 적절한 것을 고르시오.

① 거실을 청소하기
② 집 안에 머무르기
③ 집 안을 환기시키기
④ 엄마의 허락을 받기
⑤ 엄마의 심부름을 하기

16

M   What a beautiful day!

W   You're right. Why don't we _____ _____ ?

M   That's a great idea. Shall we get ready now?

W   _____ _____ _____ . I think we should get Mom's permission first.

M   That's right. Let's _____ _____ now.

---

17 대화를 듣고, 두 사람이 저녁을 먹을 곳으로 가장 적절한 곳을 고르시오.

① 중국 음식점
② 친구네 집
③ 이태리 음식점
④ 공원
⑤ 일본 음식점

17

M   Kelsey, did you _____ _____ _____ ?

W   I just finished it, Dad.

M   Great. Then why don't you _____ _____ _____ ? I think your room is quite messy.

W   Okay. I will do that.

M   Good. When you are done, let's _____ _____ _____ _____ dinner at the new Chinese restaurant.

W   That sounds awesome.

18 대화를 듣고, 여자가 주말에 한 일로 가장 적절한 것을 고르시오.

① 마을을 구경하기
② 캐나다를 여행하기
③ 친척집을 방문하기
④ 과학 숙제를 끝내기
⑤ 사촌을 관광시켜 주기

18

M Naomi, you did not _____ _____ your science report today.

W I am sorry, Mr. Thomson. I am still working on it.

M Can you tell me why it is late?

W My cousin came from Canada last Friday. I had to _____ _____ _____ _____ _____ _____.

M I see, but you still have to do your homework. I will give you _____ _____ days.

W Thank you.

[19-20] 대화를 듣고, 여자의 마지막 말에 이어질 남자의 응답으로 가장 적절한 것을 고르시오.

19 Man: _____

① Good for you.
② Maybe next time.
③ They feel very comfortable.
④ What do you think?
⑤ I don't feel very well.

19 🇬🇧

M Excuse me. Can I _____ _____ _____ _____?

W Of course. They're the most popular shoes *in our store. Are they the right size for you? How about the color?

M I don't know. I will try them on first.

W _____ _____ _____ _____ _____?

M <u>They feel very comfortable.</u>

*in our [인] [아우얼] → [이나월]

20 Man: _____

① I am a freshman.
② I will try my best.
③ Don't say that.
④ I am good at sports.
⑤ I got a good grade on my test.

20

M Hello. Is anyone here?

W Please come in. _____ _____ the tennis club.

M I'd like to _____ _____ _____. Is that possible?

W Yes. What's your name?

M I'm Jack. Jack Hamilton.

W Nice to meet you, Jack. _____ _____ _____ _____ _____?

M <u>I am a freshman.</u>

A 들려주는 단어를 듣고 쓴 뒤, 괄호 안에 우리말 뜻을 쓰시오.

	영어	우리말		영어	우리말
1			6		
2			7		
3			8		
4			9		
5			10		

B 다음 문장을 잘 듣고 빈칸에 들어갈 단어를 채우시오.

1 Tomorrow, we're leaving for home _____ _____.

2 We think it will be a good time _____ _____ _____ to play.

3 We visited his house and _____ _____ _____ to help him feel better.

4 We can leave twenty minutes _____ _____ _____ _____ _____.

5 I heard you _____ _____ _____ music.

6 The bus stop is one block _____ _____ _____.

7 I am going to the library to _____ _____ _____ on the history of our city.

8 The bakery is _____ _____ _____ the supermarket.

9 Would you _____ _____ the papers?

10 They're _____ _____ _____ shoes in our store.

1 다음을 듣고, 'I'가 무엇인지 가장 적절한 것을 고르시오.

① ② ③

④ ⑤

2 대화를 듣고, 남자가 구입할 곰 인형으로 가장 적절한 것을 고르시오.

① ② ③

④ ⑤

3 다음을 듣고, 내일의 날씨로 가장 적절한 것을 고르시오.

① ② ③

④ ⑤

4 대화를 듣고, 남자의 마지막 말의 의도로 가장 적절한 것을 고르시오.

① 찬성 ② 부탁 ③ 거절
④ 축하 ⑤ 위로

5 다음을 듣고, 남자가 아빠에 대해 언급하지 <u>않은</u> 것을 고르시오.

① 나이 ② 취미 ③ 외모
④ 직업 ⑤ 성격

6 대화를 듣고, 두 사람이 만날 시각을 고르시오.

① 1:00 p.m. ② 1:30 p.m.
③ 2:00 p.m. ④ 2:30 p.m.
⑤ 3:00 p.m.

7 대화를 듣고, 남자의 장래 희망으로 가장 적절한 것을 고르시오.

① 수의사 ② 간호사
③ 경찰관 ④ 제빵사
⑤ 동물 조련사

8 대화를 듣고, 남자의 심정으로 가장 적절한 것을 고르시오.

① calm ② worried
③ satisfied ④ hopeless
⑤ regretful

9 대화를 듣고, 여자가 대화 직후에 할 일로 가장 적절한 것을 고르시오.

① 기념사진 찍기
② 기념품 구입하기
③ 신상 카메라 구입하기
④ 카메라를 가방에 넣기
⑤ 박물관 입장권 보여 주기

10 대화를 듣고, 무엇에 관한 내용인지 가장 적절한 것을 고르시오.

① 모금 ② 수술
③ 헌혈 ④ 장학금
⑤ 봉사 활동

11 대화를 듣고, 두 사람이 함께 이용할 교통수단으로 가장 적절한 것을 고르시오.
① 버스 ② 택시 ③ 자전거
④ 지하철 ⑤ 비행기

12 대화를 듣고, 남자가 옷을 환불하려는 이유로 가장 적절한 것을 고르시오.
① 몸에 맞지 않아서
② 교환이 불가능해서
③ 바지를 사기 위해서
④ 마음에 들지 않아서
⑤ 파란 얼룩이 있어서

13 대화를 듣고, 두 사람의 관계로 가장 적절한 것을 고르시오.
① 편집장 – 직원
② 헤어 디자이너 – 고객
③ 서점 직원 – 고객
④ 미술 선생님 – 학생
⑤ 패션 디자이너 – 모델

14 대화를 듣고, 신발 가게의 위치로 가장 적절한 곳을 고르시오.

15 대화를 듣고, 남자가 여자에게 부탁한 일로 가장 적절한 것을 고르시오.
① 요리하기 ② 바닥 쓸기
③ 창문 닦기 ④ 설거지하기
⑤ 세탁물 찾기

16 대화를 듣고, 남자가 여자에게 제안한 것으로 가장 적절한 것을 고르시오.
① 평소에 공부하기
② 학습 계획 세우기
③ 아침 일찍 일어나기
④ 중요한 일 먼저 하기
⑤ 시험 준비를 시작하기

17 대화를 듣고, 남자가 잃어버린 물건을 고르시오.
① 거울 ② 리모컨
③ 안경 ④ 선글라스
⑤ 콘택트렌즈

18 대화를 듣고, 남자의 직업으로 가장 적절한 것을 고르시오.
① 의사 ② 판매원
③ 소방관 ④ 경찰관
⑤ 환경미화원

[19–20] 대화를 듣고, 남자의 마지막 말에 이어질 여자의 응답으로 가장 적절한 것을 고르시오.

19 Woman: _____
① I'd be glad to help you.
② You'd better leave now.
③ I'm afraid I can't make it.
④ Let's meet at the bus station.
⑤ Please tell her to call me back.

20 Woman: _____
① Why not? It will help.
② You will do better the next time.
③ Okay. Don't be late tomorrow.
④ Let's go to the library at 2:00 p.m.
⑤ Sorry, but I forgot the name of the hotel.

● 대화를 다시 듣고, 알맞은 것을 고르시오.

1 I live both on land and in water.
☐ True   ☐ False

2 What shapes does his daughter like?
☐ heart shapes   ☐ star shapes

3 What's the weather like right now?
☐ sunny   ☐ cloudy

4 Did Suhyeon lose his dog while he was walking her?
☐ Yes   ☐ No

5 What does his father like to do for his exercise?
☐ skiing   ☐ jogging

6 Hajun had a car accident.
☐ True   ☐ False

7 Where are they going to take the bird?
☐ to the zoo   ☐ to the animal hospital

8 His daughter has just arrived home now.
☐ True   ☐ False

9 Is taking pictures in the museum allowed?
☐ Yes   ☐ No

10 Before making a donation, people have to be checked.
☐ True   ☐ False

11 When will they go to Incheon Airport?
☐ this Friday   ☐ this Saturday

12 The clerk offers to exchange the pants for some new ones.
☐ True   ☐ False

13 Does she want to get very short bangs?
☐ Yes   ☐ No

14 The shoe store is across from City Hall.
☐ True   ☐ False

15 What is her sister doing?
☐ washing dishes   ☐ sweeping the floor

16 The woman is making a study plan.
☐ True   ☐ False

17 Minkyu is jumping on the ground.
☐ True   ☐ False

18 What was stolen from the woman?
☐ a cap   ☐ a bag

19 Sarah and Seeun are supposed to meet at the park.
☐ True   ☐ False

20 Does Jeongin plan to stay on Jeju Island this weekend?
☐ Yes   ☐ No

그림 정보 파악

1 다음을 듣고, 'I'가 무엇인지 가장 적절한
것을 고르시오.

① ② ③
④ ⑤

1

M I have a short neck and four *short legs. I also have a
_____, _____ shell on my back. When danger
comes near, I can _____ _____ my shell. I
_____ _____ _____ on land, but I can swim
fast in the sea. What am I?

*short legs: [숄트][렉스] → [숄렉스]

그림 정보 파악

2 대화를 듣고, 남자가 구입할 곰 인형으로
가장 적절한 것을 고르시오.

① ② ③
④ ⑤

2

M Hello. I want to buy a _____ _____.

W Look at this! He's wearing a checkered shirt.

M That's so cute! But my daughter likes heart shapes.

W I'm afraid that we don't _____ _____ _____
_____.

M Then I'll buy the one with the _____ _____
_____.

그림 정보 파악

3 다음을 듣고, 내일의 날씨로 가장 적절한
것을 고르시오.

① ② ③
④ ⑤

3 🇬🇧

W Now, it's _____ _____ the weather report. It's
sunny and warm outside. It will start to rain this afternoon,
and the rain will _____ _____ _____
_____. Tomorrow, the rain will stop, and it is _____
_____ _____ cloudy. The fog will be very thick. Be
careful when you drive.

의도 파악

4 대화를 듣고, 남자의 마지막 말의 의도로
가장 적절한 것을 고르시오.

① 찬성　　② 부탁　　③ 거절
④ 축하　　⑤ 위로

4

W Suhyeon, I have to _____ _____ _____
_____.

M What happened? You look sad.

W I got a phone call from my sister a while ago.

M *What did she say?

W She said my puppy is _____. I have to _____
_____ _____.

M I'm sorry to hear the bad news.

*What did she [왓] [디드] [쉬] → [왓디쉬]

언급 유무 파악

5 다음을 듣고, 남자가 아빠에 대해 언급하지 않은 것을 고르시오.

① 나이   ② 취미   ③ 외모
④ 직업   ⑤ 성격

5

M   Hello, everyone. I want to tell you about my father. He is 45 years old but _____ _____ because he likes to _____ _____ _____. He has a big voice and a large body. He is _____ and smiles every day.

숫자 정보 파악

6 대화를 듣고, 두 사람이 만날 시각을 고르시오.

① 1:00 p.m.
② 1:30 p.m.
③ 2:00 p.m.
④ 2:30 p.m.
⑤ 3:00 p.m.

6

M   Did you hear that Hajun is in the hospital?

W   Really? What's the _____ _____ him?

M   He had a _____ _____. We should *visit him.

W   I agree. What time should we _____ _____?

M   How about tomorrow at 1:00 p.m.?

W   I think that's _____. Let's meet one hour later.

M   That's a better idea.

*visit him [비지트] [힘] → [비지팀]

장래 희망 파악

7 대화를 듣고, 남자의 장래 희망으로 가장 적절한 것을 고르시오.

① 수의사
② 간호사
③ 경찰관
④ 제빵사
⑤ 동물 조련사

7 🇬🇧

M   There's a _____ _____ on the street.

W   I think it is _____. It can't fly.

M   Oh, poor thing. I should take it to the animal _____.

W   You are so kind. Do you like animals?

M   Yes. I want to take care of animals in my own hospital in the future.

W   I bet you can be a good _____ _____.

심정 추론

8 대화를 듣고, 남자의 심정으로 가장 적절한 것을 고르시오.

① calm
② worried
③ satisfied
④ hopeless
⑤ regretful

8

W   Honey, you _____ _____ _____. Is something wrong?

M   Our daughter is not home yet. It's already 10:00 p.m.

W   Come on. She's all _____ _____.

M   Not yet. She is just a teenager.

W   She is _____ _____ _____ _____. Wait for a while.

M   How do you know that? Did she call you?

할 일 파악

9 대화를 듣고, 여자가 대화 직후에 할 일로 가장 적절한 것을 고르시오.

① 기념사진 찍기
② 기념품 구입하기
③ 신상 카메라 구입하기
④ 카메라를 가방에 넣기
⑤ 박물관 입장권 보여 주기

9

M   Excuse me, but could you put your camera away?

W   _____ me?

M   You can't take any pictures in this _____.

W   _____ _____ _____? I'm sorry.

M   Look at the _____ over there. Will you put your camera in your bag, please?

W   Yes, I will.

화제 · 주제 파악

10 대화를 듣고, 무엇에 관한 내용인지 가장 적절한 것을 고르시오.

① 모금
② 수술
③ 헌혈
④ 장학금
⑤ 봉사 활동

10

W   Hello. I want to _____ blood.

M   Welcome. Let me *check your information first. Can you _____ _____ this form?

W   Sure. [*Pause*] Done. Here it is.

M   Hmm... You can give blood as you are _____ _____ _____.

W   Okay. I'm glad to hear that.

M   Sit here and _____ _____ _____ _____.

*check your [체크] [유얼] → [체큐얼]

교통수단 파악

11 대화를 듣고, 두 사람이 함께 이용할 교통수단으로 가장 적절한 것을 고르시오.

① 버스   ② 택시   ③ 자전거
④ 지하철   ⑤ 비행기

11 🇬🇧

M   _____ _____ we go to Incheon Airport this Saturday?

W   We can take a bus. It'll take thirty minutes.

M   However, we *should arrive early in the morning.

W   Then we have no _____ _____ _____ _____ a taxi.

M   Okay. Let's _____ _____ _____.

*should arrive [슈드] [어라이브] → [슈더라이브]

이유 추론

12 대화를 듣고, 남자가 옷을 환불하려는 이유로 가장 적절한 것을 고르시오.

① 몸에 맞지 않아서
② 교환이 불가능해서
③ 바지를 사기 위해서
④ 마음에 들지 않아서
⑤ 파란 얼룩이 있어서

♥ **What about ~?**

: 어떤 것을 제안할 때 쓰는 표현으로, '~는 어때?'라는 뜻이다.
= How about ~?
= Why don't you ~?

12

W Hello. What can I do for you?

M I bought these pants yesterday, but I want to _____ _____ _____ on them.

W Can you tell me why?

M There's a _____ _____ on these pants. I *haven't even _____ them _____ yet.

W Oh, I'm sorry. ♥ What about exchanging these pants for some new ones?

M I _____ _____ _____.

*haven't even [헤븐트] [이븐] → [헤브니븐]

관계 추론

13 대화를 듣고, 두 사람의 관계로 가장 적절한 것을 고르시오.

① 편집장 – 직원
② 헤어 디자이너 – 고객
③ 서점 직원 – 고객
④ 미술 선생님 – 학생
⑤ 패션 디자이너 – 모델

13 🇬🇧

M Good morning. How would you like _____ _____ _____?

W What is a _____ hairstyle these days?

M Look at this magazine.

W Okay. [*Page-turning sound*] I want to get my hair _____.

M _____ _____ do you want?

W Dark brown, please. In addition, give me some bangs, but don't *make them _____ _____.

M Got it.

*make them [메이크] [뎀] → [메익뎀]

그림 정보 파악

14 대화를 듣고, 신발 가게의 위치로 가장 적절한 곳을 고르시오.

14

M Chaewon, let's meet at 6:00 p.m. in _____ of the shoe store.

W I got it. But I don't know how to get there.

M Go _____ _____ _____. Then, turn _____.

W And?

M You will see the shoe store on your right. It's _____ the gas station and City Hall.

W Okay. _____ _____ _____ _____, I'll call you.

M Sure. See you later.

15 대화를 듣고, 남자가 여자에게 부탁한 일로 가장 적절한 것을 고르시오.

① 요리하기
② 바닥 쓸기
③ 창문 닦기
④ 설거지하기
⑤ 세탁물 찾기

♥ **Let me see.**

: 잠시 생각할 시간을 요청하기 위해 혼잣말 하듯 쓰는 표현으로, '어디 보자.'라는 뜻이다.
= Let me think.
= Just a moment.

15

W Dad, what are you doing now?

M I'm sweeping the floor. Today is _____ _____.

W Right. Is there _____ _____ _____
    _____ ?

M ♥Let me see. Your sister is washing the _____. Can you
    pick up the _____ ?

W But Jamie already did that.

M Then why don't you clean the windows?

W Sure.

---

16 대화를 듣고, 남자가 여자에게 제안한 것으로 가장 적절한 것을 고르시오.

① 평소에 공부하기
② 학습 계획 세우기
③ 아침 일찍 일어나기
④ 중요한 일 먼저 하기
⑤ 시험 준비를 시작하기

16 🇬🇧

W I forgot to _____ _____ the math test.

M Did you? I recommend you make your study plan.

W *Doesn't it _____ _____ _____ _____ ?

M Not at all. It also _____ you _____ important
    things.

W Okay. I'll try it.

*Doesn't it [더즌트] [잇] → [더즌팃]

---

17 대화를 듣고, 남자가 잃어버린 물건을 고르시오.

① 거울
② 리모컨
③ 안경
④ 선글라스
⑤ 콘택트 렌즈

17

W Minkyu, why are you crawling on the ground?

M I tried to put one of my contacts in my eye, but I _____
    _____.

W Do you need my help _____ _____ _____
    _____ ?

M Yes, please.

W [*Pause*] I found it. It is _____ _____ _____.

직업 추론

18 대화를 듣고, 남자의 직업으로 가장 적절한 것을 고르시오.

① 의사
② 판매원
③ 소방관
④ 경찰관
⑤ 환경미화원

18

[*A door slams.*]

W   I need help.

M   You are safe. You are in the _____ _____. What happened?

W   Someone stole my bag from me right _____ _____ _____.

M   Are you all right? Are you hurt anywhere?

W   I think I'm okay. Please _____ my bag.

M   _____ _____. Did you see how the thief looked?

W   No. He ran off so fast.

적절한 응답 찾기

[19-20] 대화를 듣고, 남자의 마지막 말에 이어질 여자의 응답으로 가장 적절한 것을 고르시오.

19   Woman: _____

① I'd be glad to help you.
② You'd better leave now.
③ I'm afraid I can't make it.
④ Let's meet at the bus station.
⑤ Please tell her to call me back.

19

[*Telephone rings.*]

W   Hello. Can I speak to Seeun?

M   May I ask _____ _____ _____?

W   This is Sarah. I called her cell phone, but she did not _____ _____ _____.

M   Oh, I think she is still sleeping.

W   I _____ _____ _____ meet her at the park now.

M   I will wake her up now. Would you like to leave a message?

W   Please tell her to call me back.

적절한 응답 찾기

20   Woman: _____

① Why not? It will help.
② You will do better the next time.
③ Okay. Don't be late tomorrow.
④ Let's go to the library at 2:00 p.m.
⑤ Sorry, but I forgot the name of the hotel.

20

W   Donghyun, what are you _____ _____?

M   Hi, Jeongin. I'm _____ _____ a place to stay on Jeju Island.

W   I actually visited Jeju Island last weekend.

M   Can you help me to make a plan?

W   There are many places to visit. Ah, I have a tour book.

M   Good! May I _____ your book?

W   Why not? It will help.

A 들려주는 단어를 듣고 쓴 뒤, 괄호 안에 우리말 뜻을 쓰시오.

	영어	우리말			영어	우리말
1				6		
2				7		
3				8		
4				9		
5				10		

B 다음 문장을 잘 듣고 빈칸에 들어갈 단어를 채우시오.

1 I'm _____ _____ _____ .

2 I'm _____ _____ _____ the bad news.

3 I am _____ _____ _____ her at the park now.

4 How would you like _____ _____ _____ ?

5 Someone _____ _____ _____ from me right on the street.

6 Why are you _____ _____ _____ _____ ?

7 You can give blood as you are _____ _____ _____ .

8 Excuse me, but could you _____ _____ camera _____ ?

9 When danger comes near, I can _____ _____ my shell.

10 Tomorrow, the rain will stop, and it is _____ _____ _____ cloudy.

MEMO